108課綱 林熹老師帶你

學測英文 拿高分

林熹、Luke Farkas 著

目次

模擬試題

模擬試題解析

　　新課綱時代，除了課綱內容改變，升大學制度也跟著巨大的變化，過去學測與指考考科皆有英文科，如今英文科只剩學科能力測驗一次考試，英文科成績的重要性對高中生而言，可謂是一次定勝負。掌握新課綱，首先掌握學測的命題趨勢，我們看到很多學生並沒有真正了解新課綱的命題趨勢，只是一味地埋頭苦讀，這樣表面看似努力，但到頭來也是無法在學測中拿到高分的！

　　英文科要在學測拿高分，試題教材是關鍵。比起專研歷屆舊制考古題，選擇一本符合最新課綱趨勢的模擬試題更為重要。林熹老師的試題皆為新課綱設計的 19 項議題的延伸，例如：多元文化、防災教育、法治人權等，包含相關議題的英文單字、片語、主題概念等，真正能幫助你在準備學測上有精準明確的方向。

　　除此之外，新課綱的非選題重視學生在生活中更實用的實踐能力，例如：寫一封英文請願書，像這樣的相關技巧你都可以在本書中學到。在準備學測之際，更是儲備終身受用的能力！

　　方向正確才不會徒勞無功，方法正確才能夠事半功倍！詳讀這本書就是帶你學測英文拿高分的第一步。

　　現在還來得及嗎？現在就開始，永遠不會遲！只要透過書中的方法，每一回紮實地練習、複習、吸收，我相信一定能夠再次提高自己的學測英文實力，祝福每一位手中擁有這本書的你，在學測英文中勇奪高分！

李宏緯
新北市補習教育暨品保協會理事

首先，恭喜我的補教好友林熹老師出書了！非常榮幸受到林老師的邀請寫此序。我始終相信：讀書雖然無法一蹴可幾，但絕對有捷徑！面對範圍浩瀚無垠的學測英文考科，好的老師能給你方向，甚至能拍著胸脯自信地和你說：「老師教的課、寫的教材，就是考試要考的範圍。」在我眼裡，林熹老師就是這樣勤勤懇懇的教育工作者。

林老師的這本著作，絕非只是一般的解題參考書而已，老師將對新課綱的熟稔，鉅細靡遺地作類別建檔、主題式編排，不管是能切中核心的命題，真實生活情境的親筆擬答，亦或是精彩生動的影音解說，都能讓這本書紮紮實實地帶你迎戰學測英文考科，輕鬆笑傲試場。

筆者與林熹老師同樣從事教育工作，深知學生與家長面對新課綱的迷惘及不安。應試得意吾認為有兩大關鍵：首先要建立自信心，我相信考生在練習完本書的試題後，下筆一定有如神助，得分絕對「熹」利；再者，去除不必要的雜訊，許多考生總喜歡道聽塗說一些「偏方」，買了一堆試題或課程，最後大腦中的資訊越理越亂，在考試時反而無法發揮平常的實力，實在可惜。因此，100%信任這套為你量身打造的教材吧！本書將引導你前往正確的方向，在通往成功的道路上少走彎路。

最後，預祝林熹老師的這本大作暢銷！在教育這條路上，永遠不減熱情。

洪晏
國文科補教老師、作家

這是一本很不一樣的語言學習教材。

「工欲善其事，必先利其器」，同樣身為語言教育者，對於教材的要求一直很高。除了基本編排需簡明易懂，圖文豐富外，更重要的是，要能掌握住考生的痛點，並對症下藥。

與林熹老師認識多年，她在教學上認真投入的程度，十分令我佩服。林熹老師總是能即時更新資訊，提供學生最新最豐富的英文知識，也能將英文教學融入到生活當中，讓英文學習不再枯燥乏味，而是貼近生活。

她將此份教學熱忱轉化到書籍上，從架構到範文都是親自編撰，這本《108 課綱 林熹老師帶你學測英文拿高分：6 回試題＋詳解》充分掌握了參考書該有的重點，更提供大量的考試訣竅，並著重於目前潮流的情境題型，提供大量實用的情境作文題，迎合現在 108 課綱的出題趨勢，能讓考生在上戰場前，有充分練習的機會。

寫作題在語言科目中一直是考生的致命傷，林熹老師透過此本書，補充了學生的不足，除了引導式的寫作題，還包含中翻英。書中的情境題皆相當實用且生活化，可看見林熹老師的用心與巧思，也可從林熹老師的範文中學習到寫作要領。

更特別的是，此書結合了 QR Code，考生如有對章節有較不理解的部分，還能透過影片來說明，這是一個很棒的巧思，讓書籍結合影音，增加本書的附加價值，也是此書勝過其他坊間參考書的地方。

不論哪種語言學習，都是透過不斷累積與練習，才能立竿見影。Practice makes perfect. 相信各位考生透過這本融合 108 課綱精神的學測英文參考書，都可以快速累積英文實力，考出好成績。

詹芸
詹芸國文總監

本書的創作源起說來其實是場圓夢之旅。一直以來我都想撰寫一本能讓高中生自主學習及試題演練的書籍。剛好乘著 108 新課綱的浪潮，又巧逢 EZ 叢書館邀約，讓我有這個機會實現自己長期的願望，便二話不說動筆撰寫。

我在升學補教機構任教高中英文多年，而 108 學年度公布之新課綱所強調的資訊整理、解構、分析與總結，恰好是我一直以來教學的核心。108 新課綱的變革，代表台灣語言學習將面臨巨大轉變，**學測試題內容與舊制相比，新增「篇章結構」與「混合題型」兩大題**，不只是將以往指考的大題搬來學測，更額外以簡答題測試考生對閱讀題組的理解，對不熟悉新制答題方式的考生來說，無疑是一大挑戰。

因此，我根據大考中心公布的新制學測參考試卷，並參考新課綱公布的六大素養主題：**生涯規劃、多元文化、自然科技、防災課題、法治人權**及**國際視野**，以此方向設計本書的所有題目，包含選擇題、中翻英與作文題目，希望能同時擴展學生在這六大領域的單字閱讀量。

108 課綱的另一大重點為「跨科整合」，英文科是相當容易跨科整合的科目，有鑑於此，此書一共包含了**克漏字、文意選填、篇章結構、中翻英和作文**，唯漏詞彙題以及混合題型。我的想法是：**單字為英文基本功，透過閱讀文章就能加強字彙**。此外，**混合題型本質是閱讀測驗，若學生能掌握本書的這幾個大題的英文學習要點，單就讀懂文章來說，就有很大助益**。

其中，非選擇題的作文是我撰寫本書的最主要目的，而這也是許多考生的致命傷。在大考中心公布的數據中顯示，約有五成學生在非選擇題部分只能獲得一半或更低的分數，這代表光這個部分，若沒有好好把握，英文就可能被扣 14 分。以往寫作題目多以經驗分享或（看圖）記敘寫作為主，而新課綱非常強調「整合輸出」及「生活實踐」的能力，故我在設計題目時也特別讓作文題目更為實用，包括請願書、求職信函等。另外，中翻英及作文皆附上我自撰之範文及解說。

學生在練習完各單元之後，更可以掃描每一回的 QR Code，觀看我親錄的每一回重點，增強英文實力，快速掌握章節精華。

這本書雖然不能稱作是集大成，卻是我夢想集結之作。希望學生可以藉由試寫書中試題熟悉新制學測的主題與方向，若各位能夠學習到其中的心法關鍵，對我已是無比的鼓舞。感謝手裡握著這本書的您。

111 年新制學測 —— 英文科的變革

因應 108 年新課綱的頒佈，111 年的新制學測作了兩方面的變革，首先是新增題型並調整配分：

舊制學測		
選擇題	詞彙題	15 分
	綜合測驗	15 分
	文意選填	10 分
	閱讀測驗	32 分
非選擇題	中譯英	8 分
	英文作文	20 分

111 新制學測		
選擇題	詞彙題	10 分
	綜合測驗	10 分
	文意選填	10 分
	篇章結構	8 分
	閱讀測驗	24 分
混合題	題組一篇	10 分
非選擇題	中譯英	8 分
	英文作文	20 分

新增兩個題型：「篇章結構」與「混合題」，並重新調整配分，將詞彙與綜合測驗各減少 5 分，閱讀測驗減少 8 分，將配分挪到新增的兩個題型上。

- 篇章結構：為選擇題形式的閱讀理解測驗，**重視前後文意的邏輯連結**。
- 混合題：為**簡答題**形式的閱讀測驗，測驗學生們對英文文章的**整體理解能力、資訊整理能力、細節推論能力、及延伸發想能力**。

另一個是在答案卷上作了更動，改成「卷卡合一」的答案卷，以因應新增的「混合題型」：

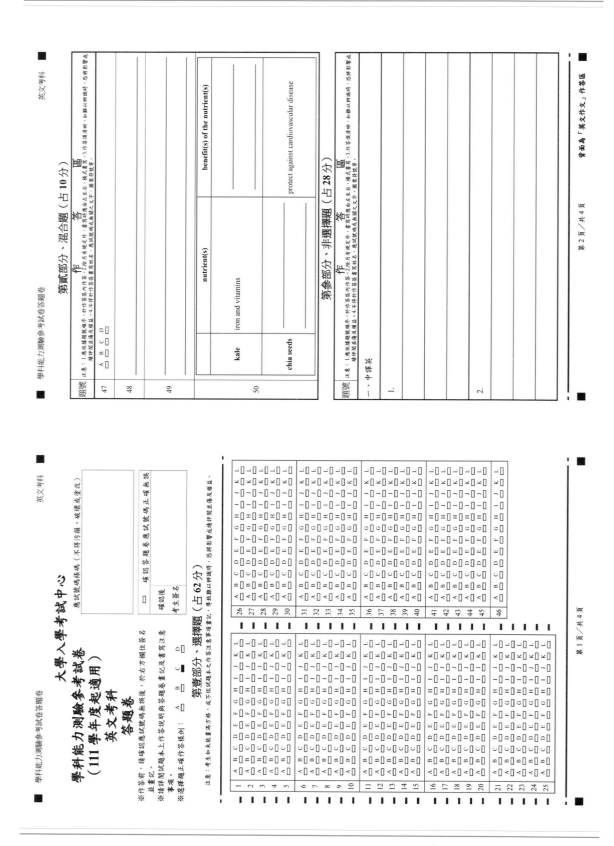

學科能力測驗參考試卷答題卷

第貳部分、混合題（占 10 分）

作　　　答　　　區

注意：1.應依題號標明作答。於作答區之外、書寫或塗改之作答不予計分。2.合字母考區由左至右、橫式書寫，填補評閱時應由左至右。3.作答須清晰，如欲以鉛筆清楚，忽將影響成績。4.不得於作答區書寫姓名，應試號碼等無關之文字、圖案符號。

題號	benefit(s) of the nutrient(s)
47	A B C D □ □ □ □
48	
49	nutrient(s)
50	kale — iron and vitamins chia seeds — protect against cardiovascular disease

第參部分、非選擇題（占 28 分）

作　　　答　　　區

注意：1.應依題號標明作答。於作答區之外、書寫或塗改之作答不予計分。2.合字母考區由左至右、橫式書寫，填補評閱時應由左至右。3.作答須清晰，如欲以鉛筆清楚，忽將影響成績。4.不得於作答區書寫姓名，應試號碼等無關之文字、圖案符號。

題號	作　答　區
一、中譯英	
1.	
2.	

學科能力測驗參考試卷答題卷

大學入學考試中心

學科能力測驗參考試卷
（111 學年度起適用）

英文考科
答 題 卷

應試號碼條碼（不得污損、破壞或塗改）

□　應試號碼條碼應貼於此

核對後　考生簽名

※作答前，請確認應試號碼條碼無誤後，於右方欄位簽名。
※作答前：請確認應試號碼條碼無誤後，於右方欄位簽名。
※請持閱試題本上作答說明與答題卷畫記及書寫注意事項：
※選擇題正確作答樣例：　A ■ C □

第壹部分、選擇題（占 62 分）

注意：考生如未能畫滿方格、或不依試題本之作答注意事項畫記，導致無法辨識，忽將影響成績或辨識，忽將影響成績或機讀評閱主偏及補益。

	A B C D E F G H I J K L
1	□ □ □ □ □ □ □ □ □ □ □ □
2	□ □ □ □ □ □ □ □ □ □ □ □
3	□ □ □ □ □ □ □ □ □ □ □ □
4	□ □ □ □ □ □ □ □ □ □ □ □
5	□ □ □ □ □ □ □ □ □ □ □ □
6	□ □ □ □ □ □ □ □ □ □ □ □
7	□ □ □ □ □ □ □ □ □ □ □ □
8	□ □ □ □ □ □ □ □ □ □ □ □
9	□ □ □ □ □ □ □ □ □ □ □ □
10	□ □ □ □ □ □ □ □ □ □ □ □
11	□ □ □ □ □ □ □ □ □ □ □ □
12	□ □ □ □ □ □ □ □ □ □ □ □
13	□ □ □ □ □ □ □ □ □ □ □ □
14	□ □ □ □ □ □ □ □ □ □ □ □
15	□ □ □ □ □ □ □ □ □ □ □ □
16	□ □ □ □ □ □ □ □ □ □ □ □
17	□ □ □ □ □ □ □ □ □ □ □ □
18	□ □ □ □ □ □ □ □ □ □ □ □
19	□ □ □ □ □ □ □ □ □ □ □ □
20	□ □ □ □ □ □ □ □ □ □ □ □
21	□ □ □ □ □ □ □ □ □ □ □ □
22	□ □ □ □ □ □ □ □ □ □ □ □
23	□ □ □ □ □ □ □ □ □ □ □ □
24	□ □ □ □ □ □ □ □ □ □ □ □
25	□ □ □ □ □ □ □ □ □ □ □ □

	A B C D E F G H I J K L
26	□ □ □ □ □ □ □ □ □ □ □ □
27	□ □ □ □ □ □ □ □ □ □ □ □
28	□ □ □ □ □ □ □ □ □ □ □ □
29	□ □ □ □ □ □ □ □ □ □ □ □
30	□ □ □ □ □ □ □ □ □ □ □ □
31	□ □ □ □ □ □ □ □ □ □ □ □
32	□ □ □ □ □ □ □ □ □ □ □ □
33	□ □ □ □ □ □ □ □ □ □ □ □
34	□ □ □ □ □ □ □ □ □ □ □ □
35	□ □ □ □ □ □ □ □ □ □ □ □
36	□ □ □ □ □ □ □ □ □ □ □ □
37	□ □ □ □ □ □ □ □ □ □ □ □
38	□ □ □ □ □ □ □ □ □ □ □ □
39	□ □ □ □ □ □ □ □ □ □ □ □
40	□ □ □ □ □ □ □ □ □ □ □ □
41	□ □ □ □ □ □ □ □ □ □ □ □
42	□ □ □ □ □ □ □ □ □ □ □ □
43	□ □ □ □ □ □ □ □ □ □ □ □
44	□ □ □ □ □ □ □ □ □ □ □ □
45	□ □ □ □ □ □ □ □ □ □ □ □
46	□ □ □ □ □ □ □ □ □ □ □ □

英文考科

學科能力測驗參考試卷答題卷

英文考科

學科能力測驗參考試卷答題卷

題號

作　答　區

注意：1.應依題號順序，於各題區內作答。2.除有規定外，書寫區域由左至右，橫式書寫。3.作答須清晰，加註以利辨識，塗改影格。務評閱主機辨識且不作答於各題畫寫作名、圖示號碼及圖解之文字、圖案將要負。

二、英文作文

本書使用說明

獨家 林熹老師解說影片 「學測即時充電站」

手機掃 QR Code

林熹老師針對每個大題分享解題技巧,搭配每回試題,考生能輕鬆透過本書自主學習。

這個陳情請願

即時充電站 01

新式作文解題技巧

第壹部分:選擇題

一、綜合測驗

第 1 至 10 題為題組 —— 校園生活

Students all around the world are excited and nervous __1__ returning to school each year. Many cultures have traditions to celebrate this day and ease students through the transition from carefree summer fun to school year __2__.

In the countries __3__ were formerly part of the Soviet Union— __4__ Russia, Ukraine, and Belarus–September 1st is known __5__ Knowledge Day. It is a time of celebration and entertainment, to welcome children back. If September 1st falls on a weekend, Knowledge Day is moved to the closest weekday. Students and their parents gather to __6__ the ceremonies. Russian students also bring their teachers flowers, and the teacher gives them balloons __7__.

In Japan, students often pack a special lunch on the first day. This meal of seaweed sauce, quail eggs, and rice is thought to bring good luck for the coming year of study. German children are given a *Schultuete* on the first day of school. *Schultuete* roughly translates to "school cone," and it is a large, colorful paper cone __8__ treats, toys, and school supplies.

For many children, back-to-school time is fun and enjoyable. __9__ may find it stressful and miss the days of summer vacation. But for all students, the return to class is an important occasion, __10__ another year along the path to adulthood.

譯文

全世界的學生每年都對開學日既期待又緊張。許多文化都有著慶祝這一天的傳統,舒緩學生從無憂無慮的快樂暑假到嚴守紀律的學校生活間的過渡心情。

在部分前蘇聯國家,例如俄羅斯、烏克蘭和白羅斯,9 月 1 號為知識日。這天是來慶祝、歡迎小孩回到學校的娛樂活動,如果 9 月 1 號是週末的話,知識日會移到最接近的平日。學生及長家會一起參與慶祝活動,俄羅斯的學生也會給老師花,而老師會回送氣球。

在日本,學生會在第一天帶特別的便當,內容包含海苔醬、鵪鶉蛋和白飯,象徵著為新的學年帶來好運。德國孩子會在開學日收到 "Schultuete",Schultuete 按字面翻譯為「學校甜筒」,是一個五彩繽紛且大型的紙布甜筒,裡面放滿了零食、玩具和學校用品。

對很多孩子來說,開學期間是充滿歡樂及有趣的;有些人或許會覺得充滿壓力,想念著暑假的日子,但對每個學生而言,回校上課是重要的階段,讓來年繼續往成人邁進。

三、 NEW 108 課綱 | 篇章結構

第 31 至 35 題為題組 —— 人際關係

Being thought of as a likable person can help open many doors. People will be enthusiastic about working with you. You don't have to act like someone you are not or put on an act. In fact, it's better to be genuine, but reconsider some of your habits when interacting with others. __31__ First, you should look for good things about other people and their work and tell them you appreciate those things. There is something positive that can be said about everybody. This is not fake flattery, but a genuine change in your outlook. By expressing positive things about others, they'll be happier about themselves and happier to cooperate with you.

__32__ Every person has a story to tell and a life they have lived. Everyone has something to say that is worth hearing. You can learn something from anyone, but only if you are open to the experience. On the other hand, don't hesitate to ask others for advice. __33__ This will make them respect you more, too. Keep in mind that no one feels happy and social all the time. __34__ If you can, take a break and have some time to yourself. You'll likely feel refreshed soon. Last but not least, find pleasure in everything around you. __35__ The more you allow yourself to like others, the more you'll like yourself!

譯文

被認為是一個人見人愛的人能夠幫助你拓展很多機會,人們會熱衷於與你共事,你不用表現得不像自己或是裝模作樣。事實上,真誠待人比較好,但當與他人互動時,還是要多加考慮自己的一些習慣。(C) **在以下祕訣的幫助下,好人緣是一項你可以使用以及精進的技能。** 首先,你應找到別人的優點及好的工作表現,並告訴他們你很欣賞他們的地方,每個人一定有某些值得稱讚的地方,這不是阿諛諂媚,而是發自內心改變自己對別人的看法,說別人好話會讓他們過得更開心,也更樂於和你合作。

(A) **當與人談話時,問關於對方的問題。** 每個人都有著值得一提的故事和人生經驗、每個人的事蹟都是值得一聽的。你可以從任何人身上學到東西,只要你願意傾聽。另一方面,別吝惜向人詢問意見,(E) **你不僅能獲得處理問題的洞察力,人們也會感覺你看重他們的能力、智慧和經驗**,這也會讓他們對你敬重有加。你還要記住:沒有人能時時保持愉悅、愛好交際。如果可以的話,休息一下,花時間自處,很快你便會感覺恢復活力。最後,從周遭事物中找尋樂趣。(D) **藉由培養對人的興趣,你會發現隨著時間你將會獲得新的機緣、契機與朋友作為回報。** 你越喜歡他人,就會越喜歡你自己。

---

108 課綱新式題型

依照新課綱「六大主題」,設計最新學測題型。提供學生準備考試方針,提升應考信心。

必買 市售最詳盡學測英語寶典

效率擴充字彙量

各篇文章補充相關**延伸單字**、**片語**、**同義詞**、**反義詞**等。透過本書模擬試題，有效增加學生詞彙量。

---

6. **ideogram** [ˈɪdɪəˌɡræm] *(n.)* [U] 表意文字
  → 字首 ideo- 表示「觀念、思想、意識」

7. **religious** [rɪˈlɪdʒəs] *(adj.)* 宗教上的；虔誠的
  → be deeply religious 非常虔誠的
  → religious beliefs 宗教信仰
  → religion *(n.)* [C,U] 宗教

8. **forbid** [fəˈbɪd] *(vt.)* 禁止、不許 ↔ permit 允許
  → forbid sb. **to V**ᴿ **/ from Ving** 禁止某人做某事
  → 動詞三態為：forbid - forbade - forbidden

9. **shrine** [ʃraɪn] *(n.)* [C] 聖壇、神社 (+ **of/to** N)
  → pray at a/the shrine 在聖壇祈禱

10. **eternal** [ɪˈtɜnl] *(adj.)* 永久的、永恆的 ↔ momentary, temporary 暫時的
  → eternity *(n.)* [U] 無窮無盡、永恆
  → eternal truth/life/arguments 永恆的真理／永生／不停的爭吵

重要片語

1. **due to + N** 因為、由於…
2. **combine A with B** 將 A 與 B 結合在一起
3. **make sense** 有道理
4. **set out** 動身、開始

---

8. **forbid** [fəˈbɪd] *(vt.)* 禁止、不許 ↔ permit 允許
  → forbid sb. **to V**ᴿ **/ from Ving** 禁止某人做某事
  → 動詞三態為：forbid - forbade - forbidden

9. **shrine** [ʃraɪn] *(n.)* [C] 聖壇、神社 (+ **of/to** N)
  → pray at a/the shrine 在聖壇祈禱

10. **eternal** [ɪˈtɜnl] *(adj.)* 永久的、永恆的 ↔ momentary, temporary 暫時的
  → eternity *(n.)* [U] 無窮無盡、永恆
  → eternal truth/life/arguments 永恆的真理／永生／不停的爭吵

重要片語

1. **due to + N** 因為、由於…
2. **combine A with B** 將 A 與 B 結合在一起
3. **make sense** 有道理
4. **set out** 動身、開始

---

1. 「認為」的主動和被動的表達方式
(1) 主動用法：

$$\left[\begin{array}{l} \text{see} \\ \text{view} \\ \text{regard} \\ \text{look upon} \\ \text{think of} \\ \text{refer to} \end{array}\right] \text{A as B} \quad 認為 A 是 B \quad = \left[\begin{array}{l} \text{think} \\ \text{consider} \end{array}\right] \text{A (to be) B}$$

例 Fuji is a volcano. Though it hasn't erupted since 1707, many geologists consider **it to** still **be** active.
富士山是一座火山。即使它從西元 1707 年就沒有爆發過，但許多地質學家認為它仍然活躍。

(2) 被動用法：

$$\text{A be} \left[\begin{array}{l} \text{seen} \\ \text{viewed} \\ \text{regarded} \\ \text{looked upon} \\ \text{thought of} \\ \text{referred to} \end{array}\right] \text{as B} \quad \text{A 被認為是 B} \quad = \text{A be} \left[\begin{array}{l} \text{thought} \\ \text{considered} \end{array}\right] \text{(to be) B}$$

例 Bubble tea is considered (to be) the pride of Taiwan.
珍珠奶茶被認為是台灣之光。

相關文法句型

1. 「認為」的主動和被動的表達方式
(1) 主動用法：

$$\left[\begin{array}{l} \text{see} \\ \text{view} \\ \text{regard} \\ \text{look upon} \\ \text{think of} \\ \text{refer to} \end{array}\right] \text{A as B} \quad 認為 A 是 B \quad = \left[\begin{array}{l} \text{think} \\ \text{consider} \end{array}\right] \text{A (to be) B}$$

例 Fuji is a volcano. Though it hasn't erupted since 1707, many geologists consider **it to** still **be** active.
富士山是一座火山。即使它從西元 1707 年就沒有爆發過，但許多地質學家認為它仍然活躍。

(2) 被動用法：

$$\text{A be} \left[\begin{array}{l} \text{seen} \\ \text{viewed} \\ \text{regarded} \\ \text{looked upon} \\ \text{thought of} \\ \text{referred to} \end{array}\right] \text{as B} \quad \text{A 被認為是 B} \quad = \text{A be} \left[\begin{array}{l} \text{thought} \\ \text{considered} \end{array}\right] \text{(to be) B}$$

例 Bubble tea is considered (to be) the pride of Taiwan.
珍珠奶茶被認為是台灣之光。

例 Bali is seen as **the perfect vacation spot** by many foreigners because of its beautiful beaches.
峇里島因為有美麗的海灘，所以被許多外國人認為是一個完美的渡假勝地。

例 Passengers who talk loudly on trains are often thought of as **rude**.
在火車上講話很大聲的人常被視為無禮。

圖列式文法句型解析

簡明比較、快速理解常混淆之高中英語文法。句型應用強化學測翻譯與英文作文能力。

創新 生活化作文題型！貼合 108 新課綱素養精神

生活化作文題型

根據 108 課綱，林熹老師親自設計多元且貼近時事生活的作文題型，包含：**全球疫情、請願訴求、求職履歷信、生涯規劃**⋯等。

名師親撰範文

林熹老師與外國老師聯手，親筆撰寫範文，提供涉及該主題重要單字與實用句型。

Let's get started!
六回模擬試題

第壹部分：選擇題

一、綜合測驗

> 說明：第 1 題至第 20 題，每題一個空格，請依文意選出最適當的一個選項。

第 1 至 10 題為題組 —— 校園生活

Students all around the world are excited and nervous __1__ returning to school each year. Many cultures have traditions to celebrate this day and ease students through the transition from carefree summer fun to school year __2__ .

In the countries __3__ were formerly part of the Soviet Union–__4__ Russia, Ukraine, and Belarus–September 1st is known __5__ Knowledge Day. It is a time of celebration and entertainment, to welcome children back. If September 1st falls on a weekend, Knowledge Day is moved to the closest weekday. Students and their parents gather to __6__ the ceremonies. Russian students also bring their teachers flowers, and the teacher gives them balloons __7__ .

In Japan, students often pack a special lunch on the first day. This meal of seaweed sauce, quail eggs, and rice is thought to bring good luck for the coming year of study. German children are given a *Schultuete* on the first day of school. *Schultuete* roughly translates to "school cone," and it is a large, colorful paper cone __8__ treats, toys, and school supplies.

For many children, back-to-school time is fun and enjoyable. __9__ may find it stressful and miss the days of summer vacation. But for all students, the return to class is an important occasion, __10__ another year along the path to adulthood.

---

1. (A) for   (B) about   (C) with   (D) in
2. (A) discipline   (B) deficiency   (C) depression   (D) dignity
3. (A) which   (B) where   (C) what   (D) when
4. (A) regarding   (B) such as   (C) considering   (D) given
5. (A) at   (B) to   (C) for   (D) as
6. (A) get along with   (B) take part in   (C) turn down   (D) run into
7. (A) in charge   (B) in advance   (C) in return   (D) in action
8. (A) carpeted with   (B) packed with   (C) equipped with   (D) faced with
9. (A) Others   (B) Another   (C) The other   (D) The others
10. (A) marked   (B) mark   (C) to mark   (D) marking

It seems like we __11__ anxiety more and more these days. As our fast-paced world becomes increasingly demanding, it can be difficult to keep our feelings under __12__ . Maybe you or someone close to you has had the experience of tackling anxiety.

Anxiety is actually a function __13__ to the human brain. Evolution created a "fight or flight" response to help us survive the natural challenges of ancient times by preparing our bodies to __14__ combat an enemy __14__ run away. Now, fight or flight can be __15__ by daily stress, __16__ the hormone Cortisol into the brain. This pattern can become a habit our minds fall into at any sign of stress. __17__ , humans as a species have a great deal of control over their own minds and techniques for managing anxiety can be learned.

Someone __18__ anxiety should work to build a more positive self-perception. We are constantly telling a story about ourselves to ourselves and others. It is best to focus on the positive aspects of yourself and your life. After a while, you will internalize these thoughts and view yourself more positively.

It's also important to practice self-care. This means __19__ your own physical and mental needs, and trying to meet them. These can be healthy diet, exercise, enough sleep and relaxation. Soon, your body will get into this __20__ of self-care and you will find yourself thinking more clearly and better able to deal with anxiety.

11. (A) belong to (B) come up with (C) struggle with (D) rely on
12. (A) control (B) attack (C) consideration (D) development
13. (A) initial (B) intimate (C) inherent (D) interior
14. (A) either... or (B) neither... nor (C) neither... or (D) either... nor
15. (A) triumphed (B) treated (C) tricked (D) triggered
16. (A) releasing (B) released (C) release (D) to release
17. (A) Accordingly (B) Fortunately (C) Gradually (D) Eventually
18. (A) restraining from (B) dealing with (C) insisting on (D) conforming to
19. (A) recovering (B) reckoning (C) registering (D) recognizing
20. (A) reward (B) routine (C) ruin (D) request

二、文意選填

說明：第21題至第30題，每題一個空格，請依文意在文章後所提供的(A)到(J)選項中分別選出最適當者。

第 21 至 30 題為題組 —— 新年目標

There is a long tradition of setting New Year's __21__ for oneself. By tying the change we wish to make in our own __22__ to the change in the calendar, we hope to make a new self with the new year. This is a way of being disciplined about the changes we wish to make, which are often difficult.

Many New Year's resolutions are about adopting a healthier lifestyle. This is a thing many find hard to do. We must reverse bad habits we have __23__ for a long time. There are a few techniques that can be used to make this process simpler.

__24__, make a specific plan of action for exercise. Know exactly what kind of exercise you want to do, and when. Commit __25__ that schedule. If your plans are too vague, it's likely you'll never do them. In addition, make sure your goals are realistic. If they are too ambitious, you may never be able to accomplish them, and quit __26__. This could cause you to abandon the idea of changing at all. Know what you're capable __27__, and what you will enjoy doing. This will help you stay committed.

And remember to accept that you may fail occasionally. If you __28__ your resolution, don't beat yourself up or feel embarrassed. This can cause you to give up.

__29__, use each failure as an opportunity to recommit, refocus, and get back __30__. Don't worry too much about your failures; think about your goal. Congratulate yourself on a series of small gains. Don't try to take on too much at once. Ask your friends and family to support you and help you accomplish your goals. Change can be hard, but it is worth it.

(A) engaged in	(B) behavior	(C) of	(D) Firstly	(E) in frustration
(F) fall short of	(G) on track	(H) resolutions	(I) commit to	(J) Instead

說明：第 31 題至第 35 題，每題一個空格。請依文意在文章後所提供的 (A) 到 (E) 選項中分別選出最適當者，填入空格中，使篇章結構清晰有條理。

第 31 至 35 題為題組 —— 人際關係

Being thought of as a likable person can help open many doors. People will be enthusiastic about working with you. You don't have to act like someone you are not or put on an act. In fact, it's better to be genuine, but reconsider some of your habits when interacting with others. __31__ First, you should look for good things about other people and their work and tell them you appreciate those things. There is something positive that can be said about everybody. This is not fake flattery, but a genuine change in your outlook. By expressing positive things about others, they'll be happier about themselves and happier to cooperate with you.

__32__ Every person has a story to tell and a life they have lived. Everyone has something to say that is worth hearing. You can learn something from anyone, but only if you are open to the experience. On the other hand, don't hesitate to ask others for advice. __33__ This will make them respect you more, too. Keep in mind that no one feels happy and social all the time. __34__ If you can, take a break and have some time to yourself. You'll likely feel refreshed soon. Last but not least, find pleasure in everything around you. __35__ The more you allow yourself to like others, the more you'll like yourself!

(A) When speaking with others, ask them questions about themselves.

(B) It's okay to be in a negative mood occasionally, but you should try to avoid taking it out on others.

(C) With the help of the following tips, being likable is a skill you can work on and improve!

(D) By cultivating a deeper interest in people, you'll find that over time you'll be rewarded with new connections, opportunities, and friends.

(E) Not only could you potentially receive some insight into a problem, but people will feel that you respect their strengths, intelligence and experience.

第貳部分：非選擇題

一、中譯英 —— 校園生活

說明：1. 請將以下中文句子譯成正確、通順、達意的英文。
　　　2. 請依序作答，並標明子題號（1、2）。

1. 學校不僅是獲得知識的地方，也是教育的搖籃。在那我可以學到如何與不同的人相處及培育人格。

2. 我很用功並盡己所能理解課程內容，因為我不想在這個學期落後。

二、英文作文 —— 投資自我

假設你今天買樂透獲得一筆為數不小的金額，你會選擇以下哪一項？寫一篇至少 120 字的英文作文。第一段明示你的選擇及理由，第二段說明你為何不選擇另一項的考量。

赴美遊學兩個月，進入大學與國際同學一起學習交流，並在課後安排旅遊行程。

進行全身大改造，在醫美診所裡花錢讓自己擁有魔鬼般的身材及天使般的容顏。

第壹部分：選擇題

一、綜合測驗

> 說明：第 1 題至第 20 題，每題一個空格，請依文意選出最適當的一個選項。

第 1 至 10 題為題組 —— 萬國節慶

In the U.K. and Ireland, Boxing Day occurs on December 26th of each year, the day after Christmas. Many people outside of the U.K. and Ireland are __1__ this holiday. Boxing Day is a time to __2__ your daily worries and spend time with family. Often this means __3__ family, because people usually stay home with their immediate family on Christmas Day.

Guests are welcomed into the home on Boxing Day, and usually much food is enjoyed. Baked ham, cakes, and puddings __4__ from Christmas are consumed. It is a way to extend the __5__ and good cheer of the holiday season. Sporting events are enjoyed on Boxing day. Football matches and horse races are televised. Traditionally, men would hunt foxes on Boxing Day, but this tradition __6__. However, people still gather in fox hunting uniforms to honor the old traditions.

No one is quite sure why it is called "Boxing Day," but there are several theories. One is that long ago wealthy people would give their servants a day off, __7__ presents for their families, called Christmas boxes. Another is that churches would __8__ a box to collect donations during the Christmas service, and the next day the money in these boxes was __9__ the poor. No matter __10__ the name comes from, everyone loves shopping, socializing, or just relaxing on this wonderful day!

1. (A) characteristic of   (B) unaware of   (C) independent of   (D) familiar with
2. (A) break down   (B) set off   (C) put out   (D) put aside
3. (A) contended   (B) extended   (C) attended   (D) intended
4. (A) left over   (B) cut down   (C) taken over   (D) wiped out
5. (A) hostility   (B) hospitality   (C) humility   (D) humidity
6. (A) is banning   (B) has banned   (C) has been banned   (D) has been banning
7. (A) except for   (B) including   (C) as well as   (D) instead of
8. (A) let go   (B) turn down   (C) set aside   (D) stack up
9. (A) attributed to   (B) contributing to   (C) distributed to   (D) tribute
10. (A) that   (B) the place   (C) wherever   (D) where

The current Dalai Lama, named Tenzin Gyatso, is getting old. He is __11__ the ripe old age of 84. It is time to locate his __12__. However, the Chinese government believes itself to be the authority that should find the next Dalai Lama. This has created a __13__ between the Chinese government and Tibetan Buddhists.

The Dalai Lama is a __14__ spiritual leader, and is responsible for promoting Buddhist beliefs and ethics throughout the entire world. The current Dalai Lama was even __15__ The Nobel Peace Prize in 1992. Because this position is so important, the Dalia Lama's successor has traditionally been discovered by senior monks.

Tenzin Gyatso became Dalai Lama when he was only 4 years old. He __16__ be the next in line when his predecessor, the 13th Dalai Lama, died and monks interpreted religious visions to locate Tenzin Gyatso. He was __17__ to be the next on the throne because he seemed to recognize the monks, as well as objects that had belonged to the previous Dalai Lama. Tibetan Buddhists would like to select the next Dalai Lama with similar methods.

The Chinese government __18__ Tibet in 1950 and Tenzin Gyatso lives in exile. The Chinese government insists it should pick the next Lama, but many __19__ this __19__ an attempt to exert influence over Tibetan spiritual and cultural life. The current Dalai Lama has made several statements that contradict China's claims. The situation remains __20__.

11. (A) on (B) at (C) in (D) behind
12. (A) assessor (B) successor (C) succession (D) suspicion
13. (A) correspondence (B) compromise (C) coincidence (D) conflict
14. (A) prevalent (B) transient (C) prominent (D) relevant
15. (A) rewarding (B) rewarded (C) awarding (D) awarded
16. (A) bore in mind (B) had determination (C) was determined to (D) made up his mind
17. (A) confirmed (B) confessed (C) conformed (D) condemned
18. (A) invaded (B) indicated (C) initiated (D) included
19. (A) consider... as (B) regard... for (C) see... as (D) view... with
20. (A) resolved (B) unresolved (C) realistic (D) unrealistic

二、文意選填

第 21 至 30 題為題組 —— 語言學習

Learning a new language can be a(n) __21__ task. Many learners have no idea how to start this kind of __22__. There have been a few different strategies developed by others that are worth __23__. They focus on different aspects of language and how to learn it. Students can decide for themselves how to best utilize these techniques.

One approach is called "extensive reading". This is when the reader tries to __24__ as much different writing in the target language as possible. By taking in many different styles, the student gains some understanding of the full possibilities of that language. The goal is to gain fluency through __25__ to a wide range of vocabulary, grammar, and ideas. This technique works best with students who enjoy reading and are happy to seek out new reading material on their own. Critics of this style say that readers only develop a __26__ understanding of the target language this way.

A second technique is called "intensive reading". In __27__ to extensive reading, which tries to take in as much as possible, intensive reading chooses shorter texts. However, intensive reading takes a hard look at these short pieces of writing, __28__ them deeply. The reader focuses on the grammar and sentence structure. In this way, a fuller understanding of the text __29__. Critics say that focusing on one short piece can lead to boredom.

Likely, using a combination of these techniques would work best. Each student should determine how to best integrate these techniques for their own learning styles and language goals. The __30__ balance of extensive and intensive reading will lead to a well-balanced course of study.

(A) considering	(B) intimidating	(C) superficial	(D) absorb	(E) proper
(F) exposure	(G) emerges	(H) analyzing	(I) endeavor	(J) contrast

說明：第 31 題至第 35 題，每題一個空格。請依文意在文章後所提供的 (A) 到 (E) 選項中分別選出最適當者，填入空格中，使篇章結構清晰有條理。

第 31 至 35 題為題組 —— 傳統文化

Matsu is a chain of islands located in the northwest of Taiwan. __31__ Matsu lies near the mouth of the Min river, as it opens into the sea from mainland China.

Water and wind erosion have sculpted striking features upon Matsu over millions of years. The scenery can suddenly go from steep hills and high cliff faces to deep valleys and bays. The relentless surf has created unique features such as caves and rock columns.

__32__ Two of these granite mountains, Bi and Yun-Tai, are listed among Taiwan's 100 Minor Mountains.

__33__ Instead, the island relies heavily on its vast fishing resources. Due to the islands' isolation, there are many distinctive plant species here, such as the Matsu Wild Lily and the Matsu Lycoris. The islands are also temporarily home to many migratory birds each year.

Unlike most of Taiwan, Matsu has four distinct seasons. Matsu is only one degree of latitude north of Taiwan, but because it is so close to the continental climate, it is significantly cooler. __34__ In the spring, fog is often so heavy that flights must be cancelled. Spring is also monsoon season, and Matsu is strongly affected.

Fishermen began using Matsu during their expeditions centuries ago. Later it became a hideout for Japanese pirates. It wasn't really settled until around the Qing period, when fishermen began to stay permanently on the island to raise families. Matsu was under martial law during the Communist revolution of 1949. __35__

(A) Strong winds buffet Matsu during the winter months.

(B) Matsu is composed of rocky granite, and the landscape is generally mountainous.

(C) These small islands comprise only about 30 square kilometers of land.

(D) Today many military structures still stand, and may be explored by tourists.

(E) Because Matsu's terrain is so rugged, farming is difficult.

第貳部分：非選擇題

一、中譯英 —— 台灣美景

> 說明：1. 請將以下中文句子譯成正確、通順、達意的英文。
>   2. 請依序作答，並標明子題號（1、2）。

1. 太魯閣峽谷（Taroko Gorge）坐落於陡峭的台灣東部。這個大自然的奇景是台灣最多遊客造訪的國家公園。

2. 即使我已經去過四次，卻不會厭倦。我希望在不久的將來能更深入探索這個幅員遼闊的國家公園。

二、英文作文 —— 外語學習

如果你有機會學習一種除了英語之外的第三外語，你會選擇哪一項？請以此為題，寫一篇至少 120 個英文單詞的作文。說明你的選擇及理由，並舉例說明你要如何運用此語言。也請說明你不選擇另一項語言的理由或考量為何。

> **語言一**：西班牙語（Spanish）為 20 個主權獨立國家的官方語言，全球約 4.4 億人口說西班牙語。除西班牙外，大部分說西班牙語的人口主要集中在拉丁美洲（中南美）國家，因此西班牙語在美洲相當受歡迎，是美洲第一大語言。

> **語言二**：法語（French）為 29 個主權獨立國家和其他多個地區的官方語言，全球約 3.9 億人口說法文。除法國及某些歐洲國家，大部分說法文的人口主要分布於北美及非洲國家，因此法語在非洲相當流行，是僅次於阿拉伯語的非洲第二大語言。

第壹部分：選擇題

一、綜合測驗

說明：第 1 題至第 20 題，每題一個空格，請依文意選出最適當的一個選項。

第 1 至 10 題為題組 —— 名人偉事

Marie Curie is one of the most famous scientists of the 20th century. In 1867, she was born Maria Sklodowska in Poland but moved to Paris, France as a young woman to pursue educational opportunities. It was in Paris __1__ she met her husband, Pierre Curie, in 1894. The two began researching the mineral uranium and its property of __2__ invisible rays. These rays are called radiation, and have the ability __3__ through solid matter. Marie eventually __4__ polonium and radium, elements even more radioactive than uranium.

1903 was a successful year for Curie. She completed her doctorate degree and won a Nobel prize, __5__ with Pierre and another scientist. Sadly, her husband was killed in an accident in 1906, but Marie continued the work they had started together. In 1911, Marie Curie won another Nobel for __6__ a way to measure radiation. She also created new research programs for the study of radiation and cancer. During the First World War, Curie traveled to the battlefield. As Director of the Red Cross Radiological Service, she used an X-ray machine she __7__ to diagnose soldiers' injuries.

After the war ended, Curie continued working and teaching. She earned __8__ for her pioneering work in chemistry, physics and medicine. __9__ her determination and intelligence, Marie Curie continues to __10__ people interested in science throughout the world.

1. (A) and   (B) when   (C) which   (D) that
2. (A) giving off   (B) giving up   (C) giving away   (D) giving in
3. (A) pass   (B) to pass   (C) passing   (D) to passing
4. (A) discharged   (B) discovered   (C) disappeared   (D) discarded
5. (A) sharing   (B) is sharing   (C) shared   (D) was shared
6. (A) developing   (B) dedicating   (C) delivering   (D) depending
7. (A) had invented   (B) has invented   (C) had been inventing   (D) had been invented
8. (A) representation   (B) responsibility   (C) reservation   (D) recognition
9. (A) Beyond   (B) Despite   (C) Due to   (D) As
10. (A) inform   (B) imitate   (C) insult   (D) inspire

Johannes Kepler is a legend of science and astronomy. A man of many interests and talents, he revolutionized the way humans view the universe and their place within it. He was a man of __11__ , and a product of a very contrasting time.

Kepler was born in what is now Germany in 1571. He was a sickly child, and suffered lifelong __12__ to his vision as a result of smallpox. He displayed a fantastic talent for mathematics __13__ a very young age. His mother, a lover of nature, showed him the night sky, which increased his interests in astronomy.

Kepler began working with another __14__ astronomer of the time, Tycho Brahe. Though the two scientists __15__ conflict at times, their relationship was a fruitful one. After Brahe's death, Kepler gained __16__ to his extensive data on planetary movement. With this data, Kepler was able to determine that the planets' orbits aren't exactly __17__ , but elliptical, in a form of an oval. This was a revolutionary concept at the time.

Kepler made many other such scientific __18__ . He discovered that __19__ from the sun, the weaker the sun's gravitational force was on that planet. He determined that the tides were caused by the gravity of the moon. He figured out the human eye actually __20__ images upside down, and our brains correct them. Truly, Kepler is one of the greatest scientific thinkers in history.

11. (A) connections　　(B) contradictions　　(C) confusions　　(D) considerations
12. (A) impression　　(B) imprisonment　　(C) impairment　　(D) improvement
13. (A) on　　(B) at　　(C) in　　(D) with
14. (A) prominent　　(B) proficient　　(C) profound　　(D) present
15. (A) came into　　(B) came with　　(C) came on　　(D) came up
16. (A) achievement　　(B) accent　　(C) account　　(D) access
17. (A) triangular　　(B) square　　(C) circular　　(D) diamond
18. (A) breakings　　(B) breakups　　(C) breakdowns　　(D) breakthroughs
19. (A) the farther was a planet away　　(B) the farther away a planet was
　　(C) farther a planet was away from　　(D) farther away a planet was
20. (A) sees　　(B) see　　(C) saw　　(D) seeing

二、文意選填

第 21 至 30 題為題組 —— 夢的解析

Since ancient times, humans have wondered if dreams are just random images or if they hold some deeper meaning. Many have __21__ to interpret dreams over the centuries. Perhaps the most famous interpreter of dreams is psychoanalyst Sigmund Freud, whose very name is synonymous with exploring dreams as a window into a deeper level of the mind. Today, the debate over just how __22__ dreams really are continues. But that hasn't stopped several writers from publishing their own ideas about some of the most commonly __23__ dreams.

A dream about teeth falling out is very common, despite being rather __24__. The most common __25__ is that losing teeth in a dream represents anxiety about losing power, strength, or courage. To lose teeth is to lose the most basic defense mechanism.

Another dream that may be familiar is the dream of being __26__ in public, for all to see. This dream is usually interpreted as a fear of being exposed to your peers as incompetent or faulty in some other way. A related dream that many reports having is being late or unprepared __27__ an important exam. This dream is about the anxiety of being unable to cope __28__ the challenges of the real world. Sometimes these two dreams are combined and the dreamer finds himself failing an exam while naked!

Many people dream about flying. This represents freedom, adventure, and an escape from the __29__ obligations of life. This can be very exciting, and we often have this dream if we need a change in our routine.

There is no real way of knowing how much dreams actually mean. However, because dreams are such a big part of the human experience, we won't stop __30__ them any time soon!

(A) naked	(B) with	(C) meaningful	(D) analyzing	(E) bizarre
(F) occurring	(G) interpretation	(H) dull	(I) for	(J) attempted

三、 108 課綱 ｜ 篇章結構

> 說明：第 31 題至第 35 題，每題一個空格。請依文意在文章後所提供的 (A) 到 (E) 選項中分別選出最適當者，填入空格中，使篇章結構清晰有條理。

第 31 至 35 題為題組 —— 科技潮流

Live streaming is the latest online craze. As the name implies, streaming is live video, in the moment with no editing. __31__ Viewers can respond to the performer, making live streaming the ultimate in social media: immediate video interaction in real time. Streaming is very popular with teenagers and some broadcasters even earn good money for streams of comedy, playing videogames, or just chatting. __32__

When young people make themselves accessible online, they sometimes become targets for "trolls," or cruel individuals who enjoy making others feel bad. __33__ Repeated harassment is called cyber-bullying and can have psychological consequences. More dangerous are individuals online looking to take advantage of teens or children.

__34__ Some might even attempt to obtain the streamer's personal information. Underage streamers should also be aware that anything they broadcast can be recorded. __35__ The internet is a powerful tool for creativity, but young people must be made aware of its many dangers.

(A) They may engage in inappropriate contact, or attempt to provoke broadcasters into sharing sexual content.
(B) It can be broadcast to anyone who wants to tune in, or to a select audience.
(C) If they engage in offensive or embarrassing behavior in the moment during a stream, it can potentially haunt them later in life.
(D) They may bombard streamers with hurtful comments or post offensive content.
(E) However, underage individuals must be wary of the dangers of streaming.

第貳部分：非選擇題

一、中譯英 —— 電子競技

> 說明：1. 請將以下中文句子譯成正確、通順、達意的英文。
>   2. 請依序作答，並標明子題號（1、2）。

1. 運動員不一定需要抵達終點線才能贏得比賽。事實上，有些人可能是專業的電子競技運動員，他們贏得許多虛擬比賽。

2. 但大眾大多分不清電玩與電競，導致電競選手常常被批評浪費時間、不務正業。

二、英文作文 —— 哲學思考

> 說明：1. 依提示在「答案卷」上寫一篇英文作文。
>
>   2. 文長至少 120 個單詞（words）。

提示： 在電影《鐘點戰》（*In Time*）中，時間取代貨幣成為一種奢侈品，此概念類似美國詩人卡爾桑德堡（Carl Sandburg）之名言：Time is the only coin in your life. It is the only coin you have, and the only coin you can determine how it will spent. Be careful lest you let other people spend it for you. 你認為桑德堡所想表達的意思是什麼？請寫一篇英文作文，第一段詮釋這幾句話的意思，第二段舉例加以佐證。

第壹部分：選擇題

一、綜合測驗

> 說明：第 1 題至第 20 題，每題一個空格，請依文意選出最適當的一個選項。

第 1 至 10 題為題組 —— 地震

Earthquakes can strike with little or no warning. If you live in an area prone to earthquakes, it is important to take __1__. __2__, you can minimize the damage to your home and injury __3__ yourself and others. Preparation is the key.

The safety of yourself and your loved ones is of primary importance. It is wise to have a first aid kit prepared. Always make sure your phone is charged. Decide __4__ a safe location for your family to meet in case you are separated. When a quake strikes, hide beneath a __5__ table or desk. If you can't get to something like this, stand in a doorway or against an interior wall, away from windows. If you __6__, try to quickly turn off the stove.

You can take steps to make your home as earthquake-proof as possible. Make sure heavy items, __7__ refrigerators and cabinets, are fixed. Make sure bookcases, mounted televisions, and artwork are __8__ to the wall as much as possible. Don't hang heavy mirrors or picture frames above beds, so they don't fall onto people __9__ there.

After an earthquake, immediately check yourself and your loved ones for any injuries and apply first aid. Call for emergency assistance if __10__. Do not enter your home or any other building that has been damaged. Earthquakes may only last a few minutes, but the damage they can cause is serious. A little preparation can minimize their threat.

1. (A) procrastinations (B) precautions (C) processes (D) precisions
2. (A) This way (B) On the way (C) No way (D) By the way
3. (A) to (B) in (C) at (D) into
4. (A) to (B) in (C) on (D) at
5. (A) staggering (B) strategic (C) static (D) sturdy
6. (A) have cooked (B) had cooked (C) are cooking (D) are cooked
7. (A) such as (B) excluding (C) besides (D) except
8. (A) seduced (B) secluded (C) smashed (D) secured
9. (A) sleep (B) slept (C) under sleep (D) sleeping
10. (A) need (B) needed (C) needing (D) be needed

In August 2009, Typhoon Morakot struck Taiwan with brutal force. __11__, over 500 people lost their lives in the flooding and landslides __12__ by the typhoon. As the nation struggled to recover, many blamed the government for slow and __13__ response.

In Hsiao-lin village, Kaohsiung county, a severe landslide buried around 400 people. __14__, hope __15__ they would be found alive had to be abandoned. The relatives of the victims didn't want heavy digging equipment to be used, for fear their loved ones' bodies would be damaged. A park memorializing this sad incident was built on the site.

Thousands of people living in rural, mountainous, or isolated areas found themselves __16__ and cut off from resources. These residents could not access food or fresh water for days because sections of the mountain road had been destroyed. Despite their dangerous situation, government officials argued they were safe where they were.

Then-President Ma Ying-jeou was heavily criticized __17__ his refusal to accept some forms of aid from foreign governments. Some government sources claimed the reason for this refusal is that it was believed that guiding foreign rescue workers to the sites where they were needed would be an unnecessary use of resources. Ma blamed a typing error for __18__ about the need for foreign assistance. This only __19__ the public perception that rescue efforts were in disarray. __20__, the government can learn from this tragedy and be better prepared for any future disasters.

---

11. (A) Terminally   (B) Temperamentally   (C) Tragically   (D) Temporarily
12. (A) caused   (B) which caused   (C) that caused   (D) causing
13. (A) insignificant   (B) infinite   (C) inaccurate   (D) inadequate
14. (A) Effectively   (B) Eventually   (C) Efficiently   (D) Elegantly
15. (A) why   (B) where   (C) what   (D) that
16. (A) stacked   (B) stranded   (C) strained   (D) stained
17. (A) at   (B) on   (C) for   (D) with
18. (A) miscommunication (B) misbehavior   (C) mischief   (D) miracle
19. (A) reinstated   (B) respected   (C) reinforced   (D) reigned
20. (A) Hopefully   (B) Hopelessly   (C) Highly   (D) Honorably

二、文意選填

第 21 至 30 題為題組 —— 火山爆發

Japan's Mount Fuji is famous around the world. Images of this elegant landmark have come to __21__ Japan itself. The smooth, snow-capped cone of Fuji rises 3,776 meters toward the sky. This natural wonder lies near the Pacific Ocean and about 60 miles west of Japan's capital city, Tokyo. Fuji and its __22__ area were designated a UNESCO World Heritage Site in 2013.

Fuji is a volcano. Though it hasn't __23__ since 1707, many geologists consider it to still be active. The age of the mountain is unclear, but the first peaks probably began to form due to volcanic activities 600,000 years ago. It is part of the Fuji Volcanic Zone, a __24__ of volcanoes that stretches from Japan to the Mariana Islands. The base of the volcano is about 78 miles in circumference.

How Fuji got its name is unclear. It might be an ancient word for "fire" __25__ with a more modern Japanese word for "mountain." This would make sense for a volcano! When Fuji is written in kanji, which are Chinese ideograms, the name seems to be more about good luck.

The area around Fuji attracts a great deal of __26__. Many people from all over the world come to climb the mountain. Often they set out on this journey at night, in order to time their arrival at the summit with the sunrise. For some, this is more than just an adventure; it's a __27__ practice. Fuji still has spiritual __28__ for many. Until 1868, women were __29__ to climb Fuji, for religious reasons. There are even shrines at the peak of the mountain. This beautiful mountain is rich with history and sits at the center of Japanese identity. Eternal Fuji continues to __30__.

(A) erupted   (B) forbidden   (C) combined   (D) surrounding   (E) significance

(F) tourism   (G) religious   (H) represent   (I) fascinate   (J) chain

三、 NEW 108 課綱 ｜ 篇章結構

說明：第 31 題至第 35 題，每題一個空格。請依文意在文章後所提供的 (A) 到 (E) 選項中分別選出最適當者，填入空格中，使篇章結構清晰有條理。

第 31 至 35 題為題組 —— 土石流

A landslide is a frightening and potentially destructive occurrence in nature. It is when ground that is on a slope gives way and tumbles with a downward movement. __31__ There are various kinds of landslide. These include falls, topples, slides, spreads and flows. Each term describes a different kind of movement.

There are several causes of landslides. __32__ Heavy rainfall over a short period of time can create fast-moving floods of mud and other debris. Longer periods of rainfall contribute to a slower movement of ground. Exposed rock can be fractured or layered, and may finally split apart. The roots of trees and other vegetation often work to hold the soil together. After deforestation or a forest fire, an area can be much more vulnerable to landslides. Some terrain is more likely to experience landslides. __33__ The western United States endures a good deal of landslides. This is the home of the steep Rocky Mountain range.

Other mountainous nations must deal with landslides. These include Switzerland, with its famous Alps, and the countries that contain the towering Himalayas, such as Pakistan, Nepal, and India. __34__ After heavy rains in Uganda, part of Mount Elgon collapsed, killing 34 people, also in 2018. __35__ Early detection systems continue to improve, but landslides remain a risk in mountainous areas.

(A) In 2018, an earthquake in Hokkaido, Japan triggered a landslide that crushed nearby homes and killed sixteen citizens
(B) Mountainous areas prone to heavy rain are particularly dangerous.
(C) This can cause destruction of property, blockage of roadways, injuries, and even death
(D) Volcanic activity can cause the land to shift and begin to slide.
(E) A year earlier, in Xinmo, China, giant rocks destroyed homes and a hotel. Tragically, over 100 people died.

第貳部分：非選擇題

一、中譯英 —— 食物耗損

> 說明：1. 請將以下中文句子譯成正確、通順、達意的英文。
> 　　　2. 請依序作答，並標明子題號（1、2）。

1. 在已開發國家，多達三分之一的食物可能會被浪費並且最後落入掩埋場。

2. 這是一個嚴重的經濟和環境問題，因為被浪費的食物花了資源來生產，包括大量的水、土地和肥料。

二、英文作文 —— 氣候變遷

> 說明：1. 依提示在「答案卷」上寫一篇英文作文。
>
>   2. 文長至少 120 個單詞（words）。

請看以下圖片，試述全球暖化可能會對地球和我們的生活造成什麼影響，以及你對全球暖化有什麼樣的看法、建議等。

第壹部分：選擇題

一、綜合測驗

> 說明：第 1 題至第 20 題，每題一個空格，請依文意選出最適當的一個選項。

第 1 至 10 題為題組 —— 交通守則

All around the world, drunk driving is considered a serious __1__. Drunk driving can cause __2__ damage, injuries, and death. Most countries __3__ heavy penalties for driving while drunk, though the punishments vary.

Drunk driving is frowned upon in Asia. Many Asian countries have a "zero tolerance" policy, meaning drivers are not allowed to __4__ any alcohol before driving. Despite the long history of drinking culture in Europe, many countries also __5__ zero tolerance. Any trace of alcohol in a driver's blood will result in fines, suspension of driver's license, and even time in jail.

Australia's legal BAC (blood alcohol concentration) is 0.05%. The United States, Canada, and Mexico are a little more __6__ at 0.08% BAC. However, all these countries use checkpoints and sobriety tests to catch drunk drivers __7__ the act.

Drunk driving in South Africa can earn the offender up to six years in jail. Many countries in the Middle East ban alcohol altogether. __8__, their penalties for drunk driving can be very __9__, including up to ten years in prison. In the United Arab Emirates, an offender can even receive 80 lashes.

Driving after consuming alcohol is dangerous, and these punishments are meant to __10__ people who may feel like they can risk it. Clearly, no matter where you are in the world, drunk driving is simply not worth it!

1. (A) crisis   (B) crime   (C) crash   (D) chaos
2. (A) personality   (B) prospect   (C) property   (D) prosperity
3. (A) impose   (B) impress   (C) improve   (D) induce
4. (A) be consume   (B) been consumed   (C) have consumed   (D) had consumed
5. (A) enroll   (B) endure   (C) enforce   (D) entail
6. (A) forgiving   (B) forcing   (C) forming   (D) facing
7. (A) in   (B) on   (C) with   (D) at
8. (A) Otherwise   (B) Therefore   (C) However   (D) In contrast
9. (A) hasty   (B) hardy   (C) handy   (D) harsh
10. (A) delegate   (B) derive   (C) depict   (D) deter

第 11 至 20 題為題組 —— 青少年犯罪

For decades, parents have been concerned that the violent imagery of some video games is negatively affecting their own children's behavior. But is this really the case? The debate is ongoing.

Home video gaming __11__ poplar since the 1980s. The latest craze is *Fortnite*. Although *Fortnite's* design is cartoonish and fun, as opposed to other more __12__ games, the action still consists of shooting as many opponents as possible. Many parents are shocked by this focus on firearms violence.

Different studies __13__ conflicting data. In 2015, The American Psychiatric Association published a statement that research showed violent games directly lead to an increase in aggressive behavior __14__ players. But many who research __15__ health disagreed, and sent a strong response to the APA. 230 scholars __16__ the APA's statement as "misleading and alarmist." More recently, a subdivision of the APA itself which focuses on the media cautioned news outlets __17__ blaming real-world violence on games.

More recent studies have not found any significant link between violent games and real violence or other negative behavior. __18__, some studies show that the popularity of games, even violent ones, might be linked to a decrease in real __19__ of aggression. There may be a publication bias in __20__ studies stating that video games lead to violent behavior, because games are an easy target to blame. It is wise to keep in mind that with the problem of violence, the causes may be complex.

---

11. (A) is   (B) was   (C) has been   (D) had been
12. (A) gracious   (B) greedy   (C) guilty   (D) grim
13. (A) yearn   (B) yield   (C) yell   (D) yawn
14. (A) in   (B) on   (C) at   (D) with
15. (A) adolescent   (B) adult   (C) activist   (D) addict
16. (A) demanded   (B) determined   (C) dismissed   (D) disrupted
17. (A) upon   (B) against   (C) beyond   (D) without
18. (A) Therefore   (B) However   (C) In fact   (D) Since
19. (A) incentives   (B) infections   (C) incidents   (D) institutions
20. (A) previous   (B) primary   (C) probable   (D) profound

二、文意選填

第 21 至 30 題為題組 —— 貪汙誠信

Corruption is a problem that affects all governments. Once it is allowed to take hold, its negative __21__ spread to all aspects of the government as if it is __22__. Public policies become less fair and effective. Citizens sense that the government is no longer working for them and lose faith in its leaders. Corruption must be dealt with seriously as it arises.

Countries with higher levels of corruption collect less tax __23__. This is because powerful individuals pay __24__ to avoid paying taxes. Less taxes collected means projects __25__ to benefit the public go underfunded. When citizens realize this, they may seek to avoid paying taxes themselves, as they can't see any benefit in doing so. Another form of corruption is spending taxpayers' money on unnecessary or __26__ products or services. This can lead to substandard work on crucial things such as roads, buildings, and bridges. The safety of those who must use these things may be __27__.

This leads to public mistrust of government, which undermines the entire society. Fortunately, there are ways to minimize corruption, through robust __28__ designed to monitor and root out misdeeds. The public must be able to report on the government. Citizens must have a way to express their concerns, free __29__ fear of punishment. Several South American countries provide an online platform through which corruption in public projects can be reported. A free press, without government oversight, is crucial.

Old institutions __30__ government should usually be reformed if they are found to harbor corruption. As the nations of the world become more interconnected, international anti-corruption organizations should be created. Corruption is an ongoing problem, but the risks of letting it go unchecked are far too great.

(A) consequences	(B) within	(C) revenue	(D) intended	(E) inefficient
(F) bribes	(G) disregarded	(H) institutions	(I) from	(J) contagious

第 31 至 35 題為題組 —— 爭取人權

Taiwan has perhaps been the most gay-friendly country in Asia for over a decade. Taipei is home to a thriving gay community and hosts Asia's largest gay pride parade. In 2019, the parade was even more festive than usual, because lawmakers made Taiwan the first Asian nation to legalize same-sex marriage.

Since then, thousands of gay couples have wed. Many heterosexuals also support gay marriage, stating that having one's union legally recognized is a human right for everyone. __31__

Not everyone is celebrating, though. __32__ Immediately after Taiwan's Constitutional Court made gay marriage legal, several groups organized in opposition to the ruling. Religious and conservative groups favored same-sex unions that were limited in nature as opposed to true marriage. __33__ Those opposed to marriage equality warned President Tsai Ing-wen that she would be voted out in the January elections. __34__

Still, gay marriage in Taiwan is not exactly equivalent to heterosexual marriage. Gay couples can not adopt children, though they may raise any biological children they may have. __35__ But many are still excited for the future of gay rights in Taiwan.

Legalizing gay marriage is just a part of many socially progressive policies Taiwan has instituted in recent years. Taiwan is seen as an example of democracy in action within the region.

(A) But most voters were more concerned with economic issues and Taiwan's strained relationship with China.

(B) As in the United States and elsewhere, many people are deeply opposed to gay marriage.

(C) They launched legal challenges, but were defeated in parliament.

(D) Many of the newly-wed gay couples were among Taipei's recent parade and celebration, with attendance estimated to be over 200,000.

(E) Also, Taiwan will not recognize marriage if one of the partners is a foreigner from a country that does not have gay marriage.

第貳部分：非選擇題

一、中譯英 —— 政治腐敗

> 說明：1. 請將以下中文句子譯成正確、通順、達意的英文。
>   2. 請依序作答，並標明子題號（1、2）。

1. 如同眾所周知的，絕對的權力導致絕對的腐敗，也因此，強大的政府很難擺脫掉貪汙的指控。

2. 如果這種混亂的政治風氣不改變的話，政府不只無法為人民服務，同時也會讓大眾對政府失去信心。

二、英文作文 —— 求職履歷

畢業季即將來臨，許多社會新鮮人及學生將陸續投入職場或工讀行列。網路大型求職平台廣大徵才，為多項專業領域開立職缺及廣泛開放人才招募。假設你是一位今年大學剛畢業的新鮮人，請在徵才平台上投遞英文求職信函，職務不拘。第一段簡單作自我介紹，並表明要應徵的職位，第二段表明為何你適任這份工作。信末署名請遵照規範，男生用 Xiao Ming，女生用 Hui Mei。文長至少 120 個單詞（words）。

第壹部分：選擇題

一、綜合測驗

說明：第 1 題至第 20 題，每題一個空格，請依文意選出最適當的一個選項。

第 1 至 10 題為題組 —— 生態保育

The leopard cat, commonly __1__ "shi hu" in Chinese, is the only remaining wild cat in Taiwan now that the Formosan clouded leopard is thought to be extinct. Leopard cats are roughly the size of housecats with black-spotted fur and thrive at elevations of around 500 meters. Sadly, leopard cats are frequently lost to road kills and poisoning, and there are now approximately 500 animals __2__ in Taiwan.

The habitats of leopard cats are at risk partly __3__ economic development. In Chuolan, an urban town in Miaoli County, __4__, a wetland park was established to provide space for locals to relax in their free time. As it turns out, however, the park was built __5__ this endangered species of wild cat. The greatest __6__ of this situation is that the public is calling this "nature park" a "memorial park" for leopard cats, __7__ part of their habitat was destroyed in the process of creating a recreation space for humans.

Aside from habitat destruction, leopard cats also suffer from pesticide ingested through their prey, as well as road deaths __8__ increased traffic in rural areas. Perhaps the most shocking deaths are those __9__ hunting and trapping, especially in Miaoli, where the cats pose a threat to farmers' free-range chickens. When these chickens become part of leopard cats' diet, farmers set up traps and hire hunters to kill these predators, __10__ understanding the negative impact their actions may have on the natural world.

---

1. (A) known   (B) called as   (C) known as   (D) called for
2. (A) leave   (B) left   (C) leaving   (D) having left
3. (A) because of   (B) in spite of   (C) instead of   (D) regardless of
4. (A) on the contrary   (B) in addition   (C) for instance   (D) after all
5. (A) in accordance with   (B) with the exception of   (C) in terms of   (D) at the expense of
6. (A) irony   (B) insight   (C) prospect   (D) provision
7. (A) on   (B) in   (C) with   (D) as
8. (A) accused of   (B) associated with   (C) removed from   (D) mistaken for
9. (A) resulting from   (B) resulting in   (C) resulted from   (D) resulted in
10. (A) for   (B) without   (C) beyond   (D) upon

Visitors to top hotels in India encounter __11__ has now become a daily routine: a body scan and a __12__ inspection of their belongings. For those who arrive by car, guards look inside the vehicle's trunk and under the hood. These __13__ were put in place after Nov. 26, 2008, when terrorists attacked several of Mumbai's most famous sites, including the city's iconic Taj Mahal Palace Hotel.

The 2008 attacks, widely __14__ to members of one of the most notorious terrorist organizations in South Asia, Lashkar-e-Taiba, __15__ in the news again because of the recent suicide bombings in Sri Lanka, which __16__ more than 300 lives. India's 2008 experience is also back in the public consciousness because of the new film *Hotel Mumbai*. Starring famous international actors and actresses, the movie provides a powerful __17__ of the assault that gripped the country's financial capital for nearly 72 hours. __18__ the attacks targeted several locations—a crowded railway __19__ , a Jewish community center, and two hotels—the movie focuses on three days and nights of horror mostly within one hotel, the glamorous Taj. __20__ the bravery of local police officers and the selfless deeds of the Taj's staff, the death toll of the attacks could have been much higher.

11. (A) which   (B) that   (C) what   (D) where
12. (A) through   (B) thought   (C) though   (D) thorough
13. (A) practices   (B) effects   (C) strategies   (D) approaches
14. (A) attributed   (B) contributed   (C) admitted   (D) referred
15. (A) is   (B) are   (C) being   (D) has been
16. (A) claimed   (B) reared   (C) stated   (D) pained
17. (A) account   (B) division   (C) conduct   (D) harmony
18. (A) While   (B) However   (C) Besides   (D) Since
19. (A) arrival   (B) denial   (C) terminal   (D) commercial
20. (A) Were it not for (B) Had it not been for (C) Should it not for (D) Were it to be

二、文意選填

第 21 至 30 題為題組 —— 年長者照護

When it comes to home care for the elderly, there are several factors that should be taken into   21   . First, every senior has their own needs. It's common knowledge that the greater a person's   22   , the greater his or her needs. When seniors have needs that can't be met by themselves or their caregivers, they may become impatient and irritated. Some seniors, however,   23   that they are content with what they have, though this is less common. All in all, there is a large gap that caregivers have to   24   .

Second, when faced with the task of caring for a senior citizen, you should bear in mind that every senior is human and should be treated as such. They are   25   to the same level freedom that adults enjoy. That is the   26   you should take when providing care to the elderly. You can help them   27   their dignity by always treating them with respect. Elder people should be encouraged to complete tasks on their own when possible, but shouldn't be criticized when they fail. Moreover, make it a   28   to be understanding. They may sometimes act like babies, but this kind of behavior is never   29   .

Finally, you should try to be a good confidant to the senior you care for. Make sure to spend time talking to them and be a good listener when they share things with you. It is vital to be like a friend to the person you are caring for. Caring for the elderly can be challenging, but if you listen to their needs and are   30   , you're sure to have a rewarding experience.

(A) fill   (B) entitled   (C) consideration   (D) priority   (E) perspective

(F) disability   (G) retain   (H) intentional   (I) indicate   (J) reliable

說明：第 31 題至第 35 題，每題一個空格。請依文意在文章後所提供的 (A) 到 (E) 選項中分別選出最適當者，填入空格中，使篇章結構清晰有條理。

第 31 至 35 題為題組 —— 氣候變遷

Time is running out for the inhabitants of Pacific Island nations. Research suggests that climate change will spell disaster for the islands—, and many others—by the end of this century. __31__ But the famously scenic islands may face an even more immediate threat.

As sea levels rise, more salt water will enter the islands' aquifers. __32__ It acts as a kind of reservoir and can be tapped into via wells. When the aquifer is inundated with ocean water, its purity is affected, and the water is rendered undrinkable. This is bad news for those who depend on this source of fresh water.

If this bleak projection proves true, islanders will be forced to collect rainfall or rely on expensive imported freshwater. __33__ Many will be forced to leave their homelands behind and emigrate to distant countries. This disturbance in the lives of Pacific Islanders will be a great climate injustice. The Pacific Island nations are small and have contributed only 0.03 percent of the greenhouse gasses which are causing climate change. __34__

Climate experts say this doomsday scenario is not yet inevitable. But we must act soon. __35__ The collective human race must stage a global intervention on behalf of all humanity. The clock is ticking.

(A) An aquifer is a mass of porous rock that collects freshwater when it falls as rain.

(B) Yet, they are among the first countries to be dramatically endangered.

(C) The more powerful nations of the world must cooperate with a decisive plan of action.

(D) Rising sea levels means waves will ravage more of the inland areas, and some of the low-lying islands will be submerged completely.

(E) Likely, water will become a scarce commodity, and the standard of living on the islands will deteriorate.

第貳部分：非選擇題

一、中譯英 —— 替代能源

> 說明：1. 請將以下中文句子譯成正確、通順、達意的英文。
> 　　　2. 請依序作答，並標明子題號（1、2）。

1. 科學家們一直在尋求各種環保的方法來替代石油和煤炭，一些常見的方法包括了太陽能以及風力發電。

2. 然而，這些方法並不是沒有缺點的。舉例來說，核能發電廠會產生大量的廢料，而太陽能需要非常昂貴的器材。

二、英文作文 —— 陳情訴求

以下是一個國際疾病救治網站，請參考網頁上的訊息，然後在下一頁的表格中，寫一封陳情書，為一個世界傳染病的防治發聲。寫陳情書時，請依據第一個箭號提示處的建議（Use strong language...），填入陳情書的標題，並依據第二個箭號提示處的建議（Describe what happened, why you're concerned, and what you want to happen now.），以 120 字寫一封陳情書。

EPIDEMIC PETITIONS

It's time to stand together on epidemic prevention!

Epidemics have threatened humans even before history, but the "precautions" and "conversations" that bring about a collective response are a relatively new phenomenon. International concerns help shape the global health landscape. And our actions today have a tremendous impact on the earth and our future!

Start a Petition

DENGUE FEVER

Worsening threats of global warming and climate change have made the insect rage on fiercely! Our actions today have a tremendous impact on the earth and our future!

33,437 SUPPORTING Sign NOW

RABIES

A vaccine-preventable viral disease. Dogs are the main source of human rabies deaths.

35,248 SUPPORTING Sign NOW

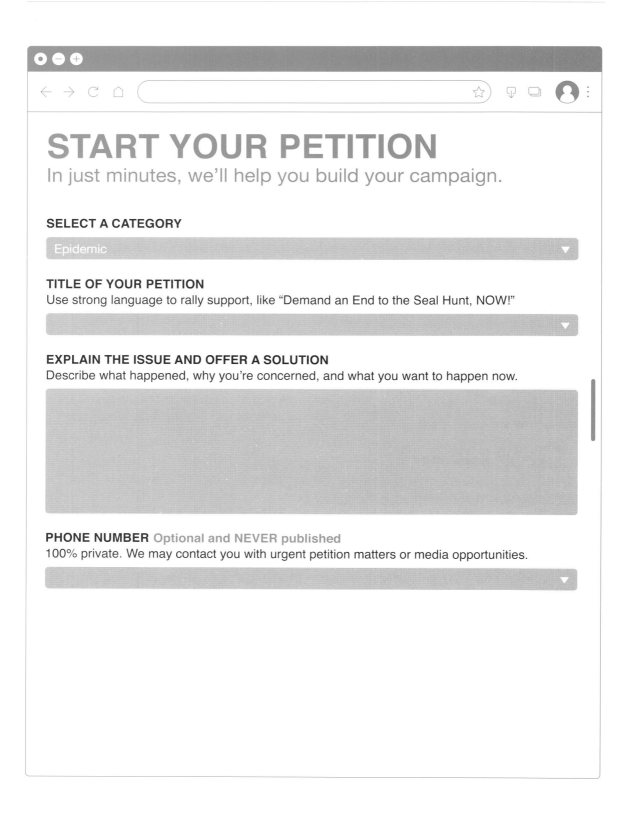

START YOUR PETITION

In just minutes, we'll help you build your campaign.

SELECT A CATEGORY

Epidemic ▼

TITLE OF YOUR PETITION

Use strong language to rally support, like "Demand an End to the Seal Hunt, NOW!"

▼

EXPLAIN THE ISSUE AND OFFER A SOLUTION

Describe what happened, why you're concerned, and what you want to happen now.

PHONE NUMBER Optional and NEVER published

100% private. We may contact you with urgent petition matters or media opportunities.

▼

NOTE

解 答

第 1 回

第壹部分：選擇題

一、綜合測驗

1. (B)　2. (A)　3. (A)　4. (B)　5. (D)　6. (B)　7. (C)　8. (A)　9. (A)　10. (D)
11. (C)　12. (A)　13. (C)　14. (A)　15. (D)　16. (A)　17. (B)　18. (B)　19. (D)　20. (B)

二、文意選填

21. (H)　22. (B)　23. (A)　24. (D)　25. (I)　26. (E)　27. (C)　28. (F)　29. (J)　30. (G)

三、篇章結構

31. (C)　32. (A)　33. (E)　34. (B)　35. (D)

第貳部分：非選擇題

※ 參考答案請直接看解析頁 P.78-79

第 2 回

第壹部分：選擇題

一、綜合測驗

1. (B)　2. (D)　3. (B)　4. (A)　5. (B)　6. (C)　7. (C)　8. (C)　9. (C)　10. (D)
11. (B)　12. (B)　13. (D)　14. (C)　15. (D)　16. (C)　17. (A)　18. (A)　19. (C)　20. (B)

二、文意選填

21. (B)　22. (I)　23. (A)　24. (D)　25. (F)　26. (C)　27. (J)　28. (H)　29. (G)　30. (E)

三、篇章結構

31. (C)　32. (B)　33. (E)　34. (A)　35. (D)

第貳部分：非選擇題

※ 參考答案請直接看解析頁 P.102-103

第 3 回

第壹部分：選擇題

一、綜合測驗

1. (D)   2. (A)   3. (B)   4. (B)   5. (C)   6. (A)   7. (A)   8. (D)   9. (C)   10. (D)
11. (B)   12. (C)   13. (B)   14. (A)   15. (A)   16. (D)   17. (C)   18. (D)   19. (B)   20. (A)

二、文意選填

21. (J)   22. (C)   23. (F)   24. (E)   25. (G)   26. (A)   27. (I)   28. (B)   29. (H)   30. (D)

三、篇章結構

31. (B)   32. (E)   33. (D)   34. (A)   35. (C)

第貳部分：非選擇題

※ 參考答案請直接看解析頁 P.126-127

第 4 回

第壹部分：選擇題

一、綜合測驗

1. (B)   2. (A)   3. (A)   4. (C)   5. (D)   6. (C)   7. (A)   8. (D)   9. (D)   10. (B)
11. (C)   12. (A)   13. (D)   14. (B)   15. (D)   16. (B)   17. (C)   18. (A)   19. (C)   20. (A)

二、文意選填

21. (H)   22. (D)   23. (A)   24. (J)   25. (C)   26. (F)   27. (G)   28. (E)   29. (B)   30. (I)

三、篇章結構

31. (C)   32. (D)   33. (B)   34. (A)   35. (E)

第貳部分：非選擇題

※ 參考答案請直接看解析頁 P.151-152

第 5 回

第壹部分：選擇題

一、綜合測驗

1. (B)　　2. (C)　　3. (A)　　4. (C)　　5. (C)　　6. (A)　　7. (A)　　8. (B)　　9. (D)　　10. (D)

11. (C)　　12. (D)　　13. (B)　　14. (A)　　15. (A)　　16. (C)　　17. (B)　　18. (C)　　19. (C)　　20. (A)

二、文意選填

21. (A)　　22. (J)　　23. (C)　　24. (F)　　25. (D)　　26. (E)　　27. (G)　　28. (H)　　29. (I)　　30. (B)

三、篇章結構

31. (D)　　32. (B)　　33. (C)　　34. (A)　　35. (E)

第貳部分：非選擇題

※ 參考答案請直接看解析頁 P.178-179

第 6 回

第壹部分：選擇題

一、綜合測驗

1. (C)　　2. (B)　　3. (A)　　4. (C)　　5. (D)　　6. (A)　　7. (D)　　8. (B)　　9. (A)　　10. (B)

11. (C)　　12. (D)　　13. (A)　　14. (D)　　15. (B)　　16. (A)　　17. (A)　　18. (A)　　19. (C)　　20. (B)

二、文意選填

21. (C)　　22. (F)　　23. (I)　　24. (A)　　25. (B)　　26. (E)　　27. (G)　　28. (D)　　29. (H)　　30. (J)

三、篇章結構

31. (D)　　32. (A)　　33. (E)　　34. (B)　　35. (C)

第貳部分：非選擇題

※ 參考答案請直接看解析頁 P.201-208

解析

第壹部分：選擇題

一、綜合測驗

第 1 至 10 題為題組 —— 校園生活

Students all around the world are excited and nervous __1__ returning to school each year. Many cultures have traditions to celebrate this day and ease students through the transition from carefree summer fun to school year __2__.

In the countries __3__ were formerly part of the Soviet Union–__4__ Russia, Ukraine, and Belarus–September 1st is known __5__ Knowledge Day. It is a time of celebration and entertainment, to welcome children back. If September 1st falls on a weekend, Knowledge Day is moved to the closest weekday. Students and their parents gather to __6__ the ceremonies. Russian students also bring their teachers flowers, and the teacher gives them balloons __7__.

In Japan, students often pack a special lunch on the first day. This meal of seaweed sauce, quail eggs, and rice is thought to bring good luck for the coming year of study. German children are given a *Schultuete* on the first day of school. *Schultuete* roughly translates to "school cone," and it is a large, colorful paper cone __8__ treats, toys, and school supplies.

For many children, back-to-school time is fun and enjoyable. __9__ may find it stressful and miss the days of summer vacation. But for all students, the return to class is an important occasion, __10__ another year along the path to adulthood.

譯文

全世界的學生每年都對開學日既期待又緊張。許多文化都有著慶祝這一天的傳統，舒緩學生從無憂無慮的快樂暑假到嚴守紀律的學校生活間的過渡心情。

在部分前蘇聯國家，例如俄羅斯、烏克蘭和白俄羅斯，9 月 1 號為知識日。這天是來慶祝、歡迎小孩回到學校的娛樂活動，如果 9 月 1 號是週末的話，知識日會移到最接近的平日。學生及家長會一起參與慶祝活動，俄羅斯的學生也會給老師花，而老師會回送氣球。

在日本，學生會在第一天帶特別的便當，內容包含海苔醬、鵪鶉蛋和白飯，象徵著為新的學年帶來好運。德國孩子會在開學日收到 *Schultuete*，*Schultuete* 按字面翻譯為「學校甜筒」，是一個五彩繽紛且大型的紙作甜筒，裡面放滿了零食、玩具和學校用品。

對很多孩子來說，開學期間是充滿歡樂及有趣的；有些人或許會覺得充滿壓力，想念暑假的日子，但對每個學生而言，回學校上課是重要的階段，讓來年繼續往成人邁進。

1. (A) for   **(B) about**   (C) with   (D) in

> **解說** be nervous about 對…感到緊張

2. **(A) discipline**   (B) deficiency   (C) depression   (D) dignity
   (A) 紀律   (B) 缺乏   (C) 沮喪   (D) 尊嚴

3. **(A) which**   (B) where   (C) what   (D) when

> **解說** which 為關係代名詞，修飾前方先行詞 countries，也可以使用 that。關係副詞 where，when 後方都必須接上完整子句；what 前方不可有先行詞。

4. (A) regarding   **(B) such as**   (C) considering   (D) given
   (A) 關於   **(B) 例如**   (C) 就…而論、如果考量到   (D) 假定、考慮到…

5. (A) at   (B) to   (C) for   **(D) as**

> **解說** be known as 是「以某身分出名」

6. (A) get along with   **(B) take part in**   (C) turn down   (D) run into
   (A) 與…和睦相處   **(B) 參加**   (C) 拒絕   (D) 偶然碰到

7. (A) in charge   (B) in advance   **(C) in return**   (D) in action
   (A) 負責   (B) 預先   **(C) 作為回報**   (D) 在運轉中

8. **(A) carpeted with**   (B) packed with   (C) equipped with   (D) faced with
   (A) 被…覆蓋   (B) 塞滿著   (C) 配有、有著（能力）   (D) 面對

9. **(A) Others**   (B) Another   (C) The other   (D) The others

> **解說** 前文提及「對很多小孩來說」，後文繼續論述「其他」小孩，為不指定的複數名詞用法，故選 (A) Others。

10. (A) marked   (B) mark   (C) to mark   **(D) marking**

> **解說** 分詞構句，原句型為 ..., and marks another... 因兩句主詞一致，省略第二句的主詞及連接詞，動詞 mark 為主動，轉為現在分詞 marking。

原文

Students all around the world **are** excited and **nervous about** returning to school each year. Many cultures have traditions to celebrate this day and [1]**ease** students through the [2]**transition** from carefree summer fun to school year [3]**discipline**.

In the countries which were formerly part of the Soviet Union—such as Russia, Ukraine, and Belarus—September 1st **is known as** Knowledge Day. It is a time of celebration and [4]**entertainment**, to welcome children back. If September 1st falls on a weekend, Knowledge Day is moved to the closest weekday. Students and their parents gather to **take part in** the [5]**ceremonies**. Russian students also bring their teachers flowers, and the teacher gives them balloons **in return**.

In Japan, students often pack a special lunch on the first day. This meal of seaweed sauce, [6]**quail** eggs, and rice is thought to bring good luck for the coming year of study. German children are given a *Schultuete* on the first day of school. *Schultuete* [7]**roughly** translates to "school cone," and it is a large, colorful paper cone packed with treats, toys, and school [8]**supplies**.

For many children back-to-school time is fun and enjoyable. Others may find it stressful and miss the days of summer vacation. But for all students, the return to class is an important occasion, marking another year along the path to adulthood.

重要單字

1. **ease** [iz] *(vt.)* 減輕、緩和 = (improve), relieve, soothe, assuage, alleviate, mitigate
   (n.) 輕鬆、容易、不費力
   → with (great/considerable) ease 非常輕鬆、不費吹灰之力
   → at ease 輕鬆自在地

2. **transition** [træn`zɪʃən] *(n.)* [C, U] 過渡（期）(+ from A to B) *(vi.)* 過渡到…(+ to/into)

3. **discipline** [`dɪsəplɪn] *(n.)* [U] 紀律 *(vt.)* 使有紀律、訓導
   → self-discipline *(n.)* 自我規範、自律
   → well-disciplined *(adj.)* 紀律嚴明的

4. **entertainment** [ˌɛntəˈtenmənt] *(n.)* [U] 娛樂
   → entertain *(vt.)* 娛樂、使歡樂；招待、款待
   → entertain sb. with sth. 用（某物）娛樂（某人）

5. **ceremony** [`sɛrəˌmonɪ] *(n.)* [C] 儀式、典禮；禮儀
   → ceremonial *(adj.)* 正式的、禮節的

6. **quail** [kwel] *(n.)* [C] 鵪鶉

7. **roughly** [ˈrʌflɪ] *(adv.)* 粗略地、大約地 = around, about, approximately

8. **supply** [səˈplaɪ] *(n.)* [C] 補給品；[U] 供給、供應 *(vt.)* 供應、供給
   → supply sb. with sth. 供應某物給某人 = supply sth. to sb.
   → be in short supply 短缺

重要片語

1. **be nervous about** 對…感到緊張

2. **be known** as + **身分、稱號** 以某身分出名
   be known for + **特色** 以某個特色知名
   be known to + **對象** 在哪些人間知名

3. **take part in**（主動、積極）參加 = participate in, partake in

4. **in return** 作為回報

5. **be packed with** 充滿、裝滿

相關文法句型

1. **分詞片語**
   例 *Schultuete* roughly translates to "school cone," and it is a large, colorful paper cone, **packed with** treats, toys, and school supplies.
   Schultuete 按字面翻譯為「學校甜筒」，是一個五彩繽紛且大型的紙做甜筒，裡面放滿了零食、玩具和學校用品。
   → 原句型為 a large, colorful paper cone, which is packed with...，**省略形容詞子句中的關係代名詞 which，動詞一律改為現在分詞**，故為 a large, colorful paper cone, (being) packed with...。

2. **分詞構句**
   例 But for all students, **the return** to class is an important occasion, **marking** another year along the path to adulthood.
   但對每個學生而言，回學校上課是重要的階段，讓來年繼續往成人邁進。
   → 原句型為 and it marks another year...。當前後對等子句主詞相同時（the return），可刪掉連接詞 and 以及第二個子句相同的主詞，動詞一律改為現在分詞 Ving。

It seems like we __11__ anxiety more and more these days. As our fast-paced world becomes increasingly demanding, it can be difficult to keep our feelings under __12__ . Maybe you or someone close to you has had the experience of tackling anxiety.

Anxiety is actually a function __13__ to the human brain. Evolution created a "fight or flight" response to help us survive the natural challenges of ancient times by preparing our bodies to __14__ combat an enemy __14__ run away. Now, fight or flight can be __15__ by daily stress, __16__ the hormone Cortisol into the brain. This pattern can become a habit our minds fall into at any sign of stress. __17__ , humans as a species have a great deal of control over their own minds and techniques for managing anxiety can be learned.

Someone __18__ anxiety should work to build a more positive self-perception. We are constantly telling a story about ourselves to ourselves and others. It is best to focus on the positive aspects of yourself and your life. After a while, you will internalize these thoughts and view yourself more positively.

It's also important to practice self-care. This means __19__ your own physical and mental needs, and trying to meet them. These can be healthy diet, exercise, enough sleep and relaxation. Soon, your body will get into this __20__ of self-care and you will find yourself thinking more clearly and better able to deal with anxiety.

譯文

近來,我們似乎越來越常與焦慮對抗。當快速變化的世界對我們越來越嚴苛,好好控管情緒就變得很困難,也許你自己或是親近之人都有過對抗焦慮的經驗。

其實焦慮是人腦與生俱來的機制。演化過程創造了「戰鬥或逃跑」的反應,不論是奮勇抗敵或是走為上策,都可以用來幫助我們迎戰古代大自然的挑戰。如今,戰鬥或逃跑反應可能來自生活壓力,它釋放荷爾蒙皮質醇到大腦裡。當心理感知到任何壓力的徵兆時,這可能會成為一種習慣。幸好,人是一種能有效控制心理的物種,且能學會管理焦慮的方法。

處理焦慮的人應該要努力建立更正面的自我認知。我們要不斷向自己或是他人講關於自己的故事,這樣最能夠專注於正向的自我與生活。一段時間後,你將會內化這些想法,並更正面地看待自己。

練習自我照顧也相當重要,這意味著要知道自己的生理及心理需求,並試著滿足它們。這些需求可能是健康的飲食、運動、充足的睡眠以及放鬆。很快地,你的身體會漸漸習慣自我照顧的機制,而且會發現自己的思緒更清楚,更能夠處理焦慮。

11. (A) belong to   (B) come up with   **(C) struggle with**   (D) rely on
     (A) 屬於   (B) 想出   **(C) 與…抗衡**   (D) 依靠

12. **(A) control**   (B) attack
     (C) consideration   (D) development
     (A) under control 在控制之下   (B) under attack 遭受攻擊
     (C) under consideration 納入考慮   (D) under development 正在開發中

13. (A) initial   (B) intimate   **(C) inherent**   (D) interior
     (A) 最初的   (B) 親密的   **(C) 與生俱來的**   (D) 內部的、室內的

14. **(A) either... or**   (B) neither... nor   (C) neither... or   (D) either... nor

> **解說** either...or 表「二擇一」；neither...nor 表達的是「既不…也不」

15. (A) triumphed   (B) treated   (C) tricked   **(D) triggered**
     (A) 獲得勝利   (B) 對待；治療   (C) 戲弄   **(D) 觸發**

16. **(A) releasing**   (B) released   (C) release   (D) to release

> **解說** 分詞片語，原句型為「..., which releases the...」，省略主格關代 which，動詞 release 轉為 releasing。

17. (A) Accordingly   **(B) Fortunately**   (C) Gradually   (D) Eventually
     (A) 因此   **(B) 幸運地**   (C) 逐步地   (D) 最後必然地

18. (A) restraining from   **(B) dealing with**   (C) insisting on   (D) conforming to
     (A) 抑止   **(B) 處理**   (C) 堅持要求   (D) 遵照

19. (A) recovering   (B) reckoning   (C) registering   **(D) recognizing**
     (A) 恢復   (B) 認為   (C) 登記   **(D) 認清、知道**

20. (A) reward   **(B) routine**   (C) ruin   (D) request
     (A) 報答；回饋   **(B) 例行公事**   (C) 摧毀   (D) 要求

原文

It seems like we ¹⁾**struggle** with ²⁾**anxiety** more and more these days. As our fast-paced world becomes increasingly ³⁾**demanding**, it can be difficult to keep our feelings under control. Maybe you or someone close to you has had the experience of tackling anxiety.

Anxiety is actually a function ⁴⁾**inherent** to the human brain. ⁵⁾**Evolution** created a "fight or flight" response to help us ⁶⁾**survive** the natural challenges of ⁷⁾**ancient** times by preparing our bodies to either ⁸⁾**combat** an ⁹⁾**enemy** or run away. Now, fight or flight can be ¹⁰⁾**triggered** by daily stress, ¹¹⁾**releasing** the hormone Cortisol into the brain. This ¹²⁾**pattern** can become a habit our minds fall into at any sign of stress. ¹³⁾**Fortunately**, humans as a ¹⁴⁾species have a great deal of control over their own minds and ¹⁵⁾**techniques** for managing anxiety can be learned.

Someone dealing with anxiety should work to build a more positive self-concept. We are constantly telling a story about ourselves to ourselves and others. It is best to focus on the positive ¹⁶⁾**aspects** of yourself and your life. After a while, you will ¹⁷⁾**internalize** these thoughts and view yourself more positively.

It's also important to practice self-care. This means ¹⁸⁾**recognizing** your own physical and mental needs, and trying to meet them. These can be healthy diet, exercise, enough sleep and ¹⁹⁾**relaxation**. Soon, your body will get into this ²⁰⁾**routine** of self-care and you will find yourself thinking more clearly and better able to deal with anxiety.

重要單字

1. **struggle** [ˋstrʌgl] *(vi.)* 奮鬥 *(n.)* [C] 奮鬥、鬥爭
   → struggle to + V$_R$ 奮力、努力做到⋯
   → struggle with/against + N 與⋯拚搏
   → struggle for + N 奮力爭取⋯
   → struggling *(adj.)* 艱難謀生過活的

2. **anxiety** [æŋˋzaɪətɪ] *(n.)* [U] 焦慮
   → anxious *(adj.)* 焦躁的、焦慮的
   → public anxiety 社交焦慮
   → arouse/provoke/cause/create/lead to anxiety 引起恐慌

3. **demanding** [dɪˋmændɪŋ] *(adj.)* 苛求的
   = （個性）unforgiving
   = （工作、任務）laborious, arduous, tough, tortuous

4. **inherent** [ɪnˋhɪrənt] *(adj.)* 與生俱來的 = inborn, innate, intrinsic, ingrained, instinctive

---

5. **evolution** [ˌɛvə`luʃən] *(n.)* [U] 演化
  → evolutionary *(adj.)* 演化（學）的；發展的、漸進的
  → evolutionary biologist 進化生物學家

6. **survive** [sə`vaɪv] *(vt.)* 倖存於 *(vi.)* 繼續生存、存活
  → 這個動詞可當及物動詞，直接加上受詞即可。

7. **ancient** [`enʃənt] *(adj.)* 古代的

8. **combat** [`kɑmbæt] *(vt.)* 與…戰鬥 *(vi.)* 戰鬥、搏鬥 (+ with/against/between) *(n.)* 戰鬥、格鬥
  → combatant *(n.)* 戰士、鬥士

9. **enemy** [`ɛnəmɪ] *(n.)* [C] 敵人
  → 近義字 competitor *(n.)* 競爭者
       opponent *(n.)* 對手
       rival *(n.)* 勁敵

10. **trigger** [`trɪɡə] *(vt.)* 引起、觸發 *(n.)* [C] 扳機

11. **release** [rɪ`lis] *(vt./n.)* 釋放

12. **pattern** [`pætən] *(n.)* [C] 模式、形態；花樣、圖案
  → a weather pattern 天氣型態／ a behavior pattern 行為模式／ a sleep pattern 睡眠型態／
    a speech pattern 措辭談吐／ a spending pattern 消費模式

13. **fortunately** [`fɔrtʃənɪtlɪ] *(adv.)* 幸運地

14. **species** [`spiʃiz] *(n.)* 物種（單複數同型）

15. **technique** [tɛk`nik] *(n.)* [C] 方法、技巧
  → use/devise/develop/learn a technique 運用／發明／學習一門技術

16. **aspect** [`æspɛkt] *(n.)* [C] 方面 = respect, angle, dimension, facet
  → in every aspect/respect = in all aspects/respects

17. **internalize** [ɪn`tɜnlˌaɪz] *(vt.)* 內化

18. **recognize** [`rɛkəɡˌnaɪz] *(vt.)* 認清、認知到；（在一群中）認出
  → recognition *(n.)* [U] 認可、承認；讚賞、表彰
  → in recognition **of** + N = in admiration **of** + N 讚賞…、為表揚…

19. **relaxation** [ˌrilæks`eʃən] *(n.)* [U] 放鬆
  → relaxed *(adj.)* 放鬆的、自在的
  → relaxing *(adj.)* 令人放鬆的

20. **routine** [ru`tin] *(n.)* [C] 慣例 *(adj.)* 例行的、常規的；平淡乏味的
    → daily routine 例行公事、日常工作
    → as a matter of routine 作為常規、作為例行公事

重要片語

1. **keep... under control** 在控制之下，在掌控之中
2. **deal with** 處理 = handle, tackle, cope with, address
3. **focus on** 集中於 = concentrate on, center on
4. **be able to + V_R** 能夠… = be capable of + Ving

相關文法句型

1. **either... or... 與 neither... nor... 的用法**
   (1) either A or B 表示「不是 A 就是 B」，是二擇一的情況。

   例 Evolution created a "fight or flight" response to help us survive the natural challenges of ancient times by preparing our bodies to **either combat** an enemy **or run away**.
   演化過程創造了「戰鬥或逃跑」的反應，不論是奮勇抗敵或是走為上策，都可以用來幫助我們迎戰古代大自然的挑戰。

   例 I want to **either stay** home **or go to** the amusement park.
   我想要待在家，或是去遊樂園玩。
   → 若引導的詞作為主詞時，動詞需跟著 **or 後面的主詞**做變化。
   → 此外，or 為對等連接詞，因此 either 與 or 後方所接的結構需一致，如本例句皆加上動詞。

   (2) neither A nor B 表示「不是 A 也不是 B」，是兩者皆非的情況。

   例 **Neither the ancient rings nor the golden utensil** was stolen.
   被偷走的寶物既不是古老戒指，也不是鍍金餐具。
   → 引導的詞作為主詞時，動詞需跟著 **nor 後面的主詞**做變化。

2. **分詞構句**

   例 Now, fight or flight can be triggered by daily stress, **releasing** the hormone Cortisol into the brain.
   如今，戰鬥或逃跑反應可能來自生活壓力，它釋放荷爾蒙皮質醇到大腦裡。
   → 原句型為 ... by daily stress, **which releases** the...。當關係代名詞作為**主格**（fight or flight）使用時，可刪掉關係代名詞 which，動詞一律改為**現在分詞** Ving。

二、文意選填

第 21 至 30 題為題組 —— 年長者照護

There is a long tradition of setting New Year's ___21___ for oneself. By tying the change we wish to make in our own ___22___ to the change in the calendar, we hope to make a new self with the new year. This is a way of being disciplined about the changes we wish to make, which are often difficult.

Many New Year's resolutions are about adopting a healthier lifestyle. This is a thing many find hard to do. We must reverse bad habits we have ___23___ for a long time. There are a few techniques that can be used to make this process simpler.

___24___, make a specific plan of action for exercise. Know exactly what kind of exercise you want to do, and when. Commit ___25___ that schedule. If your plans are too vague, it's likely you'll never do them. In addition, make sure your goals are realistic. If they are too ambitious, you may never be able to accomplish them, and quit ___26___. This could cause you to abandon the idea of changing at all. Know what you're capable ___27___, and what you will enjoy doing. This will help you stay committed.

And remember to accept that you may fail occasionally. If you ___28___ your resolution, don't beat yourself up or feel embarrassed. This can cause you to give up.

___29___, use each failure as an opportunity to recommit, refocus, and get back ___30___. Don't worry too much about your failures; think about your goal. Congratulate yourself on a series of small gains. Don't try to take on too much at once. Ask your friends and family to support you and help you accomplish your goals. Change can be hard, but it is worth it.

譯文

為自己設定新年新希望已是長久以來的傳統。我們將對自己的期許和日曆上的日期綁在一起，希望新的一年有個嶄新的自己。這是透過自律來達到改變自我的一個方法，雖然這件事通常是很困難的。

很多新年新希望跟養成更健康的生活方式有關。這對很多人來說很困難，我們必須要徹底改變我們長久以來已根深蒂固的惡習。以下有幾個方法能夠讓這過程更加容易。

第一，制定明確的運動計畫。你要清楚知道你想從事什麼運動，跟什麼時候執行。遵守時間表。如果你的計畫太過模糊，你很有可能永遠不會去做。此外，你要確認你的目標是實際的。如果過於好高騖遠，你可能永遠沒辦法達成，進而可能感到受挫而放棄。這也可能導致你決定不去改變。知道自己的能力範圍以及喜歡做什麼，才能幫助你持之以恆。

還要記得，接受自己偶爾會失敗的事實。如果沒有達成目標，也不要太過苛求自己或是覺得尷尬，這會使你想要放棄。

你反而要把每次的失敗當作重新投入、重新專注和回到正軌的機會，別太擔心失敗，而是專注在目標上，有一點小成果就該鼓勵自己，不要試圖同時承擔太多。請你的朋友及家人支持你，幫助你達成目標，改變雖然很難，但非常值得。

(A) engaged in	(B) behavior	(C) of	(D) Firstly	(E) in frustration
(A) 從事於	(B) 行為	(C) be capable of 能夠	(D) 首先	(E) 受挫的

(F) fall short of	(G) on track	(H) resolutions	(I) commit to	(J) Instead
(F) 達不到	(G) 重回軌道	(H) 決心	(I) 致力於	(J) 反而

原文

There is a long tradition of setting New Year's 1)**resolutions** for oneself. By tying the change we wish to make in our own 2)**behavior** to the change in the calendar, we hope to make a new self with the new year. This is a way of being 3)**disciplined** about the changes we wish to make, which are often difficult.

Many New Year's resolutions are about adopting a healthier lifestyle. This is a thing many find hard to do. We must 4)**reverse** bad habits we have engaged in for a long time. There are a few techniques that can be used to make this process simpler.

Firstly, make a 5)**specific** plan of action for exercise. Know exactly what kind of exercises you want to do, and when. Commit to that schedule. If your plans are too 6)**vague**, it's likely you'll never do them. In addition, make sure your goals are 7)**realistic**. If they are too 8)**ambitious**, you may never be able to 9)**accomplish** them, and quit in frustration. This could cause you to 10)**abandon** the idea of changing at all. Know what you're capable of, and what you will enjoy doing. This will help you stay committed.

And remember to accept that you may fail 11)**occasionally**. If you fall short of your resolution, don't beat yourself up or feel embarrassed. This can cause you to give up. Instead, use each failure as an opportunity to recommit, refocus, and get back on track. Don't worry too much about your failures, instead think about your goal. Congratulate yourself on a series of small gains. Don't try to take on too much at once. Ask your friends and family to support you and help you accomplish your goals. Change can be hard, but it is worth it.

重要單字

1. **resolution** [ˌrɛzəˈluʃən] *(n.)* [C] 決心 = determination；決議；解決 (+ to N)
   → make a resolution/determination + to V$_R$ = make up one's mind + to V$_R$ 下定決心

2. **behavior** [bɪˈhevjə] *(n.)* [U] 行為、表現
   → behave *(vi.)* 表現、舉止
   → be on one's best behavior 拿出最好的表現
   → behave oneself 循規蹈矩、好好表現

---

3. **disciplined** [ˋdɪsəplɪnd] *(adj.)* 遵守紀律的、守規矩的、訓練有素的
   → discipline *(n.)* [U] 紀律、約束 *(vt.)* 訓練、教導 (discipline sb./oneself + **to V**ᵣ)
   → self-discipline *(n.)* 自律
   → self-disciplined *(adj.)* 自律的

4. **reverse** [rɪˋvɝs] *(vt.)* 徹底改變；使…反轉；推翻；倒車 (+ into)　*(adj.)* 反向的、相反的
   → reversal *(n.)* 反面 (the reverse of + N)；倒轉；推翻
   → go into reverse 出現逆轉、向反方向發展

5. **specific** [spɪˋsɪfɪk] *(adj.)* 特定的；明確的 = precise, particular
   → specifically *(adv.)* 特別地；明確地
   → be specific about + N 針對…做具體說明
   → be specific to sth. 針對、特別指定（某一族群）= be limited to sth.

6. **vague** [veg] *(adj.)* 模糊的、含糊的 = unclear, blurred, obscure
   → have a vague memory of sth. 依稀記得…
   → a vague figure 模糊的身影
   → be vague about sth. 對於某事含糊其詞

7. **realistic** [rɪəˋlɪstɪk] *(adj.)* 現實的、實際的 = practical, feasible；逼真的 = vivid
   → realistically *(adv.)* 現實地
   → realistically speaking 就現實面來說

8. **ambitious** [amˋbɪʃəs] *(adj.)* 有雄心的 = determined, aspiring
   → ambition *(n.)* [U] 雄心、抱負、志向
   → be (highly) ambitious for sb. 對某人寄予厚望

9. **accomplish** [əˋkɑmplɪʃ] *(vt.)* 完成、達到 = achieve, attain, realize, complete, fulfill
   → accomplishment *(n.)* [C] 成就、成績；才華、技能；[U] 完成、實現
   → sense of accomplishment 成就感 = sense of achievement

10. **abandon** [əˋbændən] *(vt.)* 放棄；遺棄 = desert 中止 = suspend
    → abandon oneself to sth. 使某人沉溺於某事
    → with (wild/gay) abandon 盡情、放縱

11. **occasionally** [əˋkeʒənḷɪ] *(adv.)* 偶爾 = sometimes, at times, on occasion
    → occasion *(n.)* [C]（事發的）時候；重大活動、盛會
    → occasional *(adj.)* 偶爾的、不經常的

1. **engage in** 從事於

2. **commit to + N/Ving** 投身於、承諾 = commit oneself to + N/Ving = be committed to + N/Ving
   → 也可以用被動式表達相同意思：be devoted to + N/Ving = be dedicated to+ N/Ving

3. **stay committed** 持之以恆

4. **fall short of** 達不到 ↔ **live up to (one's expectation)** 達到（某人期望）

5. **at once** 同時 = at the same time, in the meantime

相關文法句型

1. **連綴動詞**

   stay、remain、keep 作「連綴動詞」時，表示「保持…；仍是…」。

   例 Good health will help you **stay** **committed**.

   身體健康才能幫助你持之以恆。

   →主詞補語 committed 為形容詞。

   此類動詞後面不接受詞，但須接對主詞加以補充說明的**主詞補語**：

   S + ⌈ stay/remain/ ⌉ + ⌈ n. ⌉
   ⌊ keep ⌋　　⌊ adj.
   　　　　　　　　V-ing
   　　　　　　　　Vpp ⌋

   這類動詞後方須接**名詞**、**形容詞**、**現在分詞**或**過去分詞**，作為主詞補語來補充說明主詞的狀態。

2. **「instead」和「instead of」的用法及差異**

   (1) Instead 為副詞，可置於句首、句中、句尾，表「（不是…）而是…、反而…」。

   例 Mark didn't go home directly last night. **Instead**, he went to the park.

   馬克昨晚沒有直接回家。相反地，他去了公園。

   → instead 放在句首。

   (2) instead of 當**介系詞**使用，表「並非…、而不是…」，可置於句首或句中，**接名詞或動名詞**。

   例 **Instead of going** home directly, Mark went to the park last night.

   馬克昨晚沒有直接回家，而是去了公園。

   → 由於 of 為介系詞，須把後面動詞加改為動名詞，變成 going。

第 31 至 35 題為題組 —— 人際關係

Being thought of as a likable person can help open many doors. People will be enthusiastic about working with you. You don't have to act like someone you are not or put on an act. In fact, it's better to be genuine, but reconsider some of your habits when interacting with others. __31__ First, you should look for good things about other people and their work and tell them you appreciate those things. There is something positive that can be said about everybody. This is not fake flattery, but a genuine change in your outlook. By expressing positive things about others, they'll be happier about themselves and happier to cooperate with you.

__32__ Every person has a story to tell and a life they have lived. Everyone has something to say that is worth hearing. You can learn something from anyone, but only if you are open to the experience. On the other hand, don't hesitate to ask others for advice. __33__ This will make them respect you more, too. Keep in mind that no one feels happy and social all the time. __34__ If you can, take a break and have some time to yourself. You'll likely feel refreshed soon. Last but not least, find pleasure in everything around you. __35__ The more you allow yourself to like others, the more you'll like yourself!

譯文

　　被認為是一個人見人愛的人能夠幫助你拓展很多機會，人們會熱衷於與你共事，你不用表現得不像自己或是裝模作樣。事實上，真誠待人比較好，但當與他人互動時，還是要多加考慮自己的一些習慣。(C) **在以下祕訣的幫助下，好人緣是一項你可以使用以及精進的技能！** 首先，你得找到別人的優點及良好的工作表現，並告訴他們你很欣賞他們的地方，每個人一定有某些值得稱讚的地方，這不是阿諛諂媚，而是發自內心改變自己對別人的看法，說別人好話會讓他們過得更開心，也更樂於和你合作。

　　(A) **當與人談話時，問關於對方的問題。** 每個人都有著值得一提的故事和人生經驗、每個人的事蹟都是值得一聽的。你可以從任何人身上學到東西，只要你願意傾聽。另一方面，別吝惜向人詢問意見，(E) **你不僅能獲得處理問題的洞察力，人們也會感覺你重視他們的能力、智慧和經驗，** 這也會讓他們對你敬重有加。你還要記住，沒有人能時時保持愉悅、愛好交際，(B) **偶爾有負面情緒是很正常的，但你應該要試著避免遷怒他人。** 如果可以的話，休息一下，花時間自處，很快你便會感覺恢復活力。最後，從周遭事物中找尋樂趣。(D) **藉由培養對人的興趣，你會發現隨著時間你將會獲得新的機緣、契機與朋友作為回報。** 你越喜歡他人，就會越喜歡你自己。

(A) When speaking with others, ask them questions about themselves.
與他人談話時，問有關對方的問題。

(B) It's okay to be in a negative mood occasionally, but you should try to avoid taking it out on others.
偶爾有負面情緒是很正常的，但你應該要試著避免遷怒他人。

(C) With the help of the following tips, being likable is a skill you can work on and improve!
有了以下祕訣的幫助，好人緣是一項你可以使用以及精進的技能！

(D) By cultivating a deeper interest in people, you'll find that over time you'll be rewarded with new connections, opportunities, and friends.
藉由培養對人的興趣，你會發現隨著時間你將會獲得新的機緣、契機與朋友作為回報。

(E) Not only could you potentially receive some insight into a problem, but people will feel that you respect their strengths, intelligence and experience.
你不僅能獲得處理問題的洞察力，人們也會感覺你重視他們的能力、智慧和經驗。

原文

Being thought of as a likable person can help open many doors. People will be [1]enthusiastic about working with you. You don't have to act like someone you are not or put on an act. In fact, it's better to be [2]genuine, but reconsider some of your habits when interacting with others. With the help of the following tips, being likable is a skill you can work on and improve! First, you should look for good things about other people and their work and tell them you [3]appreciate those things. There is something positive that can be said about everybody. This is not fake [4]flattery, but a genuine change in your outlook. By [5]expressing positive things about others, they'll be happier about themselves and happier to [6]cooperate with you.

When speaking with others, ask them questions about themselves. Every person has a story to tell and a life they have lived. Everyone has something to say that is worth hearing. You can learn something from anyone, but only if you are open to the experience. On the other hand, don't [7]hesitate to ask others for advice. Not only could you [8]potentially receive some [9]insight into a problem, but people will feel that you respect their strengths, intelligence and experience. This will make them respect you more, too. Keep in mind that no one feels happy and social all the time. It's okay to be in a negative mood occasionally, but you should try to avoid taking it out on others. If you can, take a break and have some time to yourself. Last but not least, find pleasure in everything around you. You'll likely feel refreshed soon. By [10]cultivating a deeper interest in people, you'll find that over time you'll be rewarded with new connections, opportunities, and friends. The more you allow yourself to like others, the more you'll like yourself!

1. **enthusiastic** [ɪnˏθjuzɪˋæstɪk] *(adj.)* 熱衷的 (+ **about** N/Ving)
   → enthusiasm *(n.)* [U] 熱情、熱忱 (+ **for** N/Ving)

2. **genuine** [ˋdʒɛnjuɪn] *(adj.)* 真誠的 = sincere, candid；真正的 = authentic, bona fide
   → genuinely *(adv.)* 確實、的確 = really
   → the genuine article（貨真價實的）真品

3. **appreciate** [əˋpriʃɪˏet] *(vt.)* 欣賞；意識到 (+ that S + V)
   → appreciation *(n.)* 欣賞；感謝 (+ **of/for** N)
   → I/ We appreciate **your Ving/N** 我（們）很感激…

4. **flattery** [ˋflætərɪ] *(n.)* [U] 諂媚、奉承
   → flatter *(vt.)* 奉承、討好
   → flattery will get you nowhere 奉承是沒有用的（表達自己不會被說服）

5. **express** [ɪkˋsprɛs] *(vt.)* 表達；快遞 *(adj.)* 快速的；快遞的 *(n.)* [U] 快遞服務
   → expression *(n.)* [C] 表示、表達；表情、神色；措辭、字眼
   → express oneself (clearly)（清楚地）表達自己（想法、感受）

6. **cooperate** [koˋɑpəˏret] *(vi.)* 合作、配合 = collaborate
   → cooperation *(n.)* [U] 合作、配合
   → in cooperation with + N 與…合作

7. **hesitate** [ˋhɛzəˏtet] *(vi.)* 猶豫、懷疑 = doubt, suspect
   → hesitation *(n.)* 猶豫、懷疑
   → without hesitation 毫不猶豫
   → do not hesitate + **to V_R** 不需猶豫地做某事 = feel free + **to V_R**

8. **potentially** [pəˋtɛnʃəlɪ] *(adv.)* 可能地、潛在地 = probably, possibly
   → potential *(adj.)* 潛在的、可能的 *(n.)* [U] 潛力、潛能
   → potential buyer 潛在買家
   → have potential + **to V_R** 有潛力做某事

9. **insight** [ˋɪnˏsaɪt] *(n.)* [C] 洞察力 = perception, awareness
   → insightful *(adj.)* 有眼光的、有深刻見解的 = perceptive

10. **cultivate** [ˋkʌltəˏvet] *(vt.)* 培養、養成；耕種、栽培
    → cultivation *(n.)* [U] 耕種、栽培；培養、教化
    → cultivate a good habit **of** + N/Ving 培養…的好習慣

1. **think of ... as** 認為…是、把…看作
   = view... **as**, see... **as**, <u>look upon</u>/<u>refer to</u>... **as**
   = consider, think, deem... (to be)

2. **put on an act** 裝模作樣 = make believe

3. **work on** 從事 = be engaged in

4. **be in a** negative **mood** 處於**負面**情緒 ↔ **be in a** positive **mood** 處於**正面**情緒

5. **over time** 隨著時間

相關文法句型

1. **worth, worthy, worthwhile 的用法區別**

   (1) **worth**：「be worth **+ Ving**」表「某事值得**被做**」。
       「be worth **+ N**」，表「值得…」，後面多接時間，金錢或精力等。

   例 Everyone has something to say that is **worth hearing**.
   每個人都有值得一聽的故事。

   例 The movie is really **worth watching**.
   這部電影值得一看。

   例 That Apple stock you bought must be **worth a fortune** by now.
   你當時購買的蘋果股票現在一定已經價值不斐了。

   例 Do you think learning an ancient language is **worth your time**?
   你認為古老的語言值得花時間學習嗎？

   (2) **worthy**：「be worthy **+ to V$_R$**」，表「值得去做某事」。
       「be worthy **+ of N**」，後接除金錢，時間，精力以外的其它名詞。

   例 be worthy of note/trust/praise/news
   = be noteworthy/trustworthy/praiseworthy/newsworthy
   值得注意的／值得信賴的／值得讚許的／值得新聞報導的

   例 The project is worthy **to be done**.
   = The project is worthy **of being done**.
   = The project is worth **doing**.
   這企劃值得實行。

   (3) **worthwhile**：「**sth. + be worthwhile**」，表「某事值得花時間（去做）」。
       「**It is worthwhile + to V$_R$/Ving**」表「花時間做某事是值得的」。

2. **not only... but also... 的倒裝用法**

例 **Not only could you** potentially receive some insight into a problem, **but** people will feel that you respect their strengths, intelligence and experience.

你不僅能獲得處理問題的洞察力，人們也會感覺你重視他們的能力、智慧和經驗。

→ 若連接主要子句並且由 Not only 開頭時，則要用**倒裝用法，but 為連接詞不可省略，但 also 可省可保留。**

句型：「Not only + **助動詞** + S + V$_R$, but + S + (also) + V$_R$」
　　　「Not only + **be 動詞** + S + 補語 , but + S + (also) + be 動詞」

第貳部分:非選擇題

一、中譯英 —— 校園生活

1. 學校不僅是獲得知識的地方,也是教育的搖籃。在那我可以學到如何與不同的人相處及培育人格。

School is $\begin{bmatrix} \text{more than} \\ \text{not only} \end{bmatrix}$ a place to $\begin{bmatrix} \text{gain} \\ \text{acquire} \end{bmatrix}$ knowledge, it is also the cradle of

education $\begin{bmatrix} \text{, where} \\ \text{, in which} \\ \text{; at school} \\ \text{. At school(,)} \end{bmatrix}$ I can learn how to get along with different people and

build character.

2. 我很用功並盡己所能理解課程內容,因為我不想在這個學期落後。

I study very $\begin{bmatrix} \text{hard} \\ \text{diligently} \\ \text{industriously} \end{bmatrix}$ and $\begin{bmatrix} \text{try every means possible} \\ \text{do my (level) best} \\ \text{do my utmost} \\ \text{put my best foot forward} \\ \text{leave no stone unturned} \\ \text{spare no effort} \end{bmatrix}$

to understand the lesson because I don't want to fall behind this semester.

二、英文作文 —— 投資自我

假設你今天買樂透獲得一筆為數不小的金額，你會選擇以下哪一項？寫一篇至少 120 字的英文作文。第一段明示你的選擇及理由，第二段說明你為何不選擇另一項的考量。

赴美遊學兩個月，進入大學與國際同學一起學習交流，並在課後安排旅遊行程。

進行全身大改造，在醫美診所裡花錢讓自己擁有魔鬼般的身材及天使般的容顏。

作文範文

Wow! I just won the lottery! Now I've just got to decide what to do with the prize money... I've always wanted to be handsome, like a movie star. With my winnings I could transform myself from head to toe in an aesthetic clinic. In all walks of life, good-looking people seem to achieve more. People will tell you that the essence of success is hard work and intelligence, but beautiful people absolutely receive more attention, not to mention media coverage. I want to impose a striking impression on everyone in the hope that I'll be respected. How often have you worked hard only to be faced with your lazy but handsome co-worker being promoted before you? Therefore, I will opt to spend my lottery winnings on aesthetic medical procedures at a local clinic that is noted for its proficiency. The world is superficial and cruel, and it rewards beautiful people over plain-looking ones. It's sad, but you know what they say: "If you can't beat them, join them." And now I can afford to join them!

Someone suggested that if I won, I should do a two-month study tour in the United States. But if I were to spend such a huge amount of money on a study tour for only two months, the ratio between cost and benefit would be too low. It would be a fleeting pleasure instead of the lifelong enhancement of plastic surgery. Indeed, one of my long-term goals is to be fluent in English. That said, is it really possible to authentically master English with just two short months of immersion? By the same token, I couldn't explore much of the U.S. in such a limited time frame. I wholeheartedly desire to build connections around the world, but I don't think a rushed tour of America would genuinely help me in that regard. Each person's lifetime opportunities only come in a handful, so we must choose wisely. By my definition, one's assets are only valuable if they are lasting, and aesthetic surgery would profoundly improve the rest of my life. Memories fade, and to naively assume a two-month trip would benefit me in the long term would be to waste the prize money.

譯文

哇！我剛中了彩券！現在我只要決定怎麼處理獎金…我一直想像電影明星一樣長得帥。有了獎金，我可以到醫美診所改頭換面。在各行各業中，長相好看的人似乎更有成就。大家都會說，成功的本質是勤奮和智慧，但長相好看的人絕對會得到更多關注，更別說會受到媒體報導了。我想給大家留下深刻印象，希望能藉此受到尊重。你有多少次努力工作，結果懶惰但英俊的同事卻比你先升遷？所以我會選擇將彩券獎金用在以醫術精湛著稱的本地醫美診所。這世界是膚淺而殘酷的，長相好看的人比平庸的人更有好處。這很悲哀，但你知道俗話說：「你若無法打敗他們，那就加入他們的行列。」現在我有能力加入他們了！

有人建議如果我中獎，我應該到美國進修兩個月。但我若要花大筆錢進修，卻只去兩個月，就不符合成本效益了。比起整型能讓容貌提升維持一輩子，那只是短暫的快樂。的確，我的長期目標之一是精通英語。話雖如此，在短短兩個月沉浸在英語的時間真的能讓我完全精通英語嗎？同理，在如此有限的時間內，我也無法探索美國大部分地區。我全心渴望到世界各地建立人脈，但我不認為倉促的美國之行真能在這方面幫到我。每個人一生能遇到的機會很少，所以我們要明智選擇。我指的是，個人資產只有持久才寶貴，而醫美手術能深切改善我的下半輩子。回憶會消退，天真地以為兩個月的旅行從長遠來看會對我有益，其實是浪費獎金。

作文教學

Wow! I just won the lottery! Now I've just got to decide what to do with the prize money... I've always wanted to be ¹⁾**handsome**, like a movie star. With my winnings I could ²⁾**transform** myself **from head to toe** in an ³⁾**aesthetic** clinic. In **all walks of life**, good-looking people seem to achieve more. People will tell you that the ⁴⁾**essence** of success is hard work and intelligence, but beautiful people ⁵⁾**absolutely** receive more attention, **not to mention** media ⁶⁾**coverage**. I want to ⁷⁾**impose** a ⁸⁾**striking** impression on everyone **in the hope that** I'll be respected. How often have you worked hard only to be faced with your lazy but handsome co-worker being promoted before you? Therefore, I will ⁹⁾**opt to** spend my lottery winnings on aesthetic medical procedures at a local clinic that is noted for its ¹⁰⁾**proficiency**. The world is ¹¹⁾**superficial** and cruel, and it rewards beautiful people over ¹²⁾**plain-looking** ones. It's sad, but you know what they say: "if you can't beat them, join them." And now I can afford to join them!

Someone suggested that if I won, I should do a two-month study tour in the United States. But **if I were to spend** such a huge amount of money on a study tour for only two months, **the ratio between cost and benefit would be** too low. It would be a fleeting pleasure instead of the lifelong enhancement of plastic surgery. Indeed, one of my long-term goals is to be fluent in English. **That said**, is it really possible to ¹³⁾**authentically** master English with just two short months of immersion? **By the same token**, I couldn't explore much of the U.S. in such a limited time frame. I ¹⁴⁾**wholeheartedly** desire to build connections around the world, but I don't think a rushed tour of America would genuinely help me in that regard. Each person's lifetime opportunities only **come in a handful**, so we must choose wisely. **By my**

definition, one's ¹⁵⁾**assets** are only valuable if they are lasting, and aesthetic surgery would ¹⁶⁾**profoundly** improve the rest of my life. Memories fade, and to ¹⁷⁾**naively** assume a two-month trip would benefit me in the long term would be to waste the prize money.

重要單字

1. **handsome** [ˋhænsəm] *(adj.)* 數量可觀的 = substantial, considerable；帥氣的 = good-looking, stunning

2. **transform** [trænsˋfɔrm] *(vt.)* 徹底改變、大變身

3. **aesthetic** [ɛsˋθɛtɪk] *(adj.)* 美學的

4. **essence** [ˋɛsəns] *(n.)* [U] 本質；精華

5. **absolutely** [ˏæbsəˋlutlɪ] *(adv.)* 絕對、全然地

6. **coverage** [ˋkʌvərɪdʒ] *(n.)* [U] 報導；（保險）涵蓋範圍

7. **impose** [ɪmˋpoz] *(vt.)* 強力實施；把（負擔）強加於…

8. **striking** [ˋstraɪkɪŋ] *(adj.)* 顯著的；容易被發現注意到的

9. **opt for** *(v.)* 選擇

10. **proficiency** [prəˋfɪʃənsɪ] *(n.)* [U] 精通

11. **superficial** [ˏsupɚˋfɪʃəl] *(adj.)* 膚淺的

12. **plain-looking** [plen ˋlʊkɪŋ] *(adj.)* 長相平庸的

13. **authentically** [ɔˋθɛntɪkəlɪ] *(adv.)* 真正地 = genuinely

14. **wholeheartedly** [ˏholˋhartɪdlɪ] *(adv.)* 全心全意地

15. **asset** [ˋæsɛt] *(n.)* [C] 資產

16. **profoundly** [prəˋfaʊndlɪ] *(adv.)* 深遠地、深刻地

17. **naively** [nɑˏivlɪ] *(adv.)* 天真地

重要片語

1. **from head to toe/foot** 從頭到腳
   → from womb to tomb 從出生到死亡
   → from dusk to dawn 從早到晚
   → from hand to mouth 僅能糊口
   → from A to Z 從頭到尾、徹底地

2. **all walks of life** 各行各業

3. **not to mention** 更別提、更不用說

4. **by the same token** 同樣道理地；相同地

5. **come in a handful** 屈指可數

6. **by my definition** 就（某人）的定義來說

相關文法句型

1. **in (the) hope that + S + V 希望… = in (the) hope of + N/Ving**

   例 Mike behaved well **in the hope that** Santa would give him lots of presents.
   麥克表現得很好，他希望聖誕老人可以因此而送他許多禮物。

2. **if S + were to + V_R..., S + would/could/should/might + V_R 【假設語氣】如果…（表發生機率低）**

   例 If Ellen **were to** study harder, she **would get** better grades.
   如果艾倫真的用功念書，她就會得到更好的成績。

3. **that (being) said, ... 話雖如此、儘管這麼說**

   例 Mrs. Smith is a strict teacher; **that being said**, she's very fair.
   史密斯女士是位嚴格的老師。雖然這麼說，但她卻十分公平。

NOTE

第 2 回｜解析

第壹部分：選擇題

一、綜合測驗

第 1 至 10 題為題組 —— 萬國節慶

In the U.K. and Ireland, Boxing Day occurs on December 26th of each year, the day after Christmas. Many people outside of the U.K. and Ireland are __1__ this holiday. Boxing Day is a time to __2__ your daily worries and spend time with family. Often this means __3__ family, because people usually stay home with their immediate family on Christmas Day.

Guests are welcomed into the home on Boxing Day, and usually much food is enjoyed. Baked ham, cakes, and puddings __4__ from Christmas are consumed. It is a way to extend the __5__ and good cheer of the holiday season. Sporting events are enjoyed on Boxing day. Football matches and horse races are televised. Traditionally, men would hunt foxes on Boxing Day, but this tradition __6__ . However, people still gather in fox hunting uniforms to honor the old traditions.

No one is quite sure why it is called "Boxing Day," but there are several theories. One is that long ago wealthy people would give their servants a day off, __7__ presents for their families, called Christmas boxes. Another is that churches would __8__ a box to collect donations during the Christmas service, and the next day the money in these boxes was __9__ the poor. No matter __10__ the name comes from, everyone loves shopping, socializing, or just relaxing on this wonderful day!

譯文

在英國與愛爾蘭，每年 12 月 26 日 —— 也就是聖誕節隔天 —— 是節禮日。不住在英國或愛爾蘭的人很多並不知道這個節日。節禮日是個讓人們放下日常煩憂、花時間和家人相處的日子。此處所指的家人通常是指整個大家庭，因為人們和直系親屬在聖誕節當天就會在家團圓了。

節禮日當天，人們會邀請賓客到家裡，一起享用美食，把聖誕節剩下的烤火腿、蛋糕和布丁甜點吃掉，這是一種給予聖誕節熱情與歡愉的方式。在節禮日，人們熱衷於觀賞體育賽事，電視會轉播足球比賽和賽馬。傳統上，男人會在節禮日獵狐狸，但這一傳統已被禁止。不過人們仍會穿著獵狐的服裝相聚，以紀念古老的傳統。

沒有人能確定「節禮日」這個節日名稱的由來，但有幾種說法。其中一個是，很久以前，有錢人會在這天放他們的僕人一天假，並給他們送家人的禮物，叫做「聖誕盒」。另一個說法是，教堂會在聖誕節做禮拜時設立募款盒，隔天再把這些盒子中的錢分配給窮人。無論「節禮日」究竟從何而來，每個人都享受在這個美好的日子裡，逛街購物、社交或純粹放鬆一下身心！

---

1. (A) characteristic of   **(B) unaware of**   (C) independent of   (D) familiar with
   (A) 是⋯的典型   **(B) 未察覺到的**   (C) 獨立於⋯   (D)（某人）熟悉於

2. (A) break down   (B) set off   (C) put out   **(D) put aside**
   (A) 分解；故障；簡化   (B) 出發、動身；引爆   (C) 熄滅、撲滅   **(D) 擱置、放到一邊**

3. (A) contended   **(B) extended**   (C) attended   (D) intended
   (A) 競爭的   **(B) 延伸的、擴展的**   (C) 參加的；有人照顧的   (D) 打算的、有意圖的

   > **解說** extended family 大家庭（尤指三代以上同堂）。

4. **(A) left over**   (B) cut down   (C) taken over   (D) wiped out
   (A) 留下⋯（剩下的東西）   (B) 減少   (C) 占領   (D) 消滅

   > **解說** 此句食物是「被」留下的，故選 (A) 過去分詞表被動。

5. (A) hostility   **(B) hospitality**   (C) humility   (D) humidity
   (A) 敵意   **(B) 好客、殷勤招待**   (C) 謙卑、謙遜   (D) 濕氣、濕度

6. (A) is banning   (B) has banned   **(C) has been banned**   (D) has been banning

   > **解說** ban (vt.) 禁止。用法為「人 ban（主動禁止）某法令、書、不好的行為等」或「某法令、書、或不好的行為被禁止（使用 be banned 被動形式）」。本題主詞 this tradition 為被禁物，故選唯一被動用法選項 (C)。

7. (A) except for   (B) including   **(C) as well as**   (D) instead of
   (A) 除⋯之外   (B) 包含⋯   **(C) 除⋯之外還；也；和**   (D) 只要

8. (A) let go   (B) turn down   **(C) set aside**   (D) stack up
   (A) 放開、鬆手   (B) 回絕   **(C) 留出、撥出**   (D) 堆積

9. (A) attributed to   (B) contributing to   **(C) distributed to**   (D) tribute
   (A) 把⋯歸因於   (B) 導致；捐獻奉獻給   **(C) 將⋯分發給⋯**   (D) 供品；敬意

10. (A) that   (B) the place   (C) wherever   **(D) where**

   > **解說** no matter + wh- 疑問詞 + S + V.「無論⋯」；(C) = no matter where 無論何處

原文

    In the U.K. and Ireland, Boxing Day $^{1)}$**occurs** on December 26th of each year, the day after Christmas. Many people outside of the U.K. and Ireland are $^{2)}$**unaware** of this holiday. Boxing Day is a time to put aside your daily worries and spend time with family. Often this means $^{3)}$**extended family**, because people usually stay home with their $^{4)}$**immediate family** on Christmas Day.

    Guests are welcomed into the home on Boxing Day, and usually much food is enjoyed. Baked ham, cakes, and puddings left over from Christmas are $^{5)}$**consumed**. It is a way to extend the $^{6)}$**hospitality** and good cheer of the holiday season. Sporting events are enjoyed on Boxing Day. Football $^{7)}$**matches** and horse races are $^{8)}$**televised**. Traditionally, men would hunt foxes on Boxing Day, but this tradition has been $^{9)}$**banned**. However, people still gather in fox hunting uniforms to honor the old traditions.

    No one is quite sure why it is called "Boxing Day," but there are several theories. One is that long ago wealthy people would give their servants a day off, as well as presents for their families, called Christmas boxes. Another is that churches would set aside a box to collect donations during the Christmas service, and the next day the money in these boxes was distributed to the poor. No matter where the name comes from, everyone loves shopping, $^{10)}$**socializing**, or just relaxing on this wonderful day!

重要單字

1. **occur** [əˋkɜ] *(vi.)*（事件等）發生
   → 句型：「It occurred to sb. that S + V」，指「某人想到…」

2. **unaware** [ˌʌnəˋwɛr] *(adj.)* 未意識到的、不知道的
   → be unaware **of** N/Ving / **that** S + V 未意識到…；不知道…
   → be aware **of** N/Ving / **that** S + V 意識到…；知道…

3. **extended family** [ɪkˋstɛndɪd ˋfæməlɪ] *(n.)* [C] 較遠的親屬、旁系親屬
   → extend *(vt.)* 擴大；擴展；延長；伸展

4. **immediate family** [ɪˋmidɪɪt ˋfæməlɪ] *(n.)* [C] 直系親屬
   →直系親屬即：parents 雙親、siblings 兄弟姐妹、spouses 配偶、children 子女
   → immediately *(adv.)* 立即、立刻

5. **consume** [kənˋsum] *(vt.)* 消耗；吃完、喝光
   → be consumed with jealousy/envy/passion/ambition
   　充滿某種強烈的感情，如嫉妒／羨慕／熱情／野心
   → consumer *(n.)* 消費者；顧客

6. **hospitality** [ˌhɑspɪˈtælətɪ] *(n.)* [U] 好客、殷勤招待
   → host *(n.)* 主人、東道主
   → hospitable *(adj.)* 好客的、招待周到的
   → hospital *(n.)* 醫院 → hospitalize *(v.)* 使住院治療
   → 易混淆字：hostile *(adj.)* 敵人的、敵方的 → hostility *(n.)* 敵意、敵視

7. **match** [mætʃ] *(n.)* [C] 比賽、競賽
   → **match**：通常是兩人或兩隊對打的球類比賽
      ● a soccer match 足球賽
      ● a tennis match 網球賽
      ● a boxing match 拳擊賽
   → **race**：一般用在競速的比賽
      ● a car race 賽車
      ● a horse race 賽馬
      ● a running race 賽跑
      ● a bicycle race 自行車賽
   → **contest**：多指較靜態、需特殊才藝或技巧的比賽
      ● a singing contest 歌唱比賽
      ● a speech contest 演講比賽
      ● a cooking contest 烹飪比賽
      ● a beauty contest 選美比賽
   → **competition**：較廣義，可指任何競賽，也可引申為較為抽象的各種「競爭」

8. **televise** [ˈtɛləˌvaɪz] *(vt.)* 電視播送
   → be televised live on... 由…（電視台）進行實況轉播

9. **ban** [bæn] *(vt.)* 禁止 *(n.)* [C] 禁止；禁令
   → ban sb. from doing sth. 禁止某人做某事
   → impose/lift a ban on + N/Ving 頒布／解除對…的禁令

10. **honor** [ˈɑnɚ] *(vt.)* 向…致敬 *(n.)* [U] 榮譽；名譽
    → be honored + to V$_R$ 對能做某事深感榮幸
    → give/pay honor to + N/Ving 向…致敬
    → honorable *(adj.)* 值得尊敬的，品德高尚的
    → in honor of + N 為緬懷…

11. **socialize** [ˈsoʃəˌlaɪz] *(v.)* 參與社交；交際
    → socialize with sb. 與某人來往
    → society *(n.)* 社會

1. **put aside** 把（分歧或問題）撇開不理、擱置
2. **honor the traditions** 向傳統致敬
3. **give sb. a day off** 放某人一天假
4. **collect donations** 募款

1. **No matter + 疑問詞「無論⋯」**

   例 No matter **where** the name comes from, everyone loves shopping, socializing, or just relaxing on this wonderful day!

   無論「節禮日」究竟從何而來，每個人都享受在這個美好的日子裡，逛街購物、社交或純粹放鬆一下身心！

   例 No matter **where** you travel, you should always buy travel insurance.

   無論你去哪裡旅行，你都應該購買旅平險。

   → 「**no matter + 疑問詞 what/who/when/which/where/how**」表示「無論⋯」，

   可用「**疑問詞 + ever**」代替：whatever/whoever/whenever/whichever/wherever/however。

   因此，本例句可改寫成：

   Wherever you travel, you should always buy travel insurance.

The current Dalai Lama, named Tenzin Gyatso, is getting old. He is __11__ the ripe old age of 84. It is time to locate his __12__. However, the Chinese government believes itself to be the authority that should find the next Dalai Lama. This has created a __13__ between the Chinese government and Tibetan Buddhists.

The Dalai Lama is a __14__ spiritual leader, and is responsible for promoting Buddhist beliefs and ethics throughout the entire world. The current Dalai Lama was even __15__ The Nobel Peace Prize in 1992. Because this position is so important, the Dalia Lama's successor has traditionally been discovered by senior monks.

Tenzin Gyatso became Dalai Lama when he was only 4 years old. He __16__ be the next in line when his predecessor, the 13th Dalai Lama, died and monks interpreted religious visions to locate Tenzin Gyatso. He was __17__ to be the next on the throne because he seemed to recognize the monks, as well as objects that had belonged to the previous Dalai Lama. Tibetan Buddhists would like to select the next Dalai Lama with similar methods.

The Chinese government __18__ Tibet in 1950 and Tenzin Gyatso lives in exile. The Chinese government insists it should pick the next Lama, but many __19__ this __19__ an attempt to exert influence over Tibetan spiritual and cultural life. The current Dalai Lama has made several statements that contradict China's claims. The situation remains __20__.

譯文

現任達賴喇嘛丹增嘉措日漸衰老，如今已達高齡 84 歲，是時候選定他的繼任者了。然而，中國政府認為自己才是決定下一位達賴喇嘛的權威。這件事造成了中國政府與藏傳佛教徒之間的衝突。

達賴喇嘛是重要的精神領袖，負責向全世界推廣佛教信仰與道德。現任達賴喇嘛甚至於 1992 年獲得諾貝爾和平獎。也因為這職位極為重要，達賴喇嘛的繼任者傳統上是由年長的僧侶遴選找到的。

丹增嘉措 4 歲那年就成為達賴喇嘛。在他的前任第十三世達賴喇嘛去世時，僧侶們透過解釋宗教顯化的意象找到丹增嘉措，並決定他就是繼承人。確認他為繼承人的原因是，他似乎認得那些僧侶以及前任達賴喇嘛的所有物。藏傳佛教徒希望以類似的方法選出下一位達賴喇嘛。

1950 年，中國政府入侵西藏，丹增嘉措流亡國外。中國政府堅持要選下一任喇嘛，但許多人認為，這個舉動是企圖影響西藏的精神和文化生活。現任達賴喇嘛發表了幾項與中國主張相牴觸的聲明。情況仍未解決。

11. (A) on   **(B) at**   (C) in   (D) behind

> 解說　be **at** the age of + 歲數「在⋯歲」= be **at** + 歲數
> = be 數字 (years old) = be 數字 years of age

12. (A) assessor   **(B) successor**   (C) succession   (D) suspicion
     (A) 評估師、估價員   **(B) 繼任者**   (C) 一連串；接連   (D) 懷疑

13. (A) correspondence   (B) compromise   (C) coincidence   **(D) conflict**
     (A) 信函；關聯   (B) 妥協   (C) 巧合   **(D) 衝突**

14. (A) prevalent   (B) transient   **(C) prominent**   (D) relevant
     (A) 盛行的、普遍的   (B) 短暫的   **(C) 著名的；重要的**   (D) 有關的

15. (A) rewarding   (B) rewarded   (C) awarding   **(D) awarded**
     (A)、(B) reward 報償；獎賞   (C)、**(D) award 授予（獎）**

> 解說　sb. be awarded + 獎項「獲頒⋯（獎）」

16. (A) bore in mind   (B) had determination   **(C) was determined to**   (D) made up his mind

> 解說　「決心做⋯（某事）」有多種表達方式：determine to V$_R$、have (great) determination to V$_R$、
> be determined to V$_R$、make up one's mind to V$_R$。(A) bear sth. in mind 把⋯記在心中。

17. **(A) confirmed**   (B) confessed   (C) conformed   (D) condemned
     (A) 確認   (B) 承認（錯誤或罪刑）(C) 順從；遵從 (+ to)   (D) 譴責，指責

18. **(A) invaded**   (B) indicated   (C) initiated   (D) included
     (A) 入侵   (B) 表明；顯示   (C) 開始；創始   (D) 包括

19. (A) consider... as   (B) regard... for   **(C) see... as**   (D) view... with

> 解說　「將⋯視為⋯」有多種說法：consider... (to be)...、regard/see/view... as...

20. (A) resolved   **(B) unresolved**   (C) realistic   (D) unrealistic
     (A) 堅定的   **(B) 未解決的**   (C) 現實的；實際的   (D) 不現實的；不切實際的

原文

The current Dalai Lama, named Tenzin Gyatso, is getting old. He is at the [1)]**ripe** old age of 84. It is time to locate his [2)]**successor**. However, the Chinese government believes itself to be the [3)]**authority** that should find the next Dalai Lama. This has created a [4)]**conflict** between the Chinese government and Tibetan Buddhists.

The Dalai Lama is a prominent spiritual leader, and is responsible for [5)]**promoting** Buddhist beliefs and ethics throughout the entire world. The current Dalai Lama was even awarded The Nobel Peace Prize in 1992. Because this position is so important, the Dalia Lama's successor has traditionally been discovered by senior monks.

Tenzin Gyatso became Dalai Lama when he was only 4 years old. He was determined to be the next in line when his [6)]**predecessor**, the 13th Dalai Lama, died and monks [7)]**interpreted** religious visions to locate Tenzin Gyatso. He was confirmed to be the next on the throne because he seemed to recognize the monks, as well as objects that had belonged to the [8)]**previous** Dalai Lama. Tibetan Buddhists would like to select the next Dalai Lama with similar methods.

The Chinese government [9)]**invaded** Tibet in 1950 and Tenzin Gyatso lives in exile. The Chinese government insists it should pick the next Lama, but many see this as an [10)]**attempt** to exert influence over Tibetan spiritual and cultural life. The current Dalai Lama has made several statements that contradict China's claims. The situation remains unresolved.

重要單字

1. **ripe** [raɪp] *(adj.)* 成熟的；成年的、老成的
   → at the ripe age of... 在…的高齡
   → raw *(adj.)* 生的、未煮過的；未加工的；處於自然狀態的

2. **successor** [sək`sɛsɚ] *(n.)* [C] 接替者、繼承人 (+ to)
   → successive *(adj.)* 接連的、連續的
   → three successive years 連續三年

3. **authority** [ə`θɔrətɪ] *(n.)* [C, U] 權威人士；官方；當局；權力
   → the authorities concerned 有關當局
   → have (the) authority to V$_R$ 有權做某事
   → authorize *(vt.)* 授權；委託 (+ sb. **to** V$_R$)

4. **conflict** [`kɑnflɪkt] *(n.)* [C, U] 衝突、抵觸 *(vi.)* 矛盾、衝突 (+ with)
   → avoid conflict between A and B 避免 AB 兩方的衝突
   → come into conflict with... 和…衝突

---

5. **promote** [prə`mot] *(vt.)* 宣傳、發揚、提升；促進
   → promotion *(n.)* 宣傳、推廣；促進、提升；晉升
   → promote the new product 促銷新產品
   → gain/get/win promotion 獲得升遷

6. **predecessor** [ˋprɛdɪˌsɛsə] *(n.)* [C] 前任、前輩
   → predecease *(vt.)* 死於⋯之前，先於⋯去世
   → decease *(n./vi.)* 去世、逝世
   → the deceased *(n.)* 死者

7. **interpret** [ɪn`tɝprɪt] *(v.)* 詮釋；理解；口譯
   → interpret a dream 解夢
   → interpretation *(n.)* 解釋、闡釋；理解；口譯
   → open to interpretation 可做各種詮釋

8. **previous** [ˋpriviəs] *(adj.)* 先前的，以前的 = preceding
   → the previous day 前一天
   → previous to... 在⋯之前 = prior to
   → previously *(adv.)* 在前、先前地、預先

9. **invade** [ɪn`ved] *(vt.)* 侵入、侵略
   → invasion *(n.)* 入侵、侵略

10. **attempt** [ə`tɛmpt] *(n./vt.)* 企圖、嘗試
    → attempt to V_R 試圖做某事

重要片語

1. **be responsible for...** 負責⋯

2. **be determined to V_R** 決心⋯
   = determine to V_R, have (great) determination to V_R, make up one's mind to VR

3. **in exile** 流亡

4. **exert influence over...** 對⋯施加影響

1. **at the ripe old age of + 年紀 在…的高齡**

   例 He is at the ripe old age of 84.

   他目前高齡 84 歲。

   → a ripe old age「高齡」，常用片語如 live to a ripe old age「活到很老」。

2. **insist「堅持」用法**

   (1) insist 後方可接子句，句型「S₁ insist that S₂ (should) + V_R」表「堅持…該…」。

   例 The Chinese government insists it should pick the next Lama.

   中國政府堅持要自己挑選下一任喇嘛。

   (2) insist 也可與介系詞 on/upon 連用：

   例 She insisted on/upon lending them her car.

   她堅持把她的車借給他們。

3. **remain「保持不變、仍然是」的用法**

   remain 當動詞，後常加形容詞或名詞表達一種狀態。

   例 The situation remains unresolved.

   狀況依舊無解。

二、文意選填

第 21 至 30 題為題組 ── 語言學習

Learning a new language can be a(n) __21__ task. Many learners have no idea how to start this kind of __22__. There have been a few different strategies developed by others that are worth __23__. They focus on different aspects of language and how to learn it. Students can decide for themselves how to best utilize these techniques.

One approach is called "extensive reading". This is when the reader tries to __24__ as much different writing in the target language as possible. By taking in many different styles, the student gains some understanding of the full possibilities of that language. The goal is to gain fluency through __25__ to a wide range of vocabulary, grammar, and ideas. This technique works best with students who enjoy reading and are happy to seek out new reading material on their own. Critics of this style say that readers only develop a __26__ understanding of the target language this way.

A second technique is called "intensive reading". In __27__ to extensive reading, which tries to take in as much as possible, intensive reading chooses shorter texts. However, intensive reading takes a hard look at these short pieces of writing, __28__ them deeply. The reader focuses on the grammar and sentence structure. In this way, a fuller understanding of the text __29__. Critics say that focusing on one short piece can lead to boredom.

Likely, using a combination of these techniques would work best. Each student should determine how to best integrate these techniques for their own learning styles and language goals. The __30__ balance of extensive and intensive reading will lead to a well-balanced course of study.

譯文

學習新語言可能是一項令人生畏的任務,許多學習者不知該從何著手努力。有人開發了一些不同的策略,值得參考。他們專注於語言的不同面向以及學習語言的方式,學生可以自己決定如何最妥善地使用這些技巧。

一種方法叫作「廣泛閱讀」,讀者盡可能嘗試吸收用該目標語言所寫的各種文章,透過接觸許多不同風格的文章,學生會對該語言的整體有所了解。目的是透過接觸廣泛的詞彙、文法和想法來提高流利度。這種方法最適合喜歡閱讀並樂於自己尋找新閱讀材料的學生。但批評這個方法的人認為,這個方式只會讓讀者對目標語言只有粗淺的理解。

第二種技巧叫作「密集閱讀」。與吸收越多越好的「廣泛閱讀」相反,「密集閱讀」選擇較短的文章,但會仔細閱讀這些簡短作品,對它們做深入分析,側重於文法和句子結構。藉由這種方式,人們對文章內容會有更全面的理解。但批評者則認為,專注於單一文本可能會很無聊。

將這些技巧結合使用效果可能會最好,每個學生都應該自己做決定,如何妥善將這些技巧結合,成為自己的學習風格和語言目標。在廣泛閱讀和密集閱讀間取得適當平衡,就能找到最妥善的學習方法。

(A) considering	(B) intimidating	(C) superficial	(D) absorb	(E) proper
(A) 考慮	(B) 令人生畏的	(C) 粗淺的	(D) 吸收	(E) 適當的
(F) exposure	(G) emerges	(H) analyzing	(I) endeavor	(J) contrast
(F) 暴露	(G) 發生、出現	(H) 分析	(I) 努力	(J) 對比、對照

原文

Learning a new language can be an [1]**intimidating** task. Many learners have no idea how to start this kind of [2]**endeavor**. There have been a few different strategies developed by others that are worth considering. They focus on different aspects of language and how to learn it. Students can decide for themselves how to best utilize these techniques.

One approach is called "[3]**extensive** reading". This is when the reader tries to absorb as much different writing in the [4]**target language** as possible. By taking in many different styles, the student gains some understanding of the full possibilities of that language. The goal is to gain fluency through [5]**exposure** to a wide [6]**range** of vocabulary, grammar, and ideas. This technique works best with students who enjoy reading and are happy to **seek out** new reading material on their own. Critics of this style say that readers only develop a [7]**superficial** understanding of the target language this way.

A second technique is called "[8]**intensive** reading." **In contrast to** extensive reading, which tries to take in as much as possible, intensive reading chooses shorter texts. However, intensive reading **takes a hard look at** these short pieces of writing, analyzing them deeply. The reader focuses on the grammar and sentence structure. In this way, a fuller understanding of the text [9]**emerges**. Critics say that focusing on one short piece can lead to boredom.

Likely, using a combination of these techniques would work best. Each student should determine how to best [10]**integrate** these techniques for their own learning styles and language goals. The proper balance of extensive and intensive reading will lead to well-balanced course of study.

重要單字

1. **intimidating** [ɪnˋtɪmədetɪŋ] *(adj.)* 嚇人的、令人生畏的
   → intimidate *(vt.)* 恫嚇、恐嚇
   → intimidate sb. into N/Ving 脅迫某人做某事

2. **endeavor** [ɪnˋdɛvə] *(n.)* [C, U] 努力
   → make an endeavor to V_R 努力做⋯
   → make every endeavor to V_R 盡一切努力、不遺餘力去⋯

3. **extensive** [ɪk`stɛnsɪv] *(adj.)* 廣泛的；廣大的
   → extensive reading 廣泛閱讀
   → extent *(n.)* [U] 廣度、寬度；程度；區域
   → to the extent that... 到⋯程度；到⋯地步

4. **target language** [ˋtɑrgɪt ˋlæŋgwɪdʒ] *(n.)* 目標語言（指被翻譯的語言）
   → target *(n.)* 目標、靶子
   → hit/miss the target 中靶（正中目標）／脫靶（未擊中目標）

5. **exposure** [ɪk`spoʒɚ] *(n.)* [C, U] 暴露；曝光
   → expose *(vt.)* 暴露；露出；使曝光 (+ **to** N)
   → expose one's skin to the sun 使皮膚曬到太陽

6. **range** [rendʒ] *(n.)* [C] 範圍；區域
   → a wide range of opinions 各式各樣的看法

7. **superficial** [ˋsupɚˋfɪʃəl] *(adj.)* 表面的；膚淺的
   → receive superficial injuries/cuts/wounds 受了點皮肉傷

8. **intensive** [ɪn`tɛnsɪv] *(adj.)* 加強的；密集的
   → intensive training 密集訓練
   → intensive care unit 加護病房，簡稱 ICU
   → intensify *(v.)* 加強、強化
   → intensity *(n.)* 強度；強烈、劇烈

9. **emerge** [ɪˋmɝdʒ] *(vi.)* 浮現；出現；發生 (+ from/out of)
   → emerging technology/market 新興技術／新興市場
   → emergency *(n.)* [C, U] 緊急情況；突發事件

10. **integrate** [ˋɪntəˌgret] *(vi.)* 使成一體、使結合 (+ with/into)
    → integrate oneself into the society 讓自己融入社會
    → integrate exercise into your normal life 讓運動成為日常生活的一部分

重要片語

1. **seek out** 找到、找來

2. **in contrast to** 與⋯相比

3. **take a hard look at + N** 審視、仔細考慮⋯

1. **worth 用法**

(1) be worth + Ving「值得（做）…的」

例 There have been a few different strategies... that **are worth considering**.
有不少方法值得考慮。

(2) worth 後也可加一般名詞：be worth + N「值得…的」

例 worth our attention
值得注意的

例 worth a visit
值得參觀的

2. **分詞構句**

例 Intensive reading takes a hard look at these short pieces of writing, **analyzing** them deeply.
精密閱讀需要對這些簡短作品進行細讀並深入分析。

→ 分詞構句能使句子更簡潔：本句的從屬子句原句為 **and intensive reading** analyzes them deeply，將其與主要子句相同的連接詞及主詞省略，主動動詞簡化為 Ving。

第 31 至 35 題為題組 —— 傳統文化

Matsu is a chain of islands located in the northwest of Taiwan. __31__ Matsu lies near the mouth of the Min river, as it opens into the sea from mainland China.

Water and wind erosion have sculpted striking features upon Matsu over millions of years. The scenery can suddenly go from steep hills and high cliff faces to deep valleys and bays. The relentless surf has created unique features such as caves and rock columns.

__32__ Two of these granite mountains, Bi and Yun-Tai, are listed among Taiwan's 100 Minor Mountains.

__33__ Instead, the island relies heavily on its vast fishing resources. Due to the islands' isolation, there are many distinctive plant species here, such as the Matsu Wild Lily and the Matsu Lycoris. The islands are also temporarily home to many migratory birds each year.

Unlike most of Taiwan, Matsu has four distinct seasons. Matsu is only one degree of latitude north of Taiwan, but because it is so close to the continental climate, it is significantly cooler. __34__ In the spring, fog is often so heavy that flights must be cancelled. Spring is also monsoon season, and Matsu is strongly affected.

Fishermen began using Matsu during their expeditions centuries ago. Later it became a hideout for Japanese pirates. It wasn't really settled until around the Qing period, when fishermen began to stay permanently on the island to raise families. Matsu was under martial law during the Communist revolution of 1949. __35__

譯文

馬祖是位於台灣西北方的列島，(C) **這些小島僅占地大約 30 平方公里**。馬祖鄰近閩江口，位於閩江從中國大陸通往大海之處。

數百萬年來，水和風蝕已雕塑出馬祖標誌性的特色。景觀可能從陡峭的山丘及高聳的懸崖，突然轉變為深谷和海灣，連續的碎浪創造出如洞穴和岩石柱等獨特的景觀。(B) **馬祖由堅硬的花崗岩組成，景觀多為山**。其中兩座花崗岩山——壁山和雲台山——更被列於台灣小百岳之中。

(E) **由於馬祖的地勢崎嶇陡峭，農耕相當困難**。取而代之的是，馬祖極度依賴其龐大的漁獲資源。由於馬祖島嶼的孤立性，島上有許多獨特的植物物種，例如馬祖野百合和馬祖杜鵑。而這些島嶼也是許多候鳥每年暫居的所在。

與台灣大部分地區不同，馬祖有鮮明的四季。馬祖只比台灣高 1 度緯度，但由於它非常接近大陸性氣候，因此涼爽得多。(A) **冬季時，強風吹襲馬祖**。春季時，時常大霧籠罩，必須取消航班。而春天也是季風季，馬祖會受到嚴重影響。

幾個世紀以前，漁民開始利用馬祖。後來，它成了日本海盜的藏身之處。直到清朝左右，漁民才開始永久留在島上以養家，並真正定居下來。1949 年共產主義革命期間，馬祖遵守戒嚴令。(D) **如今，許多軍事機構仍然屹立，供遊客參觀探索**。

(A) Strong winds buffet Matsu during the winter months.
　　冬季時，強風吹襲馬祖。

(B) Matsu is composed of rocky granite, and the landscape is generally mountainous.
　　馬祖由堅硬的花崗岩組成，景觀多為山。

(C) These small islands comprise only about 30 square kilometers of land.
　　這些小島僅占地大約 30 平方公里。

(D) Today many military structures still stand, and may be explored by tourists.
　　如今，許多軍事機構仍然屹立，供遊客參觀探索。

(E) Because Matsu's terrain is so rugged, farming is difficult.
　　由於馬祖的地勢崎嶇陡峭，農耕相當困難。

原文

Matsu is a chain of islands located in the northwest of Taiwan. These small islands [1)]**comprise** only about 30 square kilometers of land. Matsu lies near the mouth of the Min river, as it opens into the sea from mainland China.

Water and wind [2)]**erosion** have sculpted [3)]**striking** features upon Matsu over millions of years. The scenery can suddenly go from steep hills and high cliff faces to deep [4)]**valleys** and bays. The relentless surf has created unique features such as caves and rock columns. Matsu **is composed of** rocky [5)]**granite**, and the landscape is generally mountainous. Two of these granite mountains, Bi and Yun-Tai, are listed among Taiwan's 100 Minor Mountains.

Because Matsu's [6)]**terrain** is so [7)]**rugged**, farming is difficult. Instead the island **relies** heavily **on** its vast fishing resources. Due to the islands' isolation, there are many distinctive plant species here, such as the Matsu Wild Lily and the Matsu Lycoris. The islands are also [8)]**temporarily** home to many migratory birds each year.

Unlike most of Taiwan, Matsu has four distinct seasons. Matsu is only one degree of [9)]**latitude** north of Taiwan, but because it is so close to the continental climate, it is significantly cooler. Strong winds [10)]**buffet** Matsu during the winter months. In the spring, fog is often so heavy that flights must be cancelled. Spring is also **monsoon season**, and Matsu is strongly affected.

Fishermen began using Matsu during their [11)]**expeditions** centuries ago. Later it became a hideout for Japanese pirates. It wasn't really settled until around the Qing period, when fishermen began to stay [12)]**permanently** on the island to raise families. Matsu was under martial law during the Communist revolution of 1949. Today many military structures still stand, and may be explored by tourists.

1. **comprise** [kəmˋpraɪz] *(vt.)* 包含；由…組成
   → （主動用法）comprise + N 包含 = consist of + N
   → （被動用法）be comprised of + N 由…組成 = be composed of + N, be made up of + N

2. **erosion** [ɪˋroʒən] *(n.)* [U] 侵蝕、腐蝕；逐步破壞、削弱 = undermine
   → soil/coast erosion 水土流失／海岸侵蝕
   → (gradual) erosion of...（逐漸）侵蝕、破壞…

3. **striking** [ˋstraɪkɪŋ] *(adj.)* 引人注目的、很有魅力的 = attractive, appealing
   → bear striking similarities between A and B A 與 B 有驚人的相似性
   → be within striking distance 只差些許距離（到某地或達成某事）

4. **valley** [ˋvælɪ] *(n.)* [C] 山谷；溪谷
   → 相關字：gorge（峽谷）、canyon（峽谷）

5. **granite** [ˋgrænɪt] *(n.)* [U] 花崗岩
   → be made of granite 以花崗岩製成

6. **terrain** [təˋren] *(n.)* [U] 地形、地勢
   → rough/smooth/difficult terrain 崎嶇不平／平順／難以駕駛的地形

7. **rugged** [ˋrʌgɪd] *(adj.)* 高低不平的；粗糙的 = rough, bumpy, up-and-down
   → rugged terrain/landscape 崎嶇不平的地形／地貌

8. **temporarily** [ˋtɛmpəˏrɛrəlɪ] *(adv.)* 暫時地、臨時地 = on a temporary basis
   → temporary *(adj.)* 暫時的、短暫的 = tentative, momentary ↔ permanent 永久的
   → a temporary measure/means 暫時的解決方法

9. **latitude** [ˋlætəˏtjud] *(n.)* [U] 緯度；（言行或思維上的）自由
   → have (considerable/greater) latitude **in/for** N/Ving 在某事上有（更多的）自由
   → longitude *(n.)* [U] 經度

10. **buffet** [ˋbʌfɪt] *(vt.)* （風浪等）衝擊 *(n.)* （人生等的）打擊
      [bəˋfe] *(n.)* [C] 自助餐
    → All life's buffets should be met with dignity and good sense.
       所有人生打擊都應以尊嚴和理智處理。

11. **expedition** [ˏɛkspɪˋdɪʃən] *(n.)* [C] 遠征、探險；遠征隊、探險隊
    → on an expedition to + 地點 在去…的探險途中
    → go on a shopping expedition 去購物 = go shopping
    → expedite *(vt.)* 促進、加速完成

12. **permanently** [ˋpɝmənəntlɪ] *(adv.)* 永久地 ↔ temporarily
   → permanent *(adj.)* 永久的、恆久的；常在的、固定的
   → permanent job 固定工作 ↔ part-time job 臨時工作
   → permanent resident 永久居民
   → cause permanent damage (to N) 造成（某人或物）終身傷害

重要片語

1. **be composed of** 由…組成 = be made up of
2. **rely on** 依靠 = depend on, count on
3. **monsoon season** 季風季節

相關文法句型

1. **not... until... 直到…才…**
   (1) not until 句型中，until 後面會接某個時間點或某事件，表「直到」該時間點或該事件發生後，另一件事「才」會發生。

   例 It **wasn't** really settled **until around the Qing period**, when fishermen began to stay permanently on the island to raise families.
   直到清朝左右，漁民才開始永久留在島上養家，並真正定居下來。

   例 I did **not** get home **until midnight**.
   直到午夜我才回到家。

   例 Sam did **not** get dressed **until his mother asked him to**.
   山姆一直等到媽媽叫他，他才去著裝。

   (2) until 口語上常簡稱為 till，書寫上使用 until 較為正式。

   (3) 句型「S + V + until...」，則表「做…直到…為止」。

   例 Pauline worked as a high school teacher **until** she retired at the age of 60.
   寶琳擔任高中老師，直到她六十歲退休為止。

   (4) Not until 放句首時，須使用倒裝句：「**Not until... + 助動詞 + S + V**」。倒裝步驟如下：
   ① 先將 not until 連同其後的名詞（片語）或子句移前。
   ② 再接助動詞以及原 not 後的主要子句。

   例 **Not until** midnight **did I get** home.
   直到午夜我才回到家。

   例 **Not until** Sam's mother asked him to **did he get dressed**.
   直到山姆媽媽叫他，他才去著裝。

第貳部分：非選擇題

一、中譯英 —— 台灣美景

1. 太魯閣峽谷（Taroko Gorge）坐落於陡峭的台灣東部。這個大自然的奇景是台灣最多遊客造訪的國家公園。

Taroko Gorge [sits/lies/stands / is situated/located / is seated] in the [rugged / steep] eastern part of Taiwan.

This natural wonder is the most visited/frequented national park in Taiwan.

2. 即使我已經去過四次，卻不會厭倦。我希望在不久的將來能更深入探索這個幅員遼闊的國家公園。

Although I have been there four times, I never get tired of visiting Taroko and hope to explore more of the massive park in the near future.

二、英文作文 —— 外語學習

如果你有機會學習一種除了英語之外的第三外語，你會選擇哪一項？請以此為題，寫一篇至少 120 個英文單詞的作文。說明你的選擇及理由，並舉例說明你要如何運用此語言。也請說明你不選擇另一項語言的理由或考量為何。

語言一：西班牙語（Spanish）為 20 個主權獨立國家的官方語言，全球約 4.4 億人口說西班牙語。除西班牙外，大部分說西班牙語的人口主要集中在拉丁美洲（中南美）國家，因此西班牙語在美洲相當受歡迎，是美洲第一大語言。

語言二：法語（French）為 29 個主權獨立國家和其他多個地區的官方語言，全球約 3.9 億人口說法文。除法國及某些歐洲國家，大部分說法文的人口主要分布於北美及非洲國家，因此法語在非洲相當流行，是僅次於阿拉伯語的非洲第二大語言。

作文範文

　　I've given it some consideration and I've decided to study Spanish language. I think it would be among the most useful languages to learn. Spanish is spoken in much of the Western hemisphere. Even in the U.S., where the official language is English, Spanish is increasingly prevalent. My education will be complete around this time next year, and I plan on commencing my career in New York. I have always dreamed about moving to the Big Apple to take advantage of its endless opportunities. That same promise of opportunity has attracted millions of immigrants. Spanish-speaking people abound in the metropolis. Chances are, I will work with many of them. Although we could probably communicate using English as a lingua franca, our interactions will be more genial and precise if we can converse in their mother tongue. There are a substantial number of Spanish television and radio shows produced in America, so I could achieve a deep language immersion simply by consuming these media. Additionally, I believe Spanish would be relatively easy for me to learn due to its grammatical similarity to English. Having a good command of the three most commonly-spoken languages in the U.S.—English, Spanish, and Mandarin—may be what it takes to distinguish myself from the crowd of applicants for jobs in my field. Because of America's swiftly increasing Hispanic population, there are a multitude of employers seeking Spanish-speaking employees. I would gain a competitive advantage with fluency in Spanish.

　　I have tried to learn French. I even spent countless hours trying to understand the basics of its grammar, but it's still all Greek to me. Since my plan is to go to America, where very few people speak French, even if I did manage to learn French, I would have very few chances to use it in everyday life in the U.S. and my skills might fade. Ever since setting foot in America on a visit years ago, I knew it was where I wanted to settle down and start a career. Therefore, Spanish is a better investment of my time and effort.

譯文

　　稍做考慮之後，我決定學習西班牙語。我認為西班牙語是最實用的語言之一。西半球大部分地區都說西班牙語。即使美國的官方語言為英語，西班牙語也越來越盛行。明年大約此時我會完成學業，我計畫會在紐約展開職涯。我一直夢想著能搬到人稱「大蘋果」的都市，好好利用那裡無限的機會。這些前途無量的機會已經吸引了無數的移民。在大都會中，會講西班牙語的人比比皆是，我將有機會和他們一起工作。儘管我們可以用作為通用語的英語溝通，但若能用他們的母語交談，我們的互動將能更加親切與精確。美國有大量的西班牙語的電視和廣播節目，因此，只要我能好好運用這些媒體，我就能達到深刻的沉浸式語言學習。此外，西班牙語和英語在文法上相似，因此，我認為這點對我而言，會相對更容易學習。掌握美國三種最常用的語言──英語、西班牙語和中文──或許會讓我在同領域的眾多求職者中脫穎而出。由於美國的西裔人口正迅速增加，因此有許多雇主在尋找會說西班牙語的員工，能說一口流利西班牙語會讓我獲得競爭優勢。

　　我曾經學過法語。我甚至花了無數小時想瞭解法語的基本文法，但我對這門語言仍然一竅不通。既然我的目標是去美國，那裡很少人說法語，因此，即使我真的認真學過法語，但在美國日常中也很少有機會用到，而且法語能力也會因而退步。自從我在數年前造訪過美國後，我就知道，那裡會是我想安定下來並展開職涯的地方。因此，西班牙語是我投入時間和精力的最佳選擇。

作文教學

　　I've given it some consideration and I've decided to study Spanish language. I think it would be among the most useful languages to learn. Spanish is spoken in much of the Western hemisphere. Even in the U.S., where the official language is English, Spanish is increasingly prevalent. My education will be complete around this time next year, and I plan on [1)]**commencing** my career in New York. I have always dreamed about moving to the Big Apple to take advantage of its endless opportunities. That same promise of opportunity has attracted millions of immigrants. Spanish-speaking people [2)]**abound** in the metropolis. Chances are, I will work with many of them. Although we could probably communicate using English as a [3)]**lingua franca**, our interactions will be more [4)]**genial** and precise if we can converse in their [5)]**mother tongue**. There are a [6)]**substantial** number of Spanish television and radio shows produced in America, so I could achieve a deep [7)]**language immersion** simply by consuming these media. Additionally, I believe Spanish would be relatively easy for me to learn due to its grammatical similarity to English. **Having a good command of** the three most commonly-spoken languages in the U.S.—English, Spanish, and Mandarin—may be what it takes to distinguish myself from the crowd of applicants for jobs in my field. Because of America's [8)]**swiftly** increasing Hispanic population, there are **a multitude of** employers seeking Spanish-speaking employees. I would **gain a** competitive **advantage** with fluency in Spanish.

　　I have tried to learn French. I even spent countless hours trying to understand the basics of its grammar, but it's still all Greek to me. Since my plan is to go to America, where very few people speak French, even if I did **manage to** learn French, I would have very few chances to use it in everyday life in the U.S. and my skills might fade. Ever since setting foot in America on a visit years ago, I knew it was where I wanted to **settle down** and start a career. Therefore, Spanish is a better investment of my time and effort.

重要單字

1. **commence** [kə`mɛns] *(vt.)* 開始、著手
   → commencement *(n.)* 開始；（美）畢業典禮

2. **abound** [ə`baʊnd] *(vi.)* 大量存在、有很多

3. **lingua franca** *(n.)* [C]（不同母語人士之間交流用的）通用語
   → 指某個地區中最常被使用的語言，以國際村的觀點來看，「英文」就是廣泛被用來與世界溝通的語言，所以視為一種通用語言。

4. **genial** [`dʒinjəl] *(adj.)* 友善的、和藹的 = friendly, affable

5. **mother tongue** [`mʌðɚ tʌŋ] *(n.)* [C] 母語 = native language = the first language

6. **substantial** [səb`stænʃəl] *(adj.)* 大量的

7. **language immersion** [`læŋgwɪdʒ ɪ`mɝʒən] *(n.)* 浸潤式語言學習
   → 有一派學者認為，學習一門語言最好的方式就是「沉浸在」在充滿該語言的環境中，無論所聽所見所聞都是該門語言，如全美語學校就是典型的沉浸式語言學習。
   → be immersed/absorbed/engrossed/steeped in... 沉浸於⋯

8. **swiftly** [`swɪftlɪ] *(adv.)* 快速地 = quickly, promptly, rapidly

重要片語

1. **have a (good) command/mastery of + 語言／技能** 精通某語言／技能
2. **a multitude of** 很多⋯（後加可數名詞）
3. **have/win/gain a(n)... advantage** 取得／贏得⋯優勢
4. **manage to + V_R** 試圖去完成、做到⋯
5. **settle down** 定居；安頓下來、塵埃落定

1. **(the) chances are + that + S + V 有可能…**
   = it is (very) likely + that + S + V

   例 I'd bring an umbrella because **chances are** it's going to rain today.
   我會帶把傘，因為今天很有可能會下雨。

2. **be all Greek to + sb. 某人對…一竅不通**
   Greek 指希臘語，對許多人來說，希臘語就像外星語言一樣，因此延伸成對某事一竅不通。

   例 It**'s all Greek to** me.
   我全然不懂。

NOTE

第 3 回 │ 解析

第壹部分：選擇題

一、綜合測驗

第 1 至 10 題為題組 ── 名人偉事

Marie Curie is one of the most famous scientists of the 20th century. In 1867, she was born Maria Sklodowska in Poland but moved to Paris, France as a young woman to pursue educational opportunities. It was in Paris __1__ she met her husband, Pierre Curie, in 1894. The two began researching the mineral uranium and its property of __2__ invisible rays. These rays are called radiation, and have the ability __3__ through solid matter. Marie eventually __4__ polonium and radium, elements even more radioactive than uranium.

1903 was a successful year for Curie. She completed her doctorate degree and won a Nobel prize, __5__ with Pierre and another scientist. Sadly, her husband was killed in an accident in 1906, but Marie continued the work they had started together. In 1911, Marie Curie won another Nobel for __6__ a way to measure radiation. She also created new research programs for the study of radiation and cancer. During the First World War, Curie traveled to the battlefield. As Director of the Red Cross Radiological Service, she used an X-ray machine she __7__ to diagnose soldiers' injuries.

After the war ended, Curie continued working and teaching. She earned __8__ for her pioneering work in chemistry, physics and medicine. __9__ her determination and intelligence, Marie Curie continues to __10__ people interested in science throughout the world.

譯文

　　瑪麗居禮夫人是二十世紀最有名的科學家之一。1867 年，她以瑪麗亞斯克沃多夫斯卡之名誕生於波蘭，之後便搬到法國巴黎，以一名年輕女子的身分追求教育機會。1894 年時，她和她的丈夫皮耶居禮於巴黎相識。兩人開始研究鈾礦物及它發散出眼睛看不見的射線特性。這些射線被稱作輻射，具有穿透固態物質的能力。瑪麗後來還發現釙和鐳，這兩個元素的輻射性都比鈾來得強。

　　1903 年對居禮夫人而言是很成功的一年。她完成了博士學位，還和皮耶以及其他科學家一同獲頒諾貝爾獎。令人難過的是，她的丈夫在 1906 年的一場意外中不幸去世了，但瑪麗仍繼續兩人先前早已起步的工作。1911 年，瑪麗因為開發出一種測量輻射的方法而獲頒另一座諾貝爾獎。不僅如此，她還為了探討輻射和癌症，建立了新的研究計畫。第一次世界大戰期間，居禮夫人跋涉到戰場。身為紅十字放射服務服務部總監，她使用她之前發明的 X 光機診斷士兵傷勢。

　　戰爭結束後，居禮夫人還是不停地工作和教書。世人認可她在化學、物理及藥學的開創性成就。由於其決心和聰穎，居禮夫人現今仍持續激勵著世界各地對科學感到興趣的人們。

1. (A) and   (B) when   (C) which   **(D) that**

> 解說   It is/was + 要強調的部分 + **that** + 句子剩餘的部分

2. **(A) giving off**   (B) giving up   (C) giving away   (D) giving in
   (A) 發出   (B) 放棄   (C) 送出   (D) 勉強同意；屈服於

3. (A) pass   **(B) to pass**   (C) passing   (D) to passing

> 解說   the (in)ability **to V$_R$** 有（無）能力去做…
> = be (un)able **to V$_R$** 有（無）能力去做…
> = the (in)capability **of Ving / to V$_R$**
> = be (in)capable **of Ving** 有（無）能力去做…

4. (A) discharged   **(B) discovered**   (C) disappeared   (D) discarded
   (A) 排出   **(B) 發現**   (C) 消失   (D) 拋棄

5. (A) sharing   (B) is sharing   **(C) shared**   (D) was shared

> 解說   此句為關係子句簡化而來的分詞片語，原句為「... which was shared...」。

6. **(A) developing**   (B) dedicating   (C) delivering   (D) depending
   (A) 開發   (B) 奉獻   (C) 運送   (D) 取決於

7. **(A) had invented**   (B) has invented   (C) had been inventing   (D) had been invented

> 解說   had + Vpp 為過去完成式的主動語態，表在上戰場前已發明出機器。

8. (A) representation   (B) responsibility   (C) reservation   **(D) recognition**
   (A) 代表權   (B) 責任   (C) 預約   **(D) 認可**

9. (A) Beyond   (B) Despite   **(C) Due to**   (D) As
   (A) 超過   (B) 儘管   **(C) 因為**   (D) 作為

10. (A) inform   (B) imitate   (C) insult   **(D) inspire**
    (A) 告知   (B) 仿效   (C) 汙辱   **(D) 激勵**

原文

Marie Curie is one of the most famous scientists of the 20th century. In 1867, she was born Maria Sklodowska in Poland but moved to Paris, France as a young woman to pursue educational opportunities. It was in Paris that she met her husband, Pierre Curie, in 1894. The two began researching the ¹⁾**mineral** ²⁾**uranium** and its property of giving off ³⁾**invisible** rays. These rays are called ⁴⁾**radiation**, and have the ability to pass through solid matter. Marie eventually discovered ⁵⁾**polonium** and ⁶⁾**radium**, elements even more radioactive than uranium.

1903 was a successful year for Curie. She completed her doctorate degree and won a Nobel prize, shared with Pierre and another scientist. Sadly, her husband was killed in an accident in 1906, but Marie continued the work they had started together. In 1911, Marie Curie won another Nobel for developing a way to ⁷⁾**measure** radiation. She also created new research programs for the study of radiation and cancer. During the First World War, Curie traveled to the battlefield. As Director of the Red Cross Radiological Service, she used an X-ray machine she had invented to ⁸⁾**diagnose** soldiers' injuries.

After the war ended, Curie continued working and teaching. She earned recognition for her ⁹⁾**pioneering** work in chemistry, physics and medicine. Due to her determination and intelligence, Marie Curie continues to inspire people interested in science throughout the world.

重要單字

1. **mineral** [`mɪnərəl] *(n.)* [C] 礦物 *(adj.)* 含礦物的、有礦物質的
   → minerals and vitamins（人體所需）礦物質與維生素

2. **uranium** [ju`renɪəm] *(n.)* 鈾

3. **invisible** [ɪn`vɪzəbḷ] *(adj.)* 看不見的、隱形的
   → invisible barrier 無形的屏障、隔閡
   → be invisible to + N 無法被…偵測、看見
   → invisibility *(n.)* 隱形、不可見 *(adj.)* 無形的

4. **radiation** [ˌredɪ`eʃən] *(n.)* [U] 輻射；放射線
   → microwave/ultraviolet/electromagnetic radiation 微波／紫外線／電磁波輻射
   → radiate *(v.)*（光、熱）輻射、放射；從中心散開
   → radioactive *(adj.)* 具放射性的、有輻射性的

5. **polonium** [pə`lonɪəm] *(n.)* 釙

---

6. **radium** [ˋredɪəm] *(n.)* 鐳

7. **measure** [ˋmɛʒɚ] *(vi.)* 測量 *(n.)* [C] 方法 = approach, means, way
   → measure up to N 符合、達到… = live up to N
   → measurement *(n.)* 測量、丈量
   → measurements *(n.)* （固定用複數）尺寸；三圍

8. **diagnose** [ˋdaɪəgnoz] *(vt.)* 診斷（病症）
   → sb. be diagnosed + **with** (having) 病症 某人被診斷患有某病症
   → diagnosis *(n.)* [C] 診斷
   → make an initial diagnosis 作出初步診斷

9. **pioneering** [paɪəˋnɪərɪŋ] *(adj.)* 開創的、首創的、先導的
   → pioneering company 創新企業、新創公司 = startup
   → pioneer *(n.)* [C] 先驅、創始人；拓荒者、開發者 *(v.)* 開拓、倡導
   → pioneer (in the field) of N 某（領域）事物的開創者、先鋒

重要片語

1. **give off** 散發出（光、電、熱能、氣味或氣息）
2. **pass through** 穿過
3. **share with sb.** 與某人共享

相關文法句型

1. **It 強調句**

   例 **It was in Paris that** she met her husband, Pierre Curie, in 1894.
   1894 年她和她的丈夫皮耶居禮就是在巴黎相識的。

   句型「It is/was + 要強調的部分 + that + S + V」，用來加強語氣，步驟如下：
   ① 將要強調的部分放在 be 動詞與 that 之間，其餘的部分放在 that 後方。
   ② that 之前的先行詞若是人，則 that 也可用 who 或 whom 來代替。
   ③ 不論被強調的元素是單複數，it 後面的 be 動詞仍維持單數的 is/was。

   　　例 **Dr. White** made me fall in love with literature.
   　　　→ **It was Dr. White who/that** made me fall in love with literature.
   　　　是懷特教授讓我愛上文學。
   　　　→ 強調主詞 Dr. White。

例 The boy broke **the antique vase** accidentally.
→ **It was the antique vase that** the boy broke accidentally.
那個男孩不小心打破的是個古董花瓶。
→ 強調受詞 the antique vase。

例 Her boyfriend proposed to her **on her birthday**.
→ **It was on her birthday that** her boyfriend proposed to her.
就是在她生日那天男友和她求婚的。
→ 強調時間副詞 on her birthday。

2. **due to 表「由於」**

例 **Due to** her determination and intelligence, Marie Curie continues to inspire people interested in science throughout the world.
由於她的決心和聰穎，居禮夫人現今仍持續激勵著世界各地對科學感興趣的人。
→ due to 後面要接名詞（片語）。

其他表達「因果」的句型：

(1) because 為「從屬連接詞」，**後面要接完整句子**，等於 since 與 as。

(2) because of 為「介系詞」，**後面接名詞（片語）**，此時 because of 等於 due to、owing to、as a result of、on account of、thanks to。

例 **Because the flight was delayed**, they missed the important meeting.
= **Because of the flight delay**, they missed the important meeting.
= **Owing to the flight delay**, they missed the important meeting.
因為班機延遲，他們錯過那場重要的會議。

例 The window of the house was broken **because the wind was too strong**.
= The window of the house was broken **because of the strong wind**.
= The window of the house was broken **as a result of the strong wind**.
由於強風的緣故，房子的窗戶都破了。

例 **Because of her serious illness**, Mary had to avoid public for two weeks.
= **Since Mary suffered from a serious illness**, she had to avoid public for two weeks.
由於瑪麗病得很嚴重，這兩週她必須避免到公共場所。

Johannes Kepler is a legend of science and astronomy. A man of many interests and talents, he revolutionized the way humans view the universe and their place within it. He was a man of ___11___, and a product of a very contrasting time.

Kepler was born in what is now Germany in 1571. He was a sickly child, and suffered lifelong ___12___ to his vision as a result of smallpox. He displayed a fantastic talent for mathematics ___13___ a very young age. His mother, a lover of nature, showed him the night sky, which increased his interests in astronomy.

Kepler began working with another ___14___ astronomer of the time, Tycho Brahe. Though the two scientists ___15___ conflict at times, their relationship was a fruitful one. After Brahe's death, Kepler gained ___16___ to his extensive data on planetary movement. With this data, Kepler was able to determine that the planets' orbits aren't exactly ___17___, but elliptical, in a form of an oval. This was a revolutionary concept at the time.

Kepler made many other such scientific ___18___. He discovered that ___19___ from the sun, the weaker the sun's gravitational force was on that planet. He determined that the tides were caused by the gravity of the moon. He figured out the human eye actually ___20___ images upside down, and our brains correct them. Truly, Kepler is one of the greatest scientific thinkers in history.

譯文

約翰尼斯克卜勒是科學和天文界的傳奇人物。他興趣廣泛又極有天賦，徹底改變人類看待宇宙及周遭的觀點。他是個矛盾的人，也是矛盾時代之下的產物。

1571 年，克卜勒於現今的德國出生。他是個體弱多病的小孩，終身受到天花所造成的視力殘缺所苦。年幼時，他便展現在數學上的超群天賦。他那熱愛大自然的母親帶他去看夜空之後，更是增加他對天文學的興趣。

克卜勒便開始和當時另一位著名的天文學家第谷布拉赫一同工作。儘管兩位科學家偶爾會發生衝突，他們的合作還是產出了許多成果。布拉赫過世之後，克卜勒得到與行星運動有關的龐大資料。這些資料使克卜勒得以確定，行星運行的軌道並非精準的圓形，而是橢圓形。這在當時是全新的概念。

克卜勒在科學上做出許多諸如此類的突破。他發現某一行星距離太陽越遠，該行星所受到的太陽引力就會越小。他也確立了潮汐是受到月球引力的影響。他更發現人類的眼睛在看到影像時，其實是上下顛倒的，而是我們的腦矯正了這些影像。毫無疑問地，克卜勒是歷史上最傑出的科學思想家之一。

11. (A) connections   **(B) contradictions**   (C) confusions   (D) considerations
    (A) 關聯   **(B) 矛盾**   (C) 困惑   (D) 考慮

12. (A) impression   (B) imprisonment   **(C) impairment**   (D) improvement
    (A) 印象   (B) 拘禁   **(C) 殘缺**   (D) 改進

13. (A) on   **(B) at**   (C) in   (D) with

> **解說**   **at** a very young age 在年幼時。要表達特定的「**年齡、速度、價格、代價**」，都使用介系詞 at。

14. **(A) prominent**   (B) proficient   (C) profound   (D) present
    (A) 顯著的   (B) 擅長的   (C) 深遠的   (D) 現在的

15. **(A) came into**   (B) came with   (C) came on   (D) came up

> **解說**   come into conflict (with sb.)（與某人）發生衝突

16. (A) achievement   (B) accent   (C) account   **(D) access**
    (A) 成就   (B) 口音   (C) 帳號   **(D) 取用權**

17. (A) triangular   (B) square   **(C) circular**   (D) diamond
    (A) 三角的   (B) 方形的   **(C) 圓形的**   (D) 菱形的

18. (A) breakings   (B) breakups   (C) breakdowns   **(D) breakthroughs**
    (A) 無此用法   (B) 分手   (C) 故障   **(D) 突破**

19. (A) the farther was a planet away   **(B) the farther away a planet was**
    (C) farther a planet was away from   (D) farther away a planet was

> **解說**   表「越⋯，就越⋯」：the + **adj.-er** + S$_1$ + V$_1$, the + **adj.-er** + S$_2$ + V$_2$.

20. **(A) sees**   (B) see   (C) saw   (D) seeing

> **解說**   此句為一事實，故用現在簡單式。

原文

Johannes Kepler is a legend of science and [1)]**astronomy**. As a man of many interests and talents, he [2)]**revolutionized** the way humans view the universe and their place within it. He was a man of [3)]**contradictions**, and a product of a very contrasting time.

Kepler was born in what is now Germany in 1571. He was a sickly child, and suffered lifelong [4)]**impairment** to his vision as a result of smallpox. He displayed a fantastic talent for mathematics at a very young age. His mother, a lover of nature, showed him the night sky, which increased his interests in astronomy.

Kepler began working with another [5)]**prominent** astronomer of the time, Tycho Brahe. Though the two scientists came into conflict at times, their relationship was a [6)]**fruitful** one. After Brahe's death, Kepler gained access to his extensive data on planetary movement. With this data, Kepler was able to determine that the planets' orbits aren't exactly circular, but [7)]**elliptical**, in a form of an oval. This was a revolutionary concept at the time.

Kepler made many other such scientific breakthroughs. He discovered that the farther away a planet was from the sun, the weaker the sun's [8)]**gravitational force** was on that planet. He determined that the tides were caused by the gravity of the moon. He figured out the human eye actually sees images upside down, and our brains correct them. Truly, Kepler is one of the greatest scientific thinkers in history.

重要單字

1. **astronomy** [əsˋtrɑnəmɪ] *(n.)* [U] 天文學
   → astronomer *(n.)* [C] 天文學家
   → astronomical *(adj.)* 天文學的、天體的
   → astronaut *(n.)* [C] 太空人、宇航員
   → astrology *(n.)* [U] 占星學
   → astrologer *(n.)* [C] 占星師

2. **revolutionize** [ˌrɛvəˋluʃənˌaɪz] *(vt.)* 徹地改革、使⋯發生劇變
   → revolution *(n.)* [C] 革命
   → industrial/technological revolution 工業／科技革命
   → revolutionary *(adj.)* 革命性的、創新的

3. **contradiction** [ˌkɑntrəˋdɪkʃən] *(n.)* [C, U] 矛盾、衝突 = conflict, paradox
   → contradiction between A and B A 與 B 之間的矛盾、衝突
   → contradiction in terms 自相矛盾的說法；語句上的矛盾
   → contradictory [ˌkɑntrəˋdɪktərɪ] *(adj.)* 矛盾的 = conflicting, paradoxical

4. **impairment** [ɪmˋpɛrmənt] *(n.)* 損傷；（身體機能）障礙
    → hearing/intellectual impairment 聽力損害／智能障礙
    → impair *(vt.)* 損害、削弱

5. **prominent** [ˋprɑmənənt] *(adj.)* 重要的；著名的；顯眼的
    → play a prominent/important/crucial role (+ in sth.) 在某事上扮演重要角色
    → in a prominent position/place 在一個顯眼的位置
    → prominence *(n.)* [U] 顯著、有名

6. **fruitful** [ˋfrutfəl] *(adj.)* 富有成效的 ↔ fruitless 無成果的、無效的
    → fruitfulness *(n.)* [U] 豐收、有成果
    → fruitfully *(adv.)* 有成效地、有成果地

7. **elliptical** [ɪˋlɪptɪkl] *(adj.)* 橢圓形的

8. **gravitational force** [ˏgrævəˋteʃənḷ fors] *(n.)* 萬有引力、地心引力 = gravity
    → gravitational *(adj.)* 引力的、重力的
    → gravitation *(n.)* [U] 引力
    → the laws of gravity 萬有引力定律

重要片語

1. **increase... in...** 在（某方面）增加…
2. **come into conflict** 發生衝突
    = cause/create/provoke/lead to conflict 導致、引發、陷入衝突
    = bring sb./sth. into conflict 使…引起衝突

相關文法句型

1. 「年齡」的表達方式
    (1) 表達「（人）幾歲」：be 數字 (year(s) old) 或 be at the age of + 數字
    (2) 表達「（人）十幾歲」：be in one's 數字 **s**

2. **the way** 表示「如何…，用…方式」
    例 As a man of many interests and talents, he revolutionized **the way** **humans view the universe and their place within it**.
    他興趣廣泛且極富天賦，徹底改變人類看待宇宙及周遭的觀點。
    (1) 後方可加上 that、in which。

(2) the way 也可以使用 how 代替，注意，**the way 與 how 不會同時出現！**

例 The public was shocked by **the way** **this pet shop treated animals**.
  → The public was shocked by **the way** **(that/in which)** **this pet shop treated animals**.
  → The public was shocked by **how** **this pet shop treated animals**.
  各界對於這間寵物店對待動物的方式感到震驚。

3. 和 **time** 有關的片語

例 Though the two scientists came into conflict **at times**, their relationship was a fruitful one.
儘管兩位科學家偶爾會發生衝突，他們的合作還是產出了很多成果。

其他包含 time 的片語：
→ all the time 總是、一直
→ of all time 有史以來
→ for the time being 暫時、暫且
→ at the time 在當時
→ at one's time of life 在⋯這樣的年紀
→ in time 及時地
→ on time 準時地
→ about time 早該
→ at all times 一直、總是
→ at times 有時
→ at one time 過去；有一度

二、文意選填

第 21 至 30 題為題組 —— 夢的解析

Since ancient times, humans have wondered if dreams are just random images or if they hold some deeper meaning. Many have __21__ to interpret dreams over the centuries. Perhaps the most famous interpreter of dreams is psychoanalyst Sigmund Freud, whose very name is synonymous with exploring dreams as a window into a deeper level of the mind. Today, the debate over just how __22__ dreams really are continues. But that hasn't stopped several writers from publishing their own ideas about some of the most commonly __23__ dreams.

A dream about teeth falling out is very common, despite being rather __24__. The most common __25__ is that losing teeth in a dream represents anxiety about losing power, strength, or courage. To lose teeth is to lose the most basic defense mechanism.

Another dream that may be familiar is the dream of being __26__ in public, for all to see. This dream is usually interpreted as a fear of being exposed to your peers as incompetent or faulty in some other way. A related dream that many reports having is being late or unprepared __27__ an important exam. This dream is about the anxiety of being unable to cope __28__ the challenges of the real world. Sometimes these two dreams are combined and the dreamer finds himself failing an exam while naked!

Many people dream about flying. This represents freedom, adventure, and an escape from the __29__ obligations of life. This can be very exciting, and we often have this dream if we need a change in our routine.

There is no real way of knowing how much dreams actually mean. However, because dreams are such a big part of the human experience, we won't stop __30__ them any time soon!

譯文

　　從古至今，夢境都困惑著人類，關於究竟夢境是否僅是隨機的圖像，亦或蘊含了更深層的含意。幾個世紀以來，許多人都曾嘗試去解讀夢境。其中最具盛名的解夢家可能就屬心理分析家西格蒙德佛洛伊德了，而他的名字中也帶有把探索夢境當作一個窗口來解讀內心深處的意思。現今，關於夢境到底有沒有意義的辯論仍在進行中，但這也阻止不了一些作家發表他們對於常見夢境的相關看法。

　　作有關牙齒掉下來的夢是非常常見的，儘管這有些詭異。最常見的解釋就是掉牙齒的夢代表對於失去權力、力量或勇氣感到焦慮。掉牙齒就是失去最基本的心理防禦機制。

　　另一種常見的夢境就是夢到在大眾場合讓大家看到裸體。這種夢境經常被解讀為一個人因為能力不足或不完美而害怕在同儕前展現自己。很多人也會做到類似的夢境，像是遲到或是沒有準備好重要的考試。這種夢境是和無法應付現實中的挑戰相關。有時這兩種夢會互相結合，做夢的人會夢見自己在赤裸身軀的狀態下考試落榜！

許多人會夢到飛翔。這種夢境代表自由、冒險和逃離生活中枯燥乏味的義務。這可說是非常令人興奮的，而當我們需要改變生活中的例行公事時，常會作這類的夢。

沒有確切的方法可以得知夢境究竟代表程度多高。然而，由於夢境是人生閱歷中很重要的一環，所以我們在短期內是不會停止分析它們的。

(A) naked	(B) with	(C) meaningful	(D) analyzing	(E) bizarre
(A) 裸身的	(B) cope with 應付	(C) 有意義的	(D) 分析	(E) 詭異的
(F) occurring	(G) interpretation	(H) dull	(I) for	(J) attempted
(F) 發生的	(G) 解釋	(H) 枯燥的	(I) 沒有準備好的	(J) 嘗試

原文

Since ancient times, humans have wondered if dreams are just random images or if they hold some deeper meaning. Many have attempted to interpret dreams over the centuries. Perhaps the most famous [1]interpreter of dreams is [2]psychoanalyst Sigmund Freud, whose very name is [3]synonymous with exploring dreams as a window into a deeper level of the mind. Today, the debate over just how meaningful dreams really are continues. But that hasn't stopped several writers from publishing their own ideas about some of the most commonly occurring dreams.

A dream about teeth falling out is very common, despite being rather [4]bizarre. The most common interpretation is that losing teeth in a dream represents anxiety about losing power, strength, or courage. To lose teeth is to lose the most basic [5]defense [6]mechanism.

Another dream that may be familiar is the dream of being naked in public, for all to see. This dream is usually interpreted as a fear of being exposed to your peers as incompetent or faulty in some other way. A related dream that many report having is being late or unprepared for an important exam. This dream is about the anxiety of being unable to cope with the challenges of the real world. Sometimes these two dreams are combined and the dreamer finds himself failing an exam while naked!

Many people dream about flying. This represents freedom, adventure, and an escape from the [7]dull [8]obligations of life. This can be very exciting, and we often have this dream if we need a change in our routine.

There is no real way of knowing how much dreams actually mean. However, because dreams are such a big part of the human experience, we won't stop analyzing them any time soon!

1. **interpreter** [ɪnˋtɝprɪtɚ] *(n.)* [C] 釋義者；口譯員
   → interpret *(v.)* 解釋、闡釋；（對於作品的）演譯；翻譯 = translate
   → interpret sth. as N 把某事解釋為、看作是…
   → interpretation [ɪnˌtɝprɪˋteʃən] *(n.)* [U, C] 解釋、闡明；（音樂、戲劇等）表演
   → be open to interpretation 可作各種詮釋、有開放的討論空間

2. **psychoanalyst** [ˌsaɪkoˋænlɪst] *(n.)* [C] 精神分析學家、心理分析學家
   → psychology *(n.)* [U] 心理學
   → psychologist *(n.)* [C] 心理學家
   → psychological *(adj.)* 心理的、心理學的

3. **synonymous** [sɪˋnɑnəməs] *(adj.)* 同義的 ↔ antonymous 反義的
   → synonym *(n.)* [C] 同義字、近義詞 ↔ antonym 反義字

4. **bizarre** [bɪˋzɑr] *(adj.)* 怪異的；異於尋常的 = odd, peculiar, eccentric
   → a bizarre situation 異於尋常的情形
   → bizarrely *(adv.)* 怪異地、異於尋常地

5. **defense** [dɪˋfɛns] *(n.)* [C] 防禦；辯護
   → in one's defense 以…的立場來說
   → come/rush to one's defense（趕忙）為某人辯護
   → defend *(vt.)* 保護、防護；（法庭上）為…辯護 *(vi.)*（比賽中）防守

6. **mechanism** [ˋmɛkəˌnɪzəm] *(n.)* 機構；結構、機制
   → defense mechanism 防禦機制

7. **dull** [dʌl] *(adj.)* 乏味的、單調的 = boring, monotonous, dreary；暗淡的、陰暗的
   → be (as) dull as ditchwater 非常無聊乏味

8. **obligation** [ˌɑbləˋgeʃən] *(n.)* [C, U] 義務、責任；必須做的事
   → under no obligation + to V_R 沒有義務去做…
   → obligate *(vt.)* 使…負義務；強使 → be obligated + to V_R 有義務要去做…
   → obligatory *(adj.)*（根據法律、規範）有義務的、必須履行的

1. **attempt to V_R** 嘗試…

2. **be synonymous with** 與…同義

3. **stop sb./sth. from Ving** 使某人事物停止做該動作

4. **fall out** 掉下來

5. **cope with** 應付 = deal with, handle with

相關文法句型

1. **over 的用法**

over 當形容詞時表示「結束的、完了的」。而當介系詞時有三種主要用法：

(1) 表「在…之上」，與 above 用法相似。

(2) 表「在…期間」，常以「over + 一段時間」表示，常搭配現在完成式。

(3) 表「與…有關」，常以「over + 引起關注、擔憂、討論的原因」表示。

例 Many **have attempted** to interpret dreams over **the centuries**.

幾個世紀以來，很多人都曾嘗試去解讀夢境。

→表「在…期間」，搭配現在完成式。

例 Today, the debate over **just how meaningful dreams really are continues**.

現今，關於夢境到底有沒有意義的辯論還是在進行中。

→表「與…有關」。

2. **despite 用法**

(1) despite 和 in spite of 是介系詞（片語），後面要加名詞或動名詞 Ving。若要接子句，則須用 despite/in spite of **the fact that…**。

(2) 兩者皆能和連接詞 although、though 與 even though 代換使用，但後接一個完整子句。

例 A dream about teeth falling out is very common, despite being **rather bizarre**.

作有關牙齒掉下來的夢是非常常見的，儘管這有些詭異。

例 In spite of **setting off early in the morning**, Tim got stuck in a traffic jam.

= Despite the fact that **Tim set off early in the morning**, he got stuck in a traffic jam.

= Even though **Tim set off early in the morning**, he got stuck in a traffic jam.

儘管堤姆今天很早出門，他仍遇到塞車。

例 The singer did not cancel the concert despite **the outbreak of coronavirus**.

= The singer did not cancel the concert despite the fact that **the coronavirus broke out**.

= The singer did not cancel the concert although the coronavirus broke out.

儘管新型冠狀病毒疫情爆發，那位歌手並沒有取消演唱會。

第 31 至 35 題為題組 —— 科技潮流

Live streaming is the latest online craze. As the name implies, streaming is live video, in the moment with no editing. __31__ Viewers can respond to the performer, making live streaming the ultimate in social media: immediate video interaction in real time. Streaming is very popular with teenagers and some broadcasters even earn good money for streams of comedy, playing videogames, or just chatting. __32__

When young people make themselves accessible online, they sometimes become targets for "trolls," or cruel individuals who enjoy making others feel bad. __33__ Repeated harassment is called cyber-bullying and can have psychological consequences. More dangerous are individuals online looking to take advantage of teens or children. __34__ Some might even attempt to obtain the streamer's personal information. Underage streamers should also be aware that anything they broadcast can be recorded. __35__ The internet is a powerful tool for creativity, but young people must be made aware of its many dangers.

譯文

　　線上直播是最新的網路風潮。正如其名,線上直播以影片直播,既即時且不能編輯。(B) **線上直播可以放送給任何想觀看的人,也可以選擇特定的觀眾。** 觀看者可以給表演者回應,這也使線上直播成為社群媒體中的佼佼者:直接且即時的影片互動。直播在青少年中非常流行,有些直播主甚至可以靠著搞笑影片、遊戲實況,或只是單純的聊聊天賺取金錢。(E) **然而,未成年者一定要警惕線上直播帶來的危險。**

　　當年輕人自己上網時,他們有時就成了「酸民」的攻擊對象,他們是殘忍的人,以讓別人不舒服為樂。(D) **他們可能會以傷人的言論、張貼具有攻擊性的文章來抨擊直播主。** 重複的騷擾被稱作網路霸凌,而這也可能會造成心靈上的創傷。更危險的是有人會在線上尋找青少年或小孩並利用他們。(A) **他們可能會以不適當的方式聯繫對方,或慫恿直播主分享色情內容。** 有些人甚至會嘗試取得直播主的個人資料。未成年的直播主應該要多加提防,因為他們直播的任何東西都有可能被錄下來。(C) **假如他們在直播時做了冒犯或難堪的舉動,這些東西都有可能影響他們往後的人生。** 網路對創造力來說是個強而有力的工具,但年輕人必須要對它所挾帶的危險有所警戒。

(A) They may engage in inappropriate contact, or attempt to provoke broadcasters into sharing sexual content.
他們可能會以不適當的方式聯繫對方,或慫恿直播主分享色情內容。

(B) It can be broadcast to anyone who wants to tune in, or to a select audience.
線上直播可以放送給任何想觀看的人,也可以選擇特定的觀眾。

(C) If they engage in offensive or embarrassing behavior in the moment during a stream, it can potentially haunt them later in life.
假如他們在直播時做了冒犯或難堪的舉動,這些東西都有可能影響他們往後的人生。

(D) They may bombard streamers with hurtful comments or post offensive content.
他們可能會以傷人的言論、張貼具有攻擊性的文章來抨擊直播主。

(E) However, underage individuals must be wary of the dangers of streaming.
然而，未成年者一定要警惕線上直播帶來的危險。

原文

Live streaming is the latest online craze. As the name implies, streaming is live video, in the moment with no editing. It can be broadcast to anyone who wants to **tune in**, or to a select audience. Viewers can respond to the performer, making live streaming the [1]**ultimate** in social media: immediate video interaction in real time. Streaming is very popular with teenagers and some broadcasters even earn good money for streams of comedy, playing videogames, or just chatting. However, [2]**underage** individuals must **be** [3]**wary of** the dangers of streaming.

When young people make themselves accessible online they sometimes become targets for "[4]**trolls**," or cruel individuals who enjoy making others feel bad. They may [5]**bombard** streamers with hurtful comments or post [6]**offensive** content. Repeated [7]**harassment** is called cyber-bullying and can have psychological consequences. More dangerous are individuals online looking to **take advantage of** teens or children. They may **engage in** inappropriate contact, or attempt to **provoke** broadcasters **into** sharing sexual content. Some might even attempt to obtain the stream's personal information. Underage streamers should also be aware that anything they broadcast can be recorded. If they engage in offensive or embarrassing behavior in the moment during a stream, it can potentially haunt them later in life. The internet is a powerful tool for creativity, but young people must be made aware of its many dangers.

重要單字

1. **ultimate** [ˈʌltəmɪt] *(n.)* 極品、極致 *(adj.)* 極端的、最終的
    → the ultimate in sth. 某事物中的極品、極致
    → ultimately *(adv.)* 最終、終究

2. **underage** [ˈʌndəˋedʒ] *(adj.)* 未成年的 ↔ adult *(adj.)* 成年的 *(n.)* [C] 成年人
    → the underage 未成年的人，視為複數
    → teenage *(adj.)* 青少年的、十幾歲的
    → teenager *(n.)* [C] 青少年

3. **wary** [ˋwɛrɪ] *(adj.)* 謹慎的、小心翼翼的 = careful, cautious
   → be wary of/about +N/Ving 對於…很謹慎

4. **troll** [trol] *(n.)* 【網路用語】酸民，發布具有煽動性或帶有破壞性的言論，來挑釁或激怒他人的人

5. **bombard** [bɑmˋbɑrd] *(vt.)* 砲擊；轟炸
   → bombard sb. with sth. = sb. be bombarded with sth.
   用某物對某人疲勞轟炸（某人被某事物疲勞轟炸）

6. **offensive** [əˋfɛnsɪv] *(adj.)* 冒犯的；具有攻擊性的 = aggressive, rude, hostile
   → be offensive to sb. 冒犯到某人
   → offense [əˋfɛns] *(n.)* 冒犯、攻擊
   → No offense. 無意冒犯。
   → offend [əˋfɛnd] *(vt.)* 冒犯、攻擊
   → offended [əˋfɛndɪd] *(adj.)* 受冒犯的、受傷的

7. **harassment** [ˋhærəsmənt] *(n.)* [U] 騷擾
   → sexual harassment 性騷擾
   → harass *(vt.)* 騷擾、煩擾

重要片語

1. **tune in** 收看、收聽

2. **be wary of** 提防

3. **take advantage of** 利用

4. **engage in** 進行；參加

5. **provoke sb. into + N/Ving** 激起、引發某人做…

相關文法句型

1. 分詞片語

   例 Viewers can respond to the performer, **making** live streaming the **ultimate** in social media: immediate video interaction in real time.
   觀看者可以給表演者回應，這也使線上直播成為社群媒體中的佼佼者：直接且即時的影片互動。
   → 例句中 making 是由關係子句「..., which makes live streaming...」簡化而來。分詞片語用來修飾名詞或代名詞。**若先行詞後的動詞為先行詞產生的動作，則用**現在分詞 Ving **的形式；若非先行詞主動產生的動作，則用**過去分詞 Vpp。

2. **aware「提醒」的用法**

(1) aware 當形容詞，指「意識到的」，用句型「**be aware that + S + V**」接一個子句，提醒對方要意識到後面這件事情：

> 例 Underage streamers should also be aware that **anything they broadcast can be recorded**.
>
> 未成年的直播主應該要多加提防，因為他們直播的任何東西都有可能被錄下來。

(2) 也可以用「**be aware of N**」接名詞或名詞子句。

> 例 The internet is a powerful tool for creativity, but young people must be made aware of **its many dangers**.
>
> 網路對創造力來說是個強而有力的工具，但年輕人必須要對它所挾帶的危險有所警戒。

(3) 其他表「提醒」的字：

→**remind**：提醒某人已忘記或可能會忘記的事，用在使某人想起一件「原本就知道」的事。
- 用法：remind sb. **of** N / **to** V_R / that S + V

→**alert**：用來告知他人一個即將到來的危險情況或急需解決的問題，常用在警告、告知他人一件對方「原本不知情的緊急事件」。
- 常見用法：alert sb. **to** + N.

→**warn**：提醒他人意識到有可能發生的危險或可能出現的狀況，也可以強調提醒一個人「意識到事情的重要性」。
- 常見用法：warn sb. **about/of** N「警告某人某事」；warn sb. **against**...「警告某人遠離…」

第貳部分：非選擇題

一、中譯英 —— 電子競技

1. 運動員不一定需要抵達終點線才能贏得比賽。事實上，有些人可能是專業的電子競技運動員，他們贏得許多虛擬比賽。

   Athletes don't necessarily have to reach the finish line to win a race. In fact, some may be professional esports athletes who have won many virtual games.

2. 但大眾大多分不清電玩與電競，導致電競選手常常被批評浪費時間、不務正業。

   | However,
Nonetheless,
Nevertheless | the general public cannot |

   differentiate video games from esports games
tell the difference between video games and esports games.
distinguish video games from esports games.

   | Therefore,
Hence,
Thus,
As a result,
Consequently, | esports athletes are often criticized for wasting time and |

   fooling around.
hanging around.
goofing around.

二、英文作文 —— 哲學思考

> 說明：1. 依提示在「答案卷」上寫一篇英文作文。
> 　　　2. 文長至少 120 個單詞（words）。

> **提示**：在電影《鐘點戰》（*In Time*）中，時間取代貨幣成為一種奢侈品，此概念類似美國詩人卡爾桑德堡（Carl Sandburg）之名言：Time is the only coin in your life. It is the only coin you have, and the only coin you can determine how it will spent. Be careful lest you let other people spend it for you. 你認為桑德堡所想表達的意思是什麼？請寫一篇英文作文，第一段詮釋這幾句話的意思，第二段舉例加以佐證。

作文範文

By the time you finish reading these words, you will have lost several seconds of your life. This is the nature of time, as it continuously marches into infinity. Poet Carl Sandburg points out that time is our most valuable asset in life and that we must spend it wisely. For Sandberg, time is like a currency, in that we choose to put it to good use or let it slip down the drain. Though we can't save time up and withdraw it as needed, we can squander it away—sometimes without even realizing it. We control relatively few things in our lives, and time is our most precious possession. Time has a way of passing us by when we aren't paying attention. When we waste time, we betray ourselves. Time that we have let slip through our fingers can in no way be retrieved. Time is fleeting, its progress ruthless and unsentimental. However, if we can learn to appreciate it, we can make time our strongest ally.

If we fail to take advantage of the present moment, every time an opportunity knocks on our door—whether it's a job offer or a chance to meet someone new—we will find ourselves unprepared. If we better utilize our time, we will be available to open ourselves to new experiences. If we insist on fooling around and sitting on the sidelines, we pass up these golden opportunities. We should invest our time in nourishing the things we cherish and focusing on our current goals in relationships or careers. Those who recognize the value of each passing moment live their lives to the fullest. We don't want to look back and feel that we've missed out on the precious things in life due to chronic procrastination, laziness, or distraction. That said, we should also be sure to take time to relax. To pursue opportunities with constant ambition can lead to burnout, and taking on too many things at once means none of them getting completed. As with all things in life, a balance is necessary. We must follow Mr. Sandburg's advice and become judicious economists of time.

譯文

　　當你讀完這些字時，你將失去人生中的幾秒時間。這就是時間的本質，因為時間是永無止盡地往前走。詩人卡爾桑德堡指出，時間是生命中最寶貴的財富，我們必須善用。對桑德堡來說，時間猶如貨幣，我們可以選擇充分運用或揮霍。雖然我們無法儲存時間也無法在需要時提領，但我們還是能揮霍掉，有時甚至沒意識到自己已揮霍。我們在生活中所能控制的事物相對極少，而時間是我們最寶貴的財富。在我們不注意時，時間便已流逝。當我們浪費時間，就等於背叛自己。從指縫間流失的時間是無法挽回的。時間是轉瞬即逝的，它的進程既殘忍又無情。不過，我們若能學會體悟時間，就能讓時間成為我們最強大的盟友。

　　我們若不能利用當下，每次機會來敲門時 —— 無論是工作機會或結識新朋友的機會 —— 我們都會發現自己尚未準備好。我們若能更善用自己的時間，便能為自己帶來新體驗。我們若堅持虛度光陰和置身事外，那我們將錯過千載難逢的機會。我們應該投入時間來培養自己所珍惜的事物，並專注於目前在人際關係或職業方面的目標。認識到每時每刻有多寶貴的人會過著充實的生活。我們不想日後回首覺得自己因長年拖延、懶惰或分心而錯過了生活中的寶貴事物。儘管如此，我們也應確保花點時間放鬆。追求目標的野心不間斷會導致精疲力竭，而一次承擔太多事情會徒勞無功。與生活中的所有事物一樣，保持平衡是必要的。我們必須遵從桑德堡先生的建議，成為明智的時間經濟學家。

作文教學

　　By the time you finish reading these words, you will have lost several seconds of your life. This is the nature of time, as it continuously marches into [1]**infinity**. Poet Carl Sandburg points out that time is our most valuable [2]**asset** in life and that we must spend it wisely. For Sandberg, time is like a [3]**currency**, in that we choose to put it to good use or let it slip down the drain. Though we can't save time up and [4]**withdraw** it as needed, we can [5]**squander** it away—sometimes without even realizing it. We control [6]**relatively** few things in our lives, and time is our most precious [7]**possession**. Time has a way of passing us by when we aren't paying attention. When we waste time, we [8]**betray** ourselves. Time that we have let slip through our fingers can in no way be [9]**retrieved**. Time is [10]**fleeting**, its progress ruthless and [11]**unsentimental**. However, if we can learn to appreciate it, we can make time our strongest ally.

　　If we fail to take advantage of the present moment, every time an opportunity knocks on our door—whether it's a job offer or a chance to meet someone new—we will find ourselves unprepared. If we better [12]**utilize** our time, we will be available to open ourselves to new experiences. If we insist on fooling around and sitting on the sidelines, we pass up these golden opportunities. We should invest our time in [13]nourishing the things we cherish and focusing on our current goals in relationships or careers. Those who recognize the value of each passing moment live their lives to the fullest. We don't want to look back and feel that we've missed out on the precious things in life due to [14]chronic procrastination, laziness, or distraction. That said, we should also be sure to take time to relax. To pursue opportunities with constant ambition can lead to burnout, and taking on too many things at once means none of them getting completed. As with all things in life, a balance is necessary. We must follow Mr. Sandburg's advice and become judicious economists of time.

重要單字

1. **infinity** [ɪnˈfɪnətɪ] *(n.)* [U] 無限、無窮
   → infinite *(adj.)* 無限的

2. **asset** [ˈæsɛt] *(n.)* [C] 資產
   → fixed/liquid assets 固定／流動資產

3. **currency** [ˈkɜənsi] *(n.)* [C] 貨幣

4. **withdraw** [wɪðˈdrɔ] *(vt.)* 提領、提取；抽回、拉開；撤銷

5. **squander** [ˈskwɑndɚ] *(vt.)* 浪費、揮霍
   → squander on + N 浪費…
   → squander away... 大肆揮霍光…

6. **relatively** [ˈrɛlətɪvli] *(adv.)* 相對地

7. **possession** [pəˈzɛʃən] *(n.)* [C] 所有物、財產；[U] 擁有

8. **betray** [bɪˈtre] *(vt.)* 背叛
   → betray one's beliefs/principles/ideals 背棄某人的信念／原則／理想
   → betrayal *(n.)* [U] 背叛

9. **retrieve** [rɪˈtriv] *(vt.)* 失而復得、取回

10. **fleeting** [ˈflitɪŋ] *(adj.)* 暫時的 = passing, transient, momentary, temporary

11. **unsentimental** [ˌʌnsɛntəˈmɛntl] *(adj.)* 不感情用事的、客觀的

12. **utilize** [ˈjuɫaɪz] *(vt.)* 運用 = employ, make use of, take advantage of, draw on

13. **nourish** [ˈnɜɪʃ] *(vt.)* 滋養、培育

14. **chronic** [ˈkrɑnɪk] *(adj.)* 慢性的；長期的

1. **in that** 因為 = because

2. **down the drain** 付諸東流

3. **miss out on** 錯過 = pass up, let pass, ley go by

4. **every time** 每當 = whenever 每當
   → 不可連在一起寫成 everytime。

5. **fool around** 遊手好閒、無所事事 = fiddle around, hang around, goof around

6. **sit on the sidelines** 事不關己、隔岸觀火

7. **pass up** 放棄掉；拒絕掉
   → pass up the chance/opportunity/invitation 放棄機會／拒絕邀約

相關文法句型

1. **by the time 的用法**
   by the time 表示「在…之前」，因此主要子句所接的事情是**更早發生**，時態上也要做變化。

   例 **By the time** the sun **sets**, the kids **will have returned** home.
   到太陽下山之時，孩子們就已經到家了。
   → 孩子到家是比太陽下山更早發生的事情，因此時態使用比現在式 sets 更早發生的未來完成式 will have Vpp：will have returned。

   例 **By the time** the firefighters **arrived** at the scene, the building **had already burned down**.
   消防隊員抵達現場時，建物早已付之一炬。
   → 建物燒毀是更早發生的事情，因此時態要使用比過去式 arrived 更早發生的過去完成式 had + Vpp：had burned down。

2. **S + V (that) + 子句 1 and that + 子句 2**
   → 第一個 that 作為 V 的受詞，可以省略。但為了不讓語意混亂，之後接的 that 不可省略。

NOTE

第 4 回 | 解析

第壹部分：選擇題

一、綜合測驗

第 1 至 10 題為題組 —— 地震

Earthquakes can strike with little or no warning. If you live in an area prone to earthquakes, it is important to take __1__. __2__, you can minimize the damage to your home and injury __3__ yourself and others. Preparation is the key.

The safety of yourself and your loved ones is of primary importance. It is wise to have a first aid kit prepared. Always make sure your phone is charged. Decide __4__ a safe location for your family to meet in case you are separated. When a quake strikes, hide beneath a __5__ table or desk. If you can't get to something like this, stand in a doorway or against an interior wall, away from windows. If you __6__, try to quickly turn off the stove.

You can take steps to make your home as earthquake-proof as possible. Make sure heavy items, __7__ refrigerators and cabinets, are fixed. Make sure bookcases, mounted televisions, and artwork are __8__ to the wall as much as possible. Don't hang heavy mirrors or picture frames above beds, so they don't fall onto people __9__ there.

After an earthquake, immediately check yourself and your loved ones for any injuries and apply first aid. Call for emergency assistance if __10__. Do not enter your home or any other building that has been damaged. Earthquakes may only last a few minutes, but the damage they can cause is serious. A little preparation can minimize their threat.

譯文

　　地震來襲總是幾乎毫無預警。如果你住在常常地震的地方，做好預防措施是非常重要的。藉此，你可以盡可能地降低地震對你家園的傷害和它對你或其他人的損傷。準備是關鍵。

　　你自己和所愛之人的安全是至關重要的。把急救箱先準備好是個明智的選擇，並確保你的手機總是充飽電。要決定一個安全的地方讓你的家人會合，以免你們走散了。當地震來襲時，躲在一個堅固的桌子或椅子下。如果你沒辦法找到類似的東西，那就站在門口或靠在內牆，並遠離窗戶。如果你正在煮飯，盡可能快速關掉爐子。

　　你可以採取措施使你的家裡盡可能地防震。確保像是冰箱或衣櫥等重物是固定的；確保書櫃、壁櫃電視和藝術品盡越固定在牆上越好。還有，別在床上方掛很重的鏡子或相框，它們才不會砸在沉睡中人們的臉上。

　　地震結束後，請立即檢查你和你的親人是否受傷，並且採取緊急措施。如果需要，請尋求緊急援助。千萬別進入你的家或任何已損毀的房子。地震可能只會持續幾分鐘，但它們所造成的破壞是嚴重的。只需一點點的準備，你就能最大程度地減少它的威脅。

1. (A) procrastinations   **(B) precautions**   (C) processes   (D) precisions
   (A) 拖延   **(B) 預防（措施）**   (C) 過程   (D) 精確性

2. **(A) This way**   (B) On the way   (C) No way   (D) By the way
   (A) 這樣；如此一來   (B) 在路上   (C) 不可能   (D) 順帶一提

3. **(A) to**   (B) in   (C) at   (D) into

   > 解說　injury 搭配的介系詞為 to，「an injury to + N」對⋯的傷害

4. (A) to   (B) in   **(C) on**   (D) at

   > 解說　decide 搭配之介系詞為 on，「decide on + N」決定（事項）

5. (A) staggering   (B) strategic   (C) static   **(D) sturdy**
   (A) 令人吃驚的   (B) 有謀略的   (C) 靜態的   **(D) 堅固的**

6. (A) have cooked   (B) had cooked   **(C) are cooking**   (D) are cooked

   > 解說　這裡表示地震當下正在煮飯，故使用現在進行式。

7. **(A) such as**   (B) excluding   (C) besides   (D) except
   (A) 例如   (B) 排除掉   (C) 除了⋯還有   (D) 只有

8. (A) seduced   (B) secluded   (C) smashed   **(D) secured**
   (A) 被誘惑   (B) 被隔離   (C) 被摔爛的   **(D) 被固定住**

9. (A) sleep   (B) slept   (C) under sleep   **(D) sleeping**

   > 解說　原句為 people who sleep there，此處為分詞片語的用法。

10. (A) need   **(B) needed**   (C) needing   (D) be needed

   > 解說　if needed 表「如果需要」，原句可寫成 if it is needed。

原文

Earthquakes can ¹⁾**strike** with little or no warning. If you live in an area ²⁾**prone** to earthquakes, it is important to take ³⁾**precautions**. This way, you can ⁴⁾**minimize** the damage to your home and ⁵⁾**injury** to yourself and others. Preparation is the key.

The safety of yourself and your loved ones is of ⁶⁾**primary** importance. It is wise to have a first aid kit prepared. Always make sure your phone is ⁷⁾**charged**. Decide on a safe location for your family to meet in case you are ⁸⁾**separated**. When a quake strikes, hide beneath a sturdy table or desk. If you can't get to something like this, stand in a doorway or against an interior wall, away from windows. If you are cooking, try to quickly turn off the stove.

You can take steps to make your home as earthquake-proof as possible. Make sure heavy items, such as refrigerators and cabinets, are fixed. Make sure bookcases, ⁹⁾**mounted** televisions, and artwork are secured to the wall as much as possible. Don't hang heavy mirrors or picture ¹⁰⁾**frames** above beds, so they don't fall onto people sleeping there.

After an earthquake, immediately check yourself and your loved ones for any injuries and apply first aid. Call for emergency assistance if needed. Do not enter your home or any other building that has been damaged. Earthquakes may only last a few minutes, but the damage they can cause is serious. A little preparation can minimize their threat.

重要單字

1. **strike** [staɪk] *(vt.)* 打、擊 *(vi.)* 突然侵襲；罷工
   → 動詞三態變化：strike - struck - struck
   → a(an) disaster/disease/earthquake strikes 災難／疾病／地震襲擊
   → strike a balance between... 在…之間取得平衡
   → strike *(n.)* [C] 罷工；打、擊
   → be on strike 在罷工
   → call/**go on**/take part in a strike 發動／實行／參與罷工
   → a strike against/in protest at/in pursuit of... 對抗…的／為…抗議的／追求…的罷工

2. **prone** [pron] *(adj.)* 有…傾向的；易於…的 (+ **to** N/V$_R$)
   → be prone to depression/headaches 容易情緒抑鬱／頭痛
   → an area prone to earthquakes 一個地震頻仍的地區
   → be prone to exaggerate 有誇大其詞的傾向

3. **precaution** [prɪˋkɔʃən] *(n.)* [C,U] 預防、警惕；預防措施
   → as a precaution 以防萬一
   → take the necessary precautions 採取必要的預防措施

4. **minimize** [ˋmɪnəˌmaɪz] *(vt.)* 使減到最少、使縮到最小 ↔ maximize *(vt.)* 最大化
   → minimum *(n.)* [C] 最小值；最少量；最低限度 ↔ maximum *(n.)* [C] 最大值
   → minimal *(adj.)* 極小的；極少的 ↔ maximal *(adj.)* 極大的
   → minimize the losses/risk/impact 將損失／風險／影響降到最低

5. **injury** [ˋɪndʒərɪ] *(n.)* [C,U] 傷害、損害（ + **to** N 或受傷部位）
   → injure *(vt.)* 傷害、損害
   → be badly/seriously/critically injured 受重傷

6. **primary** [ˋpraɪˌmɛrɪ] *(adj.)* 首要的，主要的 = prime
   → (a matter) of primary importance 頭等重要的（事情）
   → primary concern 首要關心的事情
   → primarily *(adv.)* 主要地
   → be primarily concerned with... 主要關心的是…

7. **charge** [tʃɑrdʒ] *(v./n.)* 充電；收費 *(vt.)* 控告；刷卡付錢
   → charge (up) the batteries 充（電池）電
   → free of charge 免費的
   → be charged with murder 被指控謀殺
   → take charge of + N 掌管、負責…

8. **separate** [ˋsɛpəˌret] *(v.)* （使）分離 *(adj.)* 各自的、單獨的
   → separate A from B 將 A 與 B 分開；區別 A 和 B
   → go ones' (own) separate ways 分道揚鑣、各奔東西

9. **mounted** [ˋmauntɪd] *(adj.)* 架設好的
   → mount *(vt.)* 安裝；登（山） *(vi.)* 上升
   → mount the throne 即位

10. **frame** [frem] *(n.)* [C] 骨架、結構 *(vt.)* 裝框；陷害、誣陷
    → in a positive frame of mind 以積極正向的心態
    → frame sb. 陷害某人、使某人陷入圈套

重要片語

1. **in case** 萬一

2. **get to + N** 去…、跑到…
   → get to + V_R 得以…

1. (just) in case 以防萬一

(1) 放句首，後接一個完整句子，或放句尾，指出預先做一些行動的原因是以防萬一。

(2) in case 或 just in case 後面的動詞只可用簡單現在式、簡單過去式，或加上 should 助動詞，不可用未來式。

> 例 Decide on a safe location for your family to meet **in case** you are separated.
> 要決定一個安全的地方讓你的家人會合，以免你們走散了。

> 例 **In case** you need something, please don't hesitate to let me know.
> 如果你需要什麼東西，請不客氣地對我說。

> 例 I don't think I'll need any money, but I'll bring some **just in case**.
> 我想我不會用到錢的，不過我還是帶一些以防萬一。

(3) in case of 則是指「如果、假如」，後面加上名詞，指如果出現隨後的情況。

> 例 **In case of emergency**, break the glass.
> 如果發生緊急情況，打破玻璃。

> 例 **In case of fire**, do not use the lift.
> 如果發生火警，切勿使用升降機。

2. 有 -proof 的複合形容詞

> 例 You can take steps to make your home as **earthquake-proof** as possible.
> 你可以採取措施使你的家裡盡可能地防震。

其他複合形容詞還有：bullet-proof（防彈的）、water-proof（防水的）、error-proof（不會出錯的）、fire-proof（防火的）、sound-proof（隔音的）、wrinkle-proof（防皺的）、idiot-proof/fool-proof（傻瓜也能使用的）

第 11 至 20 題為題組 —— 颱風

In August 2009, Typhoon Morakot struck Taiwan with brutal force. __11__, over 500 people lost their lives in the flooding and landslides __12__ by the typhoon. As the nation struggled to recover, many blamed the government for slow and __13__ response.

In Hsiao-lin village, Kaohsiung county, a severe landslide buried around 400 people. __14__, hope __15__ they would be found alive had to be abandoned. The relatives of the victims didn't want heavy digging equipment to be used, for fear their loved ones' bodies would be damaged. A park memorializing this sad incident was built on the site.

Thousands of people living in rural, mountainous, or isolated areas found themselves __16__ and cut off from resources. These residents could not access food or fresh water for days because sections of the mountain road had been destroyed. Despite their dangerous situation, government officials argued they were safe where they were.

Then-President Ma Ying-jeou was heavily criticized __17__ his refusal to accept some forms of aid from foreign governments. Some government sources claimed the reason for this refusal is that it was believed that guiding foreign rescue workers to the sites where they were needed would be an unnecessary use of resources. Ma blamed a typing error for __18__ about the need for foreign assistance. This only __19__ the public perception that rescue efforts were in disarray. __20__, the government can learn from this tragedy and be better prepared for any future disasters.

譯文

2009 年 8 月,莫拉克颱風殘忍地摧殘了台灣。悲慘的是,超過 500 人因颱風造成的水災和土石流而失去性命。當國家在努力復甦時,許多人指責了政府救災緩慢且應對不足。

在高雄縣的小林村,一場嚴重的土石流沒了 400 條人命。最後,他們能被救活的希望必須被拋棄。因為擔心親人的身體會被破壞,因此受害人的家屬不希望使用重型挖掘設備。而一座紀念這個悲傷事件的公園就在此建立。

數以千計住在鄉村、山裡或孤立地區的人們發現他們自己受困且彈盡糧絕。因為山路的各個部分都被摧毀了,這些居民好幾天都無法取得食物和水。儘管他們處境危險,政府官員們卻認為他們身處之地是安全的。

時任的馬英九總統因拒絕外國政府以某種形式援助而飽受批評。一些政府消息人士稱,會拒絕的原因是,他們認為將外國救援人員引導到需要的地點會造成不必要的資源使用。而馬英九總統將此番外國救援的誤解歸咎於誤植。這件事只加重了大眾對救援工作混亂的印象。希望政府可以從這場悲劇中學到教訓,並為未來的任何災害做好準備。

11. (A) Terminally   (B) Temperamentally   **(C) Tragically**   (D) Temporarily
     (A) 晚期地；末期地   (B) 性情不定；善變地   **(C) 悲劇地**   (D) 暫時地

12. **(A) caused**   (B) which caused   (C) that caused   (D) causing

> **解說** 此處為分詞片語的用法，原句為「... which were caused by the typhoon」。

13. (A) insignificant   (B) infinite   (C) inaccurate   **(D) inadequate**
     (A) 不重要的   (B) 無限的   (C) 不準確的   **(D) 不足的**

14. (A) Effectively   **(B) Eventually**   (C) Efficiently   (D) Elegantly
     (A) 有效地   **(B) 最後地**   (C) 有效率地   (D) 優雅地

15. (A) why   (B) where   (C) what   **(D) that**

> **解說** 此處名詞子句 that they would be found alive 做前方名詞 hope 的同位語。指「他們能被救活的希望」。

16. (A) stacked   **(B) stranded**   (C) strained   (D) stained
     (A) 被堆放   **(B) 受困**   (C) 被拉緊；繃緊   (D) 遭污染

17. (A) at   (B) on   **(C) for**   (D) with

> **解說** 片語 criticize sb. for + N/Ving 表「因為某事批評某人」

18. **(A) miscommunication**   (B) misbehavior   (C) mischief   (D) miracle
     (A) 誤解；溝通不良   (B) 行為不端   (C) 淘氣   (D) 奇蹟

19. (A) reinstated   (B) respected   **(C) reinforced**   (D) reigned
     (A) 恢復   (B) 尊重   **(C) 增強**   (D) 統治

20. **(A) Hopefully**   (B) Hopelessly   (C) Highly   (D) Honorably
     (A) 希望   (B) 絕望地   (C) 非常   (D) 榮幸地

原文

In August 2009, Typhoon Morakot struck Taiwan with brutal force. Tragically, over 500 people lost their lives in the flooding and landslides caused by the typhoon. As the nation **struggled to** recover, many **blamed** the government **for** slow and 1)**inadequate** response.

In Hsiao-lin village, Kaohsiung county, a severe landslide buried around 400 people. Eventually, hope had to be 2)**abandoned** that they would be found alive. The relatives of the victims didn't want heavy digging 3)**equipment** to be used, for fear their loved ones' bodies would be damaged. A park 4)**memorializing** this sad incident was built on the site.

Thousands of people living in 5)**rural**, mountainous, or isolated areas found themselves 6)**stranded** and cut off from resources. These residents could not access food or fresh water for days because sections of the mountain road had been destroyed. Despite their dangerous situation, government officials argued they were safe where they were.

Then-President Ma Ying-jeou **was** heavily 7)**criticized for** his refusal to accept some forms of aid from foreign governments. Some government sources claimed the reason for this refusal is that it was believed that guiding foreign rescue workers to the sites where they were needed would be an unnecessary use of resources. Ma blamed a typing error for 8)**miscommunication** about the need for foreign assistance. This only reinforced the public 9)**perception** that rescue efforts were in 10)**disarray**. Hopefully, the government can learn from this tragedy and be better prepared for any future disasters.

重要單字

1. **inadequate** [ɪnˋædəkwɪt] *(adj.)* 不充分的；不適當的 ↔ adequate 合適的
   → be inadequate **to V_R/for N** 不足以做成某事／應付某事
   → inadequacy *(n.)* [C,U] 不足；劣質

2. **abandon** [əˋbændən] *(vt.)* 丟棄、拋棄
   → abandon oneself to one's emotions 使自己沉溺於情緒中、為之左右

3. **equipment** [ɪˋkwɪpmənt] *(n.)* [U] 配備，裝備，設備；用具
   → office/electrical equipment 辦公用品／電器設備
   → equip *(vt.)* 裝備，配備 (+ **with N**)
   → be well/poorly equipped 裝備齊全／簡陋

4. **memorialize** [məˋmorɪəl͵aɪz] *(vt.)* 紀念
   → memorial *(n.)* 紀念物；紀念碑 (+ **to N**) *(adj.)* 紀念的
   → a war memorial 戰爭紀念碑
   → be in memory of 紀念、緬懷 = commemorate

5. **rural** [ˋrʊrəl] *(adj.)* 農村的；鄉下的 ↔ urban *(adj.)* 城市的；居住在城市的
   → rural/urban area(s) 鄉村地區／市區

6. **stranded** [ˋstrændɪd] *(adj.)* 滯留的；被困住的
   → strand *(n.)* [C] 繩線；縷；濱岸 *(vt.)* 搓、絞（繩索等）
   → a strand of hair 一絡頭髮

7. **criticize** [ˋkrɪtɪˏsaɪz] *(vt./vi.)* 批評；批判
   → criticize sb. for N/Ving. 因某事指責某人
   → criticism *(n.)* [C, U] 批評、批判
   → make/take criticism 做／接受批評

8. **miscommunication** [ˏmɪskəˏmjunəˋkeʃən] *(n.)* [U] 溝通不良 (+ **between**)
   → communication skills 溝通技巧
   → communicate *(vt./vi.)* 交流、溝通 (+ **with** sb.)

9. **perception** [pəˋsɛpʃən] *(n.)* [U] 見解、看法；感知、感覺 (+ of N)
   → a public/general/visual perception 大眾看法／普遍見解／視覺
   → perceptive *(adj.)* 感知能力強的；觀察敏銳的；有洞察力的

10. **disarray** [ˏdɪsəˋre] *(n.)* [U] 混亂、凌亂 *(vt.)* 弄亂
    → be in (complete) disarray 凌亂不堪

重要片語

1. **struggle to + V$_R$** 努力去⋯
2. **blame sb. for sth. = blame sth. on sb.** 因某件事指責某人
3. **be criticized for N/Ving** 因⋯遭受批評

相關文法句型

1. 用到受詞補語的動詞
   受詞補語對受詞補充說明，用來完整表達句意。常見的受詞補語為形容詞、分詞、不定詞、名詞、名詞片語、介系詞片語。常見後面加上受詞補語的動詞有 find, keep, leave 等。句型為：

S +	find（覺得） keep（保持） leave（讓）	+ O +	adj./N → 補充說明受詞狀態 Ving → 表主動或進行 Vpp → 表被動

例 Thousands of people living in rural, mountainous, or isolated areas found **themselves stranded and cut off from resources**.

數以千計住鄉村、山裡或孤立地區的人們發現他們受困且彈盡糧絕。

→ 本句的受詞補語為分詞 stranded and cut off from resources。

例 I entered the library and found **my teacher reading** a magazine there.

我進入圖書館，發現我的老師在那裡看雜誌。

→ 受詞補語為 Ving reading，表主動。

例 You will find **it an interesting book**.

你會發覺那是本好書。

→ 受詞補語為名詞 an interesting book，補充說明受詞 it。

例 Keep medicines **in a locked cupboard**.

把藥放在上鎖的櫥櫃中。

→ 受詞補語為介系詞片語 in a locked cupboard。

例 Josh's defeat left **his fans sad and disappointed**.

賈許的失敗讓粉絲們很難過而且很失望。

→ 受詞補語為形容詞 sad and disappointed。

例 Owing to the sudden death of the witness, a lot of **mysteries** were left **unsolved**.

由於證人猝死，許多謎團無法解開。

→ 受詞補語為分詞 unsolved，補充說明受詞 mysteries 狀態。

例 The baby in the cradle **was** left **to cry** by her mother.

媽媽任由搖籃中的小嬰兒哭而不搭理。

→ 受詞補語為不定詞 to cry，修飾受詞 the baby 的狀態。

二、文意選填

第 21 至 30 題為題組 —— 火山爆發

Japan's Mount Fuji is famous around the world. Images of this elegant landmark have come to ___21___ Japan itself. The smooth, snow-capped cone of Fuji rises 3,776 meters toward the sky. This natural wonder lies near the Pacific Ocean and about 60 miles west of Japan's capital city, Tokyo. Fuji and its ___22___ area were designated a UNESCO World Heritage Site in 2013.

Fuji is a volcano. Though it hasn't ___23___ since 1707, many geologists consider it to still be active. The age of the mountain is unclear, but the first peaks probably began to form due to volcanic activities 600,000 years ago. It is part of the Fuji Volcanic Zone, a ___24___ of volcanoes that stretches from Japan to the Mariana Islands. The base of the volcano is about 78 miles in circumference.

How Fuji got its name is unclear. It might be an ancient word for "fire" ___25___ with a more modern Japanese word for "mountain." This would make sense for a volcano! When Fuji is written in kanji, which are Chinese ideograms, the name seems to be more about good luck.

The area around Fuji attracts a great deal of ___26___. Many people from all over the world come to climb the mountain. Often they set out on this journey at night, in order to time their arrival at the summit with the sunrise. For some, this is more than just an adventure; it's a ___27___ practice. Fuji still has spiritual ___28___ for many. Until 1868, women were ___29___ to climb Fuji, for religious reasons. There are even shrines at the peak of the mountain. This beautiful mountain is rich with history and sits at the center of Japanese identity. Eternal Fuji continues to ___30___.

譯文

日本的富士山世界聞名，而這個優雅地標的各種圖照早已代表了日本本身。富士山平滑的雪錐向天際延伸了 3776 公尺。這自然奇觀座落在太平洋附近，距離日本首都東京大概 60 英里。而在 2013 年，富士山和它的周邊地區被指定為聯合國教科文組織世界遺產。

富士山是一座火山。即使它從西元 1707 年以來就沒爆發過，但許多地質學家認為它仍然活躍。這座山的年齡不明，但最早的山峰可能是由 60 萬年前的火山運動而形成的。它是富士火山帶的一部分，富士火山帶是一條從日本延伸到馬里亞納群島的火山，而火山底部的圓周大約有 78 英里。

富士山得名的方式並不清楚。它可能是一個古老的單字「火」，被搭配一個更現代的日語單字「山」。這對於火山的命名由來是合理的！當富士山被寫成漢字時，這個名字似乎更多是關於好運的。

富士山的周圍地區吸引了大量的觀光潮。來自世界各地的許多人都來這邊爬這座山。通常他們會在晚上出發，以便到達山頂時能夠迎接日出。對某些人來說，這不只是個探險，這是一種宗教習俗。富士山對於許多人來說仍具有精神上的重要意義。直到 1868 年之前，女性因為宗教因素是禁止爬富士山的。富士山頂甚至也有神社。這座美麗的山富有悠久的歷史，也是日本人身分的核心。永恆的富士山將繼續讓世人為它著迷。

(A) erupted	(B) forbidden	(C) combined	(D) surrounding	(E) significance
(A) 爆發	(B) 被禁止的	(C) 結合	(D) 周邊的	(E) 重要意義
(F) tourism	(G) religious	(H) represent	(I) fascinate	(J) chain
(F) 觀光業	(G) 宗教的	(H) 代表	(I) 使…著迷	(J) 鏈狀

原文

Japan's Mount Fuji is famous around the world. Images of this elegant landmark have come to represent Japan itself. The smooth, snow-capped cone of Fuji rises 3,776 meters toward the sky. This natural wonder lies near the Pacific Ocean and about 60 miles west of Japan's capital city, Tokyo. Fuji and its surrounding area were 1)**designated** a UNESCO World 2)**Heritage** Site in 2013.

Fuji is a volcano. Though it hasn't 3)**erupted** since 1707, many geologists consider it to still be active. The age of the mountain is unclear, but the first peaks probably began to form **due to** eruptions 600,000 years ago. It is part of the Fuji Volcanic Zone, a chain of volcanoes that 4)**stretches** from Japan to the Mariana Islands. The base of the volcano is about 78 miles in 5)**circumference**.

How Fuji got its name is unclear. It might be an ancient word for "fire" **combined with** a more modern Japanese word for "mountain." This would **make sense** for a volcano! When Fuji is written in kanji, which are Chinese 6)**ideograms**, the name seems to be more about good luck.

The area around Fuji attracts a great deal of tourism. Many people from all over the world come to climb the mountain. Often they **set out** on this journey at night, in order to time their arrival at the summit with the sunrise. For some, this is more than just an adventure; it's a 7)**religious** practice. Fuji still has spiritual significance for many. Until 1868, women were 8)**forbidden** to climb Fuji, for religious reasons. There are even 9)**shrines** at the peak of the mountain. This beautiful mountain is rich with history and sits at the center of Japanese identity. 10)**Eternal** Fuji continues to fascinate.

重要單字

1. **designate** [ˋdɛzɪɡ͵net] *(vt.)* 標出；表明；指定
   → be designated (as/to be) N 被指定為…
   → be designated to V_R 被指派做某事

2. **heritage** [ˋhɛrətɪdʒ] *(n.)* [U] 遺產，繼承物 (+ **of** N)
   → (preserve/protect) cultural/natural heritage（保存／保護）文化／自然遺產

3. **erupt** [ɪˋrʌpt] *(vi.)* 噴出、爆發；突然發生
   → erupt into laughter/desperate sobs 爆笑／忽然開始絕望地啜泣
   → eruption *(n.)* [U] 爆發、噴出、突發

4. **stretch** [strɛtʃ] *(vt.)* 伸直、伸長、延伸、伸展
   → stretch (yourself) out 舒展四肢躺下
   → at a stretch 連續地、不間斷地
   → be fully stretched 竭盡全力

5. **circumference** [sɚˋkʌmfərəns] *(n.)* [C,U] 圓周、周長
   → (measure) waist circumference（測量）腰圍

6. **ideogram** [ˋɪdɪəˌɡræm] *(n.)* [U] 表意文字
   → 字首 ideo- 表示「觀念、思想、意識」

7. **religious** [rɪˋlɪdʒəs] *(adj.)* 宗教上的；虔誠的
   → be deeply religious 非常虔誠的
   → religious beliefs 宗教信仰
   → religion *(n.)* [C,U] 宗教

8. **forbid** [fɚˋbɪd] *(vt.)* 禁止、不許 ↔ permit 允許
   → forbid sb. **to V_R / from Ving** 禁止某人做某事
   → 動詞三態為：forbid - forbade - forbidden

9. **shrine** [ʃraɪn] *(n.)* [C] 聖壇、神社 (+ **of/to** N)
   → pray at a/the shrine 在聖壇祈禱

10. **eternal** [ɪˋtɝnl] *(adj.)* 永久的、永恆的 ↔ momentary, temporary 暫時的
    → eternity *(n.)* [U] 無窮無盡、永恆
    → eternal truth/life/arguments 永恆的真理／永生／不停的爭吵

重要片語

1. **due to + N** 因為、由於⋯
2. **combine A with B** 將 A 與 B 結合在一起
3. **make sense** 有道理
4. **set out** 動身、開始

1. 「認為」的主動和被動的表達方式

(1) 主動用法：

$$\left\{\begin{array}{l}\text{see}\\\text{view}\\\text{regard}\\\text{look upon}\\\text{think of}\\\text{refer to}\end{array}\right\} \text{A \textbf{as} B} \quad 認為 A 是 B \quad = \left\{\begin{array}{l}\text{think}\\\text{consider}\end{array}\right\} \text{A (to be) B}$$

例 Fuji is a volcano. Though it hasn't erupted since 1707, many geologists **consider** **it to** still **be** active.
富士山是一座火山。即使它從西元 1707 年就沒有爆發過，但許多地質學家認為它仍然活躍。

(2) 被動用法：

$$\text{A be} \left\{\begin{array}{l}\text{seen}\\\text{viewed}\\\text{regarded}\\\text{looked upon}\\\text{thought of}\\\text{referred to}\end{array}\right\} \text{\textbf{as} B} \quad A 被認為是 B \quad = \text{A be} \left\{\begin{array}{l}\text{thought}\\\text{considered}\end{array}\right\} \text{(to be) B}$$

例 Bubble tea **is considered** (**to be**) the pride of Taiwan.
珍珠奶茶被認為是台灣之光。

例 Bali **is seen as** <u>the perfect vacation spot</u> by many foreigners because of its beautiful beaches.
峇里島因為有美麗的海灘，所以被許多外國人認為是一個完美的渡假勝地。

例 Passengers who talk loudly on trains **are** often **thought of as** <u>rude</u>.
在火車上講話很大聲的人常被視為無禮。

第 31 至 35 題為題組 —— 土石流

A landslide is a frightening and potentially destructive occurrence in nature. It is when ground that is on a slope gives way and tumbles with a downward movement. __31__ There are various kinds of landslide. These include falls, topples, slides, spreads and flows. Each term describes a different kind of movement.

There are several causes of landslides. __32__ Heavy rainfall over a short period of time can create fast-moving floods of mud and other debris. Longer periods of rainfall contribute to a slower movement of ground. Exposed rock can be fractured or layered, and may finally split apart. The roots of trees and other vegetation often work to hold the soil together. After deforestation or a forest fire, an area can be much more vulnerable to landslides. Some terrain is more likely to experience landslides. __33__ The western United States endures a good deal of landslides. This is the home of the steep Rocky Mountain range.

Other mountainous nations must deal with landslides. These include Switzerland, with its famous Alps, and the countries that contain the towering Himalayas, such as Pakistan, Nepal, and India. __34__ After heavy rains in Uganda, part of Mount Elgon collapsed, killing 34 people, also in 2018. __35__ Early detection systems continue to improve, but landslides remain a risk in mountainous areas.

譯文

　　山崩是恐怖且具有潛在破壞性的自然界現象。山崩發生的時機，是當土壤在斜坡上塌陷且隨著重力運動滾下。(C) **它會造成財產破壞、道路癱瘓、受傷，甚至是死亡。**山崩還分為好幾種，包括了落石、崩塌、土石流、翻覆和滑動。每個專有名詞描述不同的地層運動。

　　山崩的成因有非常多種。(D) **火山運動會導致土地位移並且開始滑動。**短時間內的豪雨會造成泥漿和其他碎屑的快速移動；較長時間的降雨會造成較慢的地表移動；裸露的岩石可能會破裂或分層，最後還可能分裂；樹木的根以及植物植被通常是扮演抓住土壤的角色，歷經過森林砍伐或是森林大火的地區，會更容易發生山崩。某些地形更容易遭受山崩。(B) **容易下大雨的山區特別危險。**美國的西部會發生大量山崩，就是因為位處陡峭的洛磯山脈上。

　　其他多山的國家必須處理山崩，包括座落在著名阿爾卑斯山的瑞士，和高聳喜馬拉雅山周圍的巴基斯坦、尼泊爾和印度。(A) **在 2018 年，日本北海道發生地震，引發山崩，壓垮了附近的房子並帶走了 16 條居民的性命。**同樣在 2018 年，在豪雨後，烏干達埃爾貢山部分坍塌，帶走了 34 條人命。(E) **一年前，中國新墨有巨大岩石摧毀了家園和一棟旅館，並有超過 100 人悲劇喪命。**早期檢測系統不斷改進完善，但是山崩仍然是山區的一大風險。

(A) In 2018, an earthquake in Hokkaido, Japan triggered a landslide that crushed nearby homes and killed sixteen citizens.

在 2018 年，日本北海道發生地震，引發山崩，壓垮了附近的房子並帶走了 16 條居民的性命。

(B) Mountainous areas prone to heavy rain are particularly dangerous.

容易下大雨的山區特別危險。

(C) This can cause destruction of property, blockage of roadways, injuries, and even death.

它會造成財產破壞、道路癱瘓、受傷，甚至是死亡。

(D) Volcanic activity can cause the land to shift and begin to slide.

火山運動會導致土地位移並且開始滑動。

(E) A year earlier, in Xinmo, China, giant rocks destroyed homes and a hotel. Tragically, over 100 people died.

一年前，中國新墨有巨大岩石摧毀了家園和一棟旅館，並有超過 100 人悲劇喪命。

原文

A landslide is a [1]**frightening** and [2]**potentially** destructive occurrence in nature. It is when ground that is on a slope gives way and [3]**tumbles** with a downward movement. This can cause destruction of property, blockage of roadways, injuries, and even death. There are various kinds of landslide. These include falls, [4]**topples**, slides, spreads and flows. Each term describes a different kind of movement.

There are several causes of landslides. Volcanic activity can cause the land to shift and begin to slide. Heavy rainfall over a short period of time can create fast-moving floods of mud and other [5]**debris**. Longer periods of rainfall **contribute to** a slower movement of ground. Exposed rock can be [6]**fractured** or layered, and may finally split apart. The roots of trees and other vegetation often work to hold the soil together. After [7]**deforestation** or a forest fire, an area can be much more [8]**vulnerable to** landslides. Some [9]**terrain is** more **likely to** experience landslides. Mountainous areas prone to heavy rain are particularly dangerous. The western United States endures a good deal of landslides. This is the home of the steep Rocky Mountain range.

Other mountainous nations must deal with landslides. These include Switzerland, with its famous Alps, and the countries that contain the towering Himalayas, such as Pakistan, Nepal, and India. In 2018, an earthquake in Hokkaido, Japan triggered a landslide that crushed nearby homes and killed sixteen citizens. After heavy rains in Uganda, part of Mount Elgon collapsed, killing 34 people, also in 2018. A year earlier, in Xinmo, China, giant rocks destroyed homes and a hotel. Tragically, over 100 people died. Early [10]**detection** systems continue to improve, but landslides remain a risk in mountainous areas.

1. **frightening** [ˈfraɪtə͵nɪŋ] (adj.) 令人恐懼的；使人驚嚇的
   → frightened (adj.) 害怕的、受驚的
   → frighten (vt.) 使驚恐、使害怕
   → frighten sb. to death/out of one's wits 把某人嚇得要死／嚇得不知所措
   → be frightened **of N / that S + V / to V$_R$** 害怕…

2. **potentially** [pəˈtɛnʃəlɪ] (adv.) 潛在地；可能地
   → potential (adj.) 可能的、潛在的 (n.) [U] 可能性、潛力、潛能
   → potential customers/buyers/investors/dangers 潛在客戶／買主／投資者／危險
   → have potential to V$_R$ 有潛力做…

3. **tumble** [ˈtʌmbl] (vi.) 跌倒；滾下；墜落
   → tumble down the stairs/slope 滾下樓梯／斜坡

4. **topple** [ˈtɑpl] (vt./vi.) 使倒塌；推翻、顛覆 = overthrow
   → topple the government 推翻政府

5. **debris** [dəˈbri] (n.) [U] 殘骸；破瓦殘礫
   → clear up(away) the debris 清理殘骸

6. **fracture** [ˈfræktʃə] (vt./vi.) 破裂、斷裂；折斷
   → fracture one's leg/arm/hip/ribs 腿部／手臂／臀部／肋骨骨折

7. **deforestation** [͵difɔrəsˈteʃən] (n.) [C] 砍伐森林
   → deforest (vt.) 砍伐森林
   → air pollution 空氣汙染；greenhouse gas 溫室氣體；ecosystem 生態系

8. **vulnerable** [ˈvʌlnərəbl] (adj.) 易受傷的；脆弱的；易受責難的
   → vulnerability (n.) 脆弱
   → be vulnerable to criticism/abuse/damage 易受抨擊／虐待／損傷

9. **terrain** [təˈren] (n.) [U] 地面；地域、地帶
   → rugged/fertile/infertile terrain 崎嶇不平／肥沃／貧瘠的地面、地帶

10. **detection** [dɪˈtɛkʃən] (n.) [U] 發現；偵查
    → detect (vt.) 探測、測出；發現、察覺
    → detective (n.) [C] 偵探、密探

1. **contribute to + N** 促成；導致

2. **be vulnerable to N** 易於⋯

3. **be likely to + V_R** 很可能⋯ = be possible to + V_R

相關文法句型

1. **不完全不及物動詞的用法**

(1) 這類動詞如 remain、stay、lie，後方須接**名詞**、**形容詞**、**現在分詞**或**過去分詞**，作為主詞補語來補充說明主詞的狀態，句型為：

$$S + \begin{Bmatrix} \text{remain/sit/stay} \\ \text{stand/lie... etc} \end{Bmatrix} + \begin{Bmatrix} N \\ \text{adj.} \\ \text{V-ing} \\ \text{Vpp} \end{Bmatrix}$$

例 Early **detection** systems continue to improve, but landslides **remain a risk** in mountainous areas.
早期檢測系統不斷改進完善，但是山崩仍然是山區的一大風險。
→ 主詞補語為名詞 a risk，說明主詞 landslides。

例 People should **stay calm** when earthquake happens
當地震發生時，應該保持冷靜。
→ 主詞補語為形容詞 calm，說明主詞 People 狀態。

例 The old man **sat nodding off** in the sofa without noticing that his wife was home.
老人坐在沙發上打瞌睡，沒有留意到他的太太回來了。
→ 主詞補語為現在分詞 nodding off，說明主詞 The old man 狀態。

例 Many roads **remained blocked** after the heavy rain because the maintenance department didn't have enough people to fix them all at the same time.
大雨過後，有許多路段是堵塞的，因為修繕單位沒有足夠人手同時修理全部。
→ 主詞補語為過去分詞 blocked，說明主詞 Many roads 狀態。

(2) **連綴動詞**也屬於不完全不及物動詞的一種，**也須接主詞補語做補充說明**。但主詞補語多為**形容詞**或者「**like ＋名詞**」，且通常不用進行式或被動語態。常見的連綴動詞有 be 動詞、seem（似乎、彷彿）、appear（呈現、顯現）、become（變得）、grow（成長）、turn（變得）go（變成、成為）、get（變成；變得）與五感動詞 look（看起來）、feel（感覺起來）、smell（聞起來）、taste（嚐起來）。

例 The file **seems** <u>**very important**</u> to the boss.

這份文件似乎對老闆很重要。

→ 主詞補語為形容詞 very important，說明主詞 The file。

例 She **looks** <u>**like a princess**</u> from a fairy tale.

她看起來像是從童話故事裡走出來的公主。

→ 主詞補語為 like a princess，說明主詞 She 的狀態。

第貳部分：非選擇題

一、中譯英 —— 食物耗損

1. 在已開發國家，多達三分之一的食物可能會被浪費並且最後落入掩埋場。

   In developed countries, up to a third of food is likely to be wasted and end up in landfills.

2. 這是一個嚴重的經濟和環境問題，因為被浪費的食物花了資源來生產，包括大量的水、土地和肥料。

   It is a serious economic and environmental problem/issue
   because the food takes/consumes resources to produce/manufacture,

   [including / inclusive of] [plenty of / a lot of] water, land, and fertilizer(s).

   → 若 fertilizer 採用不可數名詞狀態，可寫 great/large amounts of 修飾 water, land, and fertilizer。

二、英文作文 —— 氣候變遷

> 說明：1. 依提示在「答案卷」上寫一篇英文作文。
> 　　　2. 文長至少 120 個單詞（words）。

請看以下圖片，試述全球暖化可能會對地球和我們的生活造成什麼影響，以及你對全球暖化有什麼樣的看法、建議等。

作文範文

　　Global warming is the ongoing increase in Earth's average surface temperature. This is caused by greenhouse gases, such as carbon dioxide, released into the atmosphere as a result of industrialization. Despite ongoing debates among the public, there is broad scientific consensus that global warming (sometimes called climate change) is occurring, and its leading driver is human use of fossil fuels. A number of global warming's negative effects are distinctly observable, including change in average temperature and glacial retreat. Melting land ice, such as mountain glaciers and polar ice sheets, are releasing liquid water into the oceans. This raises the global sea level, putting coastal and low-lying communities, where 40% of the world's population lives, at risk. The increased amount of CO_2 in the atmosphere can in turn acidify the oceans through rain, jeopardizing the delicate balance which sustains marine life. Rising temperatures may hasten the growth of crops but could create lesser yields. Because all life on the planet is interconnected, this grim picture of climate change suggests that we are not only making animal life vulnerable to extinction but digging own graves as well.

　　As climate scientists made note of the greenhouse gasses accumulating on our atmosphere over the decades, many organizations raised awareness through public information campaigns and implored individuals, corporations, and governments to make meaningful change. Yet little progress has been made. From my personal perspective, more assertive actions should be taken to curb the burning of fossil fuels and the subsequent release of harmful gasses. Together with the government, we should endeavor to scale down the pace of fossil fuel consumption, with the goal of eventually ending its used altogether. The authorities concerned should reduce emissions by modernizing our power plants or, better yet, aggressively promoting sustainable sources of energy generation. Individuals can do their part by adopting a more energy-responsible lifestyle and cutting down on prevalent misuses. Compact fluorescent bulbs, for example, are designed to use far less energy than standard ones. We should take care to switch off electronic devices when not in use and only use as much light as we need. Heating water consumes a lot of energy so we should consider taking shorter showers. We can encourage others to conserve more and waste less and share information about recycling, biking, and carpooling. Many a little makes a mickle. Only with our concerted effort can we lay a solid foundation for environmental protection. In the long run, we are protecting our own future.

譯文

　　全球暖化是地球表面平均溫度持續上升的現象，這是因工業化導致的二氧化碳等溫室氣體釋放到大氣中所造成。儘管大眾仍在爭論不休，但目前各種科學共識是全球暖化（或稱氣候變遷）正在發生，主要驅使原因是人類使用化石燃料，目前明顯可觀察到出許多全球暖化的負面影響，包括平均溫度的變化和冰川退減。岸冰消融正往海洋釋放液態水，例如高山冰川和極地冰原，促使全球海平面升高，繼而導致世界上居住在沿海和低窪地區的 40% 人口處於危險之中。大氣中增加的二氧化碳含量轉而透過雨水使海水酸化，繼而危害維持海洋生物的脆弱平衡。氣溫上升可能會加速農作物生長，但產量可能會降低。由於地球上所有生命都息息相關的，所以這種嚴峻的氣候變遷情景，代表我們不但造成動物生命容易滅絕，而且也是在自掘墳墓。

　　幾十年來氣候科學家注意到，大氣中的溫室氣體正日益累積，許多組織透過公共資訊宣傳活動提高意識，並懇請個人、公司和政府做出有意義的改變，但進展甚少。從我個人角度來看，應採取更果斷的行動來遏止燃燒化石燃料和隨之釋放的有害氣體。我們應與政府一起努力減少化石燃料的消耗速度，以最終停止使用化石燃料為目標。相關當局應透過發電廠現代化來減少廢氣排放，或更好的辦法是積極促進永續能源來生產來源。個人可透過採取更負起能源責任的生活方式並減少普遍濫用以善盡本分。例如省電燈泡是為了大幅減少一般燈泡所消耗的電力而設計。在不使用電子設備時，我們應注意將電器關閉，並只使用所需的燈。燒熱水會消耗大量能源，因此我們應該考慮縮短淋浴時間。我們可以鼓勵他人節省更多能源，減少浪費，並共享有關回收、騎自行車和共乘的資訊。積少成多，只有我們共同努力，才能為環保打下紮實的基礎。從長遠來看，我們是在保護自己的未來。

作文教學

　　Global warming is the ongoing increase in Earth's average surface temperature. This is caused by greenhouse gases, such as carbon dioxide, released into the atmosphere **as a result of** industrialization. Despite ongoing debates among the public, there is broad scientific [1]**consensus** that global warming (sometimes called climate change) is occurring, and its leading driver is human use of fossil fuels. A number of global warming's negative effects are [2]**distinctly** observable, including change in average temperature and glacial [3]**retreat**. Melting land ice, such as mountain glaciers and polar ice sheets, are releasing liquid water into the oceans. This raises the global sea level, **putting** coastal and [4]**low-lying** communities, where 40% of the world's population lives, **at risk**. The increased amount of CO_2 in the atmosphere can **in turn** [5]**acidify** the oceans through rain, [6]**jeopardizing** the delicate balance which sustains marine life. Rising temperatures may [7)]**hasten** the growth of crops but could create lesser [8)]**yields**. Because all life on the planet is interconnected, this [9)]**grim** picture of climate change suggests that we are not only making animal life [10)]**vulnerable** to extinction but digging own graves as well.

As climate scientists made note of the greenhouse gasses accumulating on our atmosphere over the decades, many organizations raised awareness through public information campaigns and [11)]**implored** individuals, corporations, and governments to make meaningful change. Yet little progress has been made. From my personal perspective, more [12)]**assertive** actions should be taken to [13)]**curb** the burning of fossil fuels and the subsequent release of harmful gasses. Together with the government, we should [14)]**endeavor** to scale down the pace of fossil fuel consumption, with the goal of eventually ending its used altogether. [15)]**The authorities concerned** should reduce [16)]**emissions** by modernizing our power plants or, better yet, aggressively promoting [17)]**sustainable** sources of energy generation. Individuals can do their part by adopting a more energy-responsible lifestyle and cutting down on [18)]**prevalent** misuses. Compact [19)]**fluorescent** bulbs, for example, are designed to use far less energy than standard ones. We should take care to switch off electronic devices when not in use and only use as much light as we need. Heating water consumes a lot of energy so we should consider taking shorter showers. We can encourage others to conserve more and waste less and share information about recycling, biking, and [20)]**carpooling**. Many a little makes a mickle. Only with our concerted effort can we lay a solid foundation for environmental protection. In the long run, we are protecting our own future.

重要單字

1. **consensus** [kənˋsɛnsəs] *(n.)* 共識
   → reach/achieve/build a consensus 達成共識

2. **distinctly** [dɪˋstɪŋktlɪ] *(adv.)* 明顯清楚地
   → distinct *(adj.)* 有所區別的；明顯的、清楚的

3. **retreat** [rɪˋtrit] *(n./v.)* 後退；撤退；引退；靜修 *(n.)* [C] 隱蔽處、休養所

4. **low-lying** [ˋloˋlaɪɪŋ] *(adj.)* 低窪的

5. **acidify** [əˋsɪdəˌfaɪ] *(vi.)* 酸化
   → acid *(adj.)* 酸的
   → acid rain 酸雨
   → acidity *(n.)* [U] 酸性

6. **jeopardize** [ˋdʒɛpəɹ͵aɪz] *(vt.)* 危及;冒…的危險

7. **hasten** [ˋhesn̩] *(vt.)* 使加速

8. **yield** [jild] *(vt.)* 結出果實;生產 *(vi.)* 使屈服、放棄
   　　　　(n.) 產量(當此定義恆用複數 yields);[C, U] 收益、利潤

9. **grim** [grɪm] *(adj.)* 無情的、殘忍的;令人生畏的、猙獰的

10. **vulnerable** [ˋvʌlnərəbl] *(adj.)* 脆弱的、易受影響的

11. **implore** [ɪmˋplor] *(vt.)* 懇求、乞求

12. **assertive** [əˋsɝtɪv] *(adj.)* 果敢的、堅定自信的

13. **curb** [kɝb] *(vt.)* 抑制、控制

14. **endeavor** [ɪnˋdɛvə] *(vi./n.)* 努力

15. **the authorities concerned** 有關當局、當權者(當此定義恆用複數)

16. **emission** [ɪˋmɪʃən] *(n.)* [C,U] 排放(量)、排放物

17. **sustainable** [səˋstenəbəl] *(adj.)* 永續的
    → sustain *(vt.)* 支撐;承擔、忍受;供養
    → sustainability *(n.)* [U] 永續性

18. **prevalent** [ˋprɛvələnt] *(adj.)* 盛行的

19. **fluorescent** [fluəˋrɛsənt] *(adj.)* 螢光的、發亮的

20. **carpool** [ˋkɑrpʊl] *(vi./n.)* 汽車共乘

重要片語

1. **as a result of** 由於、因為 = because of

2. **put N at risk** 將…置於險境
   = put N in danger = expose N. to danger = put N. under threat = leave N. vulnerable to...
   = imperil = endanger = threaten

3. **in turn** 接著;反過來

4. **dig one's own grave** 自掘墳墓

5. **raise awareness** 提升意識

6. **from one's (personal) perspective** 以某人觀點來看

7. **Many a little makes a mickle.** 聚沙成塔,積少成多。

1. **together with　與…一起，連同**

   用法等同 along with、as well as，這三組片語連接兩個詞的時候，動詞需與第一個一致，強調的重點也在前面。

   例 The wind, **along with** the dry weather in the fall, helps the noodles dry quickly, which ensures the best quality.

   風再加上秋季乾燥的天氣，有助於快速風乾米粉，確保米粉的優良品質。

2. **Better yet　更好的是…、不如…更好 = better still**

   例 A: How about driving out to the beach tomorrow?

   　　我們明天開車去海邊玩如何？

   　　B: **Better yet**, why not spend the whole weekend there?

   　　我們何不整個週末都待在那裡更好？

3. **Only 為首的倒裝句**

   句型：**Only + 副詞結構 +** $\left[\begin{array}{l} \textbf{be V + S} \\ \textbf{助動詞 + S + V}_\textbf{R} \end{array}\right.$

   例 **Only** when he apologizes sincerely **will I forgive** him.

   只有當他誠心道歉時我才會原諒他。

NOTE

第 5 回 ｜解析

第壹部分：選擇題

一、綜合測驗

第 1 至 10 題為題組 —— 交通守則

All around the world, drunk driving is considered a serious __1__. Drunk driving can cause __2__ damage, injuries, and death. Most countries __3__ heavy penalties for driving while drunk, though the punishments vary.

Drunk driving is frowned upon in Asia. Many Asian countries have a "zero tolerance" policy, meaning drivers are not allowed to __4__ any alcohol before driving. Despite the long history of drinking culture in Europe, many countries also __5__ zero tolerance. Any trace of alcohol in a driver's blood will result in fines, suspension of driver's license, and even time in jail.

Australia's legal BAC (blood alcohol concentration) is 0.05%. The United States, Canada, and Mexico are a little more __6__ at 0.08% BAC. However, all these countries use checkpoints and sobriety tests to catch drunk drivers __7__ the act.

Drunk driving in South Africa can earn the offender up to six years in jail. Many countries in the Middle East ban alcohol altogether. __8__, their penalties for drunk driving can be very __9__, including up to ten years in prison. In the United Arab Emirates, an offender can even receive 80 lashes.

Driving after consuming alcohol is dangerous, and these punishments are meant to __10__ people who may feel like they can risk it. Clearly, no matter where you are in the world, drunk driving is simply not worth it!

譯文

　　世界各國都把酒駕視為嚴重的犯罪。酒後駕車可能會導致財產損失、受傷，甚至鬧出人命。許多國家針對酒後駕車者加重刑責，雖然刑責不盡相同。

　　亞洲大多不允許酒駕的行為。很多亞洲國家採行「零容忍」原則，意指駕駛在開車前連一滴酒都不允許碰。儘管飲酒文化在歐洲有很長的歷史，許多國家也都執行零容忍政策。只要在駕駛血液中檢測到有酒精的蹤跡，就會被處以罰款、吊銷駕照，甚至拘役。

　　澳洲的合法 BAC（血液酒精濃度）是 0.05%。美國、加拿大和墨西哥則是再寬待些許，落在 0.08% BAC。然而，這些國家都設立檢測站和實施醉酒測試來當場逮捕酒駕者。

　　在南非酒駕可能會使觸法者被處以至多六年的有期徒刑。許多中東國家更完全禁止酒精。因此，這些國家對於酒駕者的懲罰可說是非常嚴厲，包含十年的入監服刑。而在阿拉伯聯合大公國，觸法者甚至會被處以鞭刑 80 下。

　　酒後開車非常危險，而這些處罰是制訂來嚇阻那些想冒險嘗試的民眾。毫無疑問的，不論你身處世界的哪個角落，酒駕就是不值得！

---

1. (A) crisis   **(B) crime**   (C) crash   (D) chaos
   (A) 危機   **(B) 犯罪**   (C) 碰撞   (D) 混亂

2. (A) personality   (B) prospect   **(C) property**   (D) prosperity
   (A) 人格特質   (B) 前景   **(C) 財產**   (D) 繁榮

3. **(A) impose**   (B) impress   (C) improve   (D) induce
   (A) 施加   (B) 使印象深刻   (C) 進步   (D) 引起

4. (A) be consume   (B) been consumed   **(C) have consumed** (D) had consumed

   解說 to + have + Vpp 表示該完成式動作比前面動詞還早發生。

5. (A) enroll   (B) endure   **(C) enforce**   (D) entail
   (A) 登記；使入學   (B) 忍耐   **(C) 執行**   (D) 使必須

6. **(A) forgiving**   (B) forcing   (C) forming   (D) facing
   (A) 寬容的   (B) 強迫   (C) 形成   (D) 面對

7. **(A) in**   (B) on   (C) with   (D) at

   解說 in the act (of) 在做…的過程中。

8. (A) Otherwise   **(B) Therefore**   (C) However   (D) In contrast
   (A) 否則   **(B) 因此**   (C) 然而   (D) 相反地

9. (A) hasty   (B) hardy   (C) handy   **(D) harsh**
   (A) 輕率的   (B) 堅強刻苦的   (C) 方便的   **(D) 嚴厲的**

10. (A) delegate   (B) derive   (C) depict   **(D) deter**
    (A) 委派   (B) 源於   (C) 描繪   **(D) 威嚇**

原文

All around the world, drunk driving is considered a serious crime. Drunk driving can cause ¹⁾**property** damage, injuries, and death. Most countries ²⁾**impose** heavy penalties for driving while drunk, though the punishments vary.

Drunk driving is frowned upon in Asia. Many Asian countries have a "zero ³⁾**tolerance**" policy, meaning drivers are not allowed to have consumed any alcohol before driving. Despite the long history of drinking culture in Europe, many countries also enforce zero tolerance. Any trace of alcohol in a driver's blood will result in fines, ⁴⁾**suspension** of driver's license, and even time in jail.

Australia's legal BAC (blood alcohol concentration) is 0.05%. The United States, Canada, and Mexico are a little more forgiving at 0.08% BAC. However, all these countries use ⁵⁾**checkpoints** and ⁶⁾**sobriety tests** to catch drunk drivers in the act.

Drunk driving in South Africa can earn the ⁷⁾**offender** up to six years in jail. Many countries in the Middle East ban alcohol altogether. Therefore, their penalties for drunk driving can be very ⁸⁾**harsh,** including up to ten years in prison. In the United Arab Emirates, an offender can even receive 80 ⁹⁾**lashes**.

Driving after consuming alcohol is dangerous, and theses punishments are meant to ¹⁰⁾**deter** people who may feel like they can risk it. Clearly, no matter where you are in the world, drunk driving is simply not worth it!

重要單字

1. **property** [ˋprɑpətɪ] *(n.)* [U] 財產、資產；所有物
   → property damage 財物損失
   → personal/private/public property 個人／私人／公共財產
   → intellectual property 智慧財產權

2. **impose** [ɪmˋpoz] *(vt.)* 把⋯強加於
   → impose sth. **on** sb. 把某事強加於某人
   → impose a ban/tax/strain **on** something 禁止做某事／對⋯課稅／對⋯帶來壓力

3. **tolerance** [ˋtɑlərəns] *(n.)* [U] 寬容、寬大；忍耐力
   → tolerance **of**/toward(s)/for... 對⋯的寬容
   → tolerance **of**/for/to heat/cold 耐熱／寒能力
   → tolerant *(adj.)* 寬容的；忍受的
   → be (less/more) tolerant **of**... （更不能／更能）容忍、忍受⋯
   → tolerate *(vt.)* 容忍、忍受

4. **suspension** [sə`spɛnʃən] *(n.)* [U] 懸吊；暫停、中止；停職；停學
   - → suspend *(vt.)* 暫停、中止；停職；懸掛；懸浮
   - → suspension **of** business/hostilities/publication 停業／休戰／休刊
   - → suspend judgment/disbelief 不作評價／對某事深信不疑
   - → be suspended **from** school 被停學

5. **checkpoint** [`tʃɛk͵pɔɪnt] *(n.)* [C] 檢查站；關卡
   - → border/military checkpoint 邊境／軍事檢查站

6. **sobriety test** [sə`braɪətɪ tɛst] *(n.)* 酒精濃度測試
   - → sobriety *(n.)* [U] 未醉、清醒；嚴肅，莊重
   - → sober *(adj.)* 未醉的、清醒的；嚴肅的 *(vi.)*（使）變得冷靜或嚴肅
   - → be/remain sober 是清醒的；保持清醒、未醉的
   - → sober (sb.) up（使某人）醒酒

7. **offender** [ə`fɛndə] *(n.)* [C] 冒犯者，惹人生氣的人；違法者
   - → offend *(vt.)* 冒犯、得罪
   - → a first/persistent offender 初犯／慣犯
   - → be offended by... 被…冒犯

8. **harsh** [hɑrʃ] *(adj.)* 嚴厲的；嚴酷的，惡劣的
   - → harsh words/criticism/punishment 難聽的話／嚴厲的批評／嚴酷的懲罰
   - → harsh winter/weather 嚴冬／惡劣的天氣

9. **lash** [læʃ] *(n.)* [C] 鞭打；鞭子；睫毛 *(vt.)* 鞭打、狠打；斥責
   - → receive lashes 挨鞭
   - → come/suffer under the lash 受到嚴厲批評，遭到痛斥
   - → lash out (sth.) 浪費、揮霍（錢財）

10. **deter** [dɪ`tɝ] *(vt.)* 威懾住，嚇住
    - → deter sb. from (doing) sth. 嚇得某人不敢做某事

重要片語

1. **frown upon** 不許；不贊成

2. **result in** 導致

3. **in the act (of)** 在做…的過程中

1. **despite 儘管；雖然**

despit 和 in spite of 都屬介系詞（片語），用來表達「儘管；雖然」，後面須接名詞或動名詞。兩者皆不可直接連接子句，若要接子句，則須在子句前加 the fact that 作為介系詞的受詞，或依句意改用從屬連接詞 although/ though。

例 Despite the long history of drinking culture in Europe, many countries also enforce zero tolerance.

儘管飲酒文化在歐洲有很長的歷史，許多國家也都執行零容忍政策。

2.「列舉」的用法

(1) including 為介系詞，後面可以接舉例的名詞，等同 such as。

例 Therefore, their penalties for drunk driving can be very harsh, including up to ten years in prison.

因此，這些國家對於酒駕者的懲罰可說是非常嚴厲，包含十年的入監服刑。

(2) 關於列舉的用法，以下是總整理的句型：

Ns, **including** N1, N2, and N3

= **such as** N1, N2, and N3

= Ns, **inclusive of** N1, N2, and N3

= N1, N2, and N3 **included**

= **such** Ns **as** N1, N2, and N3

For decades, parents have been concerned that the violent imagery of some video games is negatively affecting their own children's behavior. But is this really the case? The debate is ongoing.

Home video gaming __11__ poplar since the 1980s. The latest craze is *Fortnite*. Although *Fortnite's* design is cartoonish and fun, as opposed to other more __12__ games, the action still consists of shooting as many opponents as possible. Many parents are shocked by this focus on firearms violence.

Different studies __13__ conflicting data. In 2015, The American Psychiatric Association published a statement that research showed violent games directly lead to an increase in aggressive behavior __14__ players. But many who research __15__ health disagreed, and sent a strong response to the APA. 230 scholars __16__ the APA's statement as "misleading and alarmist." More recently, a subdivision of the APA itself which focuses on the media cautioned news outlets __17__ blaming real-world violence on games.

More recent studies have not found any significant link between violent games and real violence or other negative behavior. __18__, some studies show that the popularity of games, even violent ones, might be linked to a decrease in real __19__ of aggression. There may be a publication bias in __20__ studies stating that video games lead to violent behavior, because games are an easy target to blame. It is wise to keep in mind that with the problem of violence, the causes may be complex.

譯文

數十年來，家長都在關心，某些電動玩具的暴力畫面會對自己的小孩產生負面影響。但這是事實嗎？關於此事的討論正在進行。

家用電動自 1980 年開始流行。而近期最流行的遊戲正是《堡壘之夜》（*Fortnite*）。儘管《堡壘之夜》不像其他殘忍的遊戲，它的設計比較卡通化且有趣，但玩法還是包含擊中越多對手越好。許多家長對於這種聚焦在槍枝暴力的遊戲感到震驚。

不同研究得出了互相矛盾的數據。2015 年，美國精神醫學學會（APA）發表了一項聲明，裡頭的研究指出，暴力的遊戲會直接地增加玩家的攻擊行為。然而，許多研究青少年健康的學者並不這麼認為，他們還向 APA 提出強烈的回應。230 名學者認為 APA 的聲明是「誤導且危言聳聽」，應不予理會。而在近期，APA 自家的媒體分部警告新聞媒體，不該將現實世界的暴力行為歸咎在遊戲上。

最近的研究並沒有找到任何暴力遊戲與現實暴力或其他負面行為的重要關聯。事實上，有許多研究指出，受歡迎的遊戲中，即使是暴力的，都有可能會減少現實中的攻擊事件。之前的研究聲稱電玩會導致暴力行為的研究可能都帶有發表偏倚，因為遊戲很容易成為譴責的對象。請記住，暴力問題產生的原因可能是很複雜的。

11. (A) is   (B) was   **(C) has been**   (D) had been

> 解說　has/have + Vpp 現在完成式，表過去（1980 年代）開始的狀態，而現在還持續著。

12. (A) gracious   (B) greedy   (C) guilty   **(D) grim**
    (A) 親切的   (B) 貪婪的   (C) 有罪的   **(D) 殘忍的**

13. (A) yearn   **(B) yield**   (C) yell   (D) yawn
    (A) 渴望   **(B) 產生**   (C) 大喊   (D) 打呵欠

14. **(A) in**   (B) on   (C) at   (D) with

> 解說　... in players 玩家之間的。

15. **(A) adolescent**   (B) adult   (C) activist   (D) addict
    (A) 青少年   (B) 成人   (C) 積極分子   (D) 成癮者

16. (A) demanded   (B) determined   **(C) dismissed**   (D) disrupted
    (A) 要求   (B) 定義   **(C) 認為…而不予考慮**   (D) 妨礙

17. (A) upon   **(B) against**   (C) beyond   (D) without

> 解說　caution/warn sb. against + N 警告、告誡某人不要…

18. (A) Therefore   (B) However   **(C) In fact**   (D) Since
    (A) 因此   (B) 然而   **(C) 事實上**   (D) 自那時起

19. (A) incentives   (B) infections   **(C) incidents**   (D) institutions
    (A) 動機   (B) 感染   **(C) 事件**   (D) 機構

20. **(A) previous**   (B) primary   (C) probable   (D) profound
    (A) 先前的   (B) 主要的   (C) 可能的   (D) 深遠的

原文

For decades, parents have been concerned that the violent imagery of some video games is negatively affecting their own children's behavior. But is this really the case? The debate is ongoing.

Home video gaming has been poplar since the 1980s. The latest craze is *Fortnite*. Although *Fortnite's* design is cartoonish and fun, **as opposed to** other more [1)]**grim** games, the action still consists of shooting as many [2)]**opponents** as possible. Many parents are shocked by this focus on firearms violence.

Different studies yield conflicting data. In 2015, The American Psychiatric Association published a statement that research showed violent games directly **lead to** an increase in aggressive behavior in players. But many who research [3)]**adolescent** health disagreed, and sent a strong response to the APA. 230 scholars **dismissed** the APA's statement **as** "misleading and [4)]**alarmist**." More recently, a [5)]**subdivision** of the APA itself which focuses on the media cautioned [6)]**news outlets** against **blaming** real-world violence **on** games.

More recent studies have not found any significant link between violent games and real violence or other negative behavior. In fact some studies show that the popularity of games, even violent ones, might **be linked to** a decrease in real [7)]**incidents** of aggression. There may be a [8)]**publication bias** in previous studies stating that video games lead to violent behavior, because games are an easy target to blame. It is wise to keep in mind that with the problem of violence, the causes may be complex.

重要單字

1. **grim** [grɪm] *(adj.)* 無情的、殘忍的；嚴厲的
   - → with grim determination 破釜沉舟
   - → grim-faced *(adj.)* 表情嚴肅的
   - → hang/hold on like grim death 死死地抓住不放；咬牙堅持

2. **opponent** [ə`ponənt] *(n.)* [C] 對手、敵手、反對者 (+ **of**)
   - → oppose *(vt.)* 反對；反抗；抵制
   - → a chief/main/leading opponent 主要對手、主要反對者
   - → oppose N/Ving = be opposed **to** N/Ving 反對、不贊成⋯

3. **adolescent** [ˌædl̩`ɛsənt] *(adj.)* 青春期的；青少年的 *(n.)* [C] 青少年
   - → adolescence *(n.)* [U] 青春期
   - → an adolescent boy/girl 青春期的男孩／女孩
   - → adolescent concerns/traumas 青春期孩子關心的問題／青春期創傷

4. **alarmist** [ə`lɑrmɪst] *(adj.)* 危言聳聽的
   - → alarm *(n.)* [C] 警報；驚慌；警鈴　*(v.)* 使擔心或害怕
   - → alarmist reports of... 關於⋯的危言聳聽的報導
   - → raise/sound the alarm 發出警報／響警報
   - → ring alarm bells in one's mind 引起某人的警覺；敲響心中的警鐘

5. **subdivision** [sʌbdə`vɪʒən] *(n.)* [C] 分支；分部
   - → divide *(vt.)* （使）分開；（使）分組；分攤
   - → divide A **from** B 將 A 和 B 隔開、分開
   - → divide the class **into** small groups 把班級分成小組
   - → subdivide *(vt.)* 將⋯再分，將⋯細分
   - → subdivide sth. **into** sth. 把某物再分成⋯

6. **news outlet** [njuz`aʊˌlɛt] *(n.)* 新聞媒體
   - → outlet *(n.)* [C] 排放孔；發洩途徑 (+ for)；銷路
   - → retail outlet 零售店

7. **incident** [`ɪnsədənt] *(n.)* [C] 事件；事變
   - → without incident 平安無事地
   - → a(an) isolated/serious/unfortunate incident 獨立／嚴重／不幸的事件

8. **publication bias** [ˌpʌblɪ`keʃən baɪəs] *(n.)* 發表偏差；出版偏誤
   - → bias *(n.)* [C, U] 偏見；傾向 (+ against；+ <u>towards</u>/<u>in favor of</u>)
   - → political/gender/racial bias 政治／性別／種族偏見

重要片語

1. **as opposed to + N** 而不是⋯

2. **lead to + N** 導致⋯

3. **dismiss... as...** 認為⋯而不予考慮

4. **blame sth. on sb.** 將某事歸咎於某人

5. **be linked to** 和⋯有關聯

1. **consist of 包含、組成**

   consist of 的句型可以分為主動語態和被動語態：

   (1) **主動語態**：A（大）+ consist of, comprise, contain + B（小） A 由 B 組成、A 包含 B

   　　　　　　B（小）+ make up, compose, constitute + A（大） B 組成 A

   (2) **被動語態**：A（大）+ be made up of, be composed of, be constituted of + B（小） A 是由 B 組成

   (3) 需注意，consist of 沒有被動式。

   例 Although *Fortnite's* design is cartoonish and fun, as opposed to other more grim games, the action still **consists of** shooting as many opponents as possible.

   儘管《堡壘之夜》不像其他殘忍的遊戲，它的設計比較卡通化且有趣，但玩法還是包含擊中越多對手越好。

二、文意選填

第 21 至 30 題為題組 —— 貪汙誠信

Corruption is a problem that affects all governments. Once it is allowed to take hold, its negative __21__ spread to all aspects of the government as if it is __22__. Public policies become less fair and effective. Citizens sense that the government is no longer working for them and lose faith in its leaders. Corruption must be dealt with seriously as it arises.

Countries with higher levels of corruption collect less tax __23__. This is because powerful individuals pay __24__ to avoid paying taxes. Less taxes collected means projects __25__ to benefit the public go underfunded. When citizens realize this, they may seek to avoid paying taxes themselves, as they can't see any benefit in doing so. Another form of corruption is spending taxpayers' money on unnecessary or __26__ products or services. This can lead to substandard work on crucial things such as roads, buildings, and bridges. The safety of those who must use these things may be __27__.

This leads to public mistrust of government, which undermines the entire society. Fortunately, there are ways to minimize corruption, through robust __28__ designed to monitor and root out misdeeds. The public must be able to report on the government. Citizens must have a way to express their concerns, free __29__ fear of punishment. Several South American countries provide an online platform through which corruption in public projects can be reported. A free press, without government oversight, is crucial.

Old institutions __30__ government should usually be reformed if they are found to harbor corruption. As the nations of the world become more interconnected, international anti-corruption organizations should be created. Corruption is an ongoing problem, but the risks of letting it go unchecked are far too great.

譯文

所有政府機關都受貪汙問題影響。一旦放任貪汙發展，它的負面結果可能會遍及政府機關的每個層面，就像傳染病一樣。公共政策會失去公平及成效。公民也會察覺政府不再為他們服務，進而對領導人失去信心。貪汙問題一旦發生就得立刻嚴加處理。

貪汙情形較嚴重的國家所徵收到的稅金比較少，這是因為有權勢的人會以賄賂的方式來避免繳稅。徵收到的稅金越少就代表那些為了造福公眾的計畫會資金不足。公民發現到這個情況時，可能就會想辦法讓自己免於繳稅，因為他們看不到任何繳稅後所帶來的福利。另外一種貪汙的形式就是將納稅人的錢花在不必要或沒效率的產品或服務上。這會造成在一些重要的公共建設上偷工減料，像是公路、建物和橋樑。對於那些會使用到這些公共建設的人來說，等於是忽略了他們的安全。

上述都會導致大眾不信任政府，進而蠶食整個社會。幸好，有些減少貪汙的方法，那就是透過設立健全的機構來監督政府並根除劣行。社會大眾要能夠向政府反映。公民必須有個可以表達意見、不用怕會受到懲罰的管道。有些南美國家提供一個線上平台來讓民眾反映公共計畫中的貪汙行為。一個自由、沒有政府監管的評論管道是很重要的。

如果發現政府內部的舊制機關在包庇貪汙，就應該要重組這些機關。由於世界上國與國之間變得更緊密相連，所以應該要建立一個國際的反貪汙組織。貪汙是個正在發生的問題，而不制止它的話，它所帶來的風險將無以計量。

(A) consequences	(B) within	(C) revenue	(D) intended	(E) inefficient
(A) 結果	(B) 在內部	(C) 收入	(D) 以⋯為目的	(E) 沒效率的

(F) bribes	(G) disregarded	(H) institutions	(I) from	(J) contagious
(F) 賄賂	(G) 被忽視的	(H) 機關	(I) free from 免於	(J) 蔓延的

原文

　　[1]**Corruption** is a problem that affects all governments. Once it is allowed to **take hold**, its negative consequences spread to all aspects of the government as if it is [2]**contagious**. Public policies become less fair and effective. Citizens sense that the government is no longer working for them and lose faith in its leaders. Corruption must be **dealt with** seriously as it arises.

　　Countries with higher levels of corruption collect less tax [3]**revenue**. This is because powerful individuals **pay bribes** to avoid paying taxes. Less taxes collected means projects intended to benefit the public go underfunded. When citizens realize this, they may seek to avoid paying taxes themselves, as they can't see any benefit in doing so. Another form of corruption is spending taxpayers' money on unnecessary or inefficient products or services. This can lead to [4]**substandard** work on crucial things such as roads, buildings, and bridges. The safety of those who must use these things may be [5]**disregarded**.

　　This leads to public mistrust of government, which [6]**undermines** the entire society. Fortunately, there are ways to minimize corruption, through [7]**robust** institutions designed to monitor and **root out** [8]**misdeeds**. The public must be able to report on the government. Citizens must have a way to express their concerns, **free from** fear of punishment. Several South American countries provide an online platform through which corruption in public projects can be reported. A free press, without government [9]**oversight**, is crucial.

　　Old institutions within government should usually be reformed if they are found to [10]**harbor** corruption. As the nations of the world become more interconnected, international anti-corruption organizations should be created. Corruption is an ongoing problem, but the risks of letting it go unchecked are far too great.

1. **corruption** [kə`rʌpʃən] *(n.)* [U] 墮落；腐化；貪汙
   → corrupt *(v.)* 使腐敗、墮落
   → a corrupted society 道德敗壞的社會

2. **contagious** [kən`tedʒəs] *(adj.)* 接觸性傳染的；會蔓延、感染的
   → 近義字 infectious
   → be highly contagious 極易傳染的
   → a contagious disease 傳染病

3. **revenue** [`rɛvə,nju] *(n.)* [U, C]（政府的）稅收、歲入；（公司的）收益
   → tax revenues 稅收
   → government revenues 政府財政收入
   → annual/advertising/potential revenues 年度／廣告／潛在收益

4. **substandard** [sʌb`stændəd] *(adj.)* 未達標準的、不合規格的
   → 字首 sub- 常有「under（次要、淺下、低下、從屬）」的意思，比如 subway（地下鐵）、
      submarine（潛水艇；海底的）、suburb（郊區，城郊）
   → standard *(n.)* 標準；水準；規格 *(adj.)* 標準的；模範的
   → substandard work/goods/accommodation（做得）不合格的工作／商品／住處
   → moral standards 道德規範
   → be below standard / be up to standard 未達標準／達到標準

5. **disregard** [,dɪsrɪ`gɑrd] *(v./n.)* 不理會、不顧
   → dis- 為否定字首。
   → regard *(vt./n.)* [U] 關心；考慮；重視
   → 字首 re- 表「返回、重新」；字尾 -gard 表「看，考慮」
   → regardless *(adv.)* 不管怎樣，無論如何 (+ **of**)
   → regardless of rank or status 不管地位如何
   → regardless of the weather 無論天氣如何

6. **undermine** [,ʌndə`maɪn] *(vt.)* 逐漸損害
   → undermine one's confidence/position/credibility/reputation/health
      損傷某人的信心／地位／可靠性／名譽／健康

7. **robust** [rə`bʌst] *(adj.)* 強健的；茁壯的；健全的
   → robustly *(adv.)* 堅定地，堅決地
   → a robust man 強壯的男人
   → a robust economy 蓬勃發展的經濟

8. **misdeed** [mɪsˋdid] *(n.)* [C] 不端行為；罪行
   → 字首 mis- 表示「wrongly, badly（不好、錯誤、缺乏）」的意涵，比如 misfortune（不幸）、mistake（錯誤）、misunderstand（誤解）
   → deed *(n.)* do 的名詞形，意為「行為、事情」
   → (do/perform) good/evil/brave deeds（做）好事／壞事／勇敢的事
   → make up for / repent of / pay for one's misdeed
   彌補不端行為／為罪行懺悔／為不端行為付出代價

9. **oversight** [ˋovɚ͵saɪt] *(n.)* [U] 監督、照管；疏忽、疏漏
   → oversee *(vt.)* 監督、監察、監管
   → have oversight of sth. 有…的監管責任
   → due to / through / by (an) oversight 由於疏忽

10. **harbor** [ˋhɑrbɚ] *(vt.)* 庇護、藏匿 *(n.)* 港口、港灣
    → harbor a criminal 窩藏罪犯
    → in (the) harbor 停泊中，在港口

重要片語

1. **take hold** 增強；確認地位
2. **deal with** 處理；應付 = handle with, cope with
3. **pay a bribe** 行賄
4. **root out** 找到並根除
5. **free from** 使擺脫…；免於…

相關文法句型

1. **as 的使用方式**
   (1) as 作介系詞時，表「身為…」、「當作…」：
   例 **As** a student, I should study hard.
   身為學生，我應該要好好讀書。

   例 This problem is regarded **as** a challenge.
   這個問題被視為一個挑戰。

(2) as 作連接詞時，可用在比較級 as... as（和…一樣），也可以表「正如同…」、「當」、「因為」的意思。

例 Do in Rome as the Romans do.
入境隨俗。

例 I saw Linda as I was on my way home.
當我回家時我看見琳達。

例 As it is getting dark, I decide to go home.
因為天色漸暗，我決定回家。

(3) 片語 as if 則是「彷彿」：

例 Once it is allowed to take hold, its negative consequences spread to all aspects of the government **as if** it is contagious.
一旦放任貪汙發展，它的負面結果可能會遍及政府機關的每個層面，就像傳染病一樣。

(4) as 也有「因為、由於」之意，後面接完整子句：

例 When citizens realize this, they may seek to avoid paying taxes themselves, **as** they can't see any benefit in doing so.
公民發現到這個情況時，可能就會想辦法讓自己免於繳稅，因為他們看不到任何繳稅後所帶來的福利。

2. 後方只能接 Ving 的動詞

例 This is because powerful individuals pay bribes to **avoid** **paying** taxes.
這是因為有權勢的人會以賄賂的方式來避免繳稅。
→ avoid 後只能接 N. 或 Ving，不可接 to V$_R$。

其他後面只能接 Ving 的動詞還有：consider（考慮），dislike（不喜歡），enjoy（享受），finish（結束），forgive（原諒），keep（維持），mind（介意），miss（錯過），postpone（推延），prevent（預防），resent（怨恨），resist（堅持）等。

第 31 至 35 題為題組 —— 爭取人權

Taiwan has perhaps been the most gay-friendly country in Asia for over a decade. Taipei is home to a thriving gay community and hosts Asia's largest gay pride parade. In 2019, the parade was even more festive than usual, because lawmakers made Taiwan the first Asian nation to legalize same-sex marriage.

Since then, thousands of gay couples have wed. Many heterosexuals also support gay marriage, stating that having one's union legally recognized is a human right for everyone. __31__

Not everyone is celebrating, though. __32__ Immediately after Taiwan's Constitutional Court made gay marriage legal, several groups organized in opposition to the ruling. Religious and conservative groups favored same-sex unions that were limited in nature as opposed to true marriage. __33__ Those opposed to marriage equality warned President Tsai Ing-wen that she would be voted out in the January elections. __34__

Still, gay marriage in Taiwan is not exactly equivalent to heterosexual marriage. Gay couples can not adopt children, though they may raise any biological children they may have. __35__ But many are still excited for the future of gay rights in Taiwan.

Legalizing gay marriage is just a part of many socially progressive policies Taiwan has instituted in recent years. Taiwan is seen as an example of democracy in action within the region.

譯文

十多年來，台灣可說是亞洲國家中對同性戀最友善的國家。台北是逐漸蓬勃壯大的同性族群的所在地，而台北也是全亞洲最大同志遊行的舉辦地。2019 年的遊行比以往更歡樂，因為執法人讓台灣成為亞洲第一個同性婚姻合法化的國家。

自那時開始，上千對的同性伴侶結為夫妻。許多異性戀也都支持同性婚姻，他們表示婚姻被合法認可是每個人都應享有的權利。(D) **許多新婚的同性伴侶都現身在台北近期的遊行和慶祝活動中，出席人數估計超過 20 萬人。**

然而，並非每個人都在慶祝。(B) **就如同在美國和其他地方，很多人堅決反對同性婚姻。**就在台灣司法院通過同性婚姻合法後，許多團體反對這項判決。宗教和保守組織支持同性結合，同性結合在本質上受限，和真正的婚姻截然不同。(C) **他們提出對法律的質疑，但還是遭議會駁回了。**那些反對婚姻平權的人警告蔡英文，說她會在一月的選戰中落敗。(A) **但大多數的選民更關心經濟問題以及台灣和中國間的緊繃關係。**

同性婚姻在台灣還是和異性婚姻不完全平等。同性伴侶沒有辦法領養小孩，但他們還是可以扶養任何一方可能會有的親生子女。(E) **此外，伴侶中若有一方是外國人，且在該國的法律沒有合法化同性婚姻的情況下，台灣不會承認這對伴侶的婚姻。**然而很多人還是對未來同性戀人權在台灣的發展感到興奮。

合法化同性婚姻只是台灣近年來制定的社會發展政策中的其一。台灣在亞洲地區被視為一個將民主化為行動的典範。

(A) But most voters were more concerned with economic issues and Taiwan's strained relationship with China.
但大多數的選民更關心經濟問題以及台灣和中國間的緊繃關係。

(B) As in the United States and elsewhere, many people are deeply opposed to gay marriage.
就如同在美國和其他地方,很多人堅決反對同性婚姻。

(C) They launched legal challenges, but were defeated in parliament.
他們提出對法律的質疑,但還是遭議會駁回。

(D) Many of the newly-wed gay couples were among Taipei's recent parade and celebration, with attendance estimated to be over 200,000.
許多新婚的同性伴侶都現身在台北近期的遊行和慶祝中,出席率估計超過 20 萬人。

(E) Also, Taiwan will not recognize marriage if one of the partners is a foreigner from a country that does not have gay marriage.
此外,伴侶中若有一方是外國人,且在該國的法律沒有合法化同性婚姻的情況下,台灣不會承認這對伴侶的婚姻。

原文

Taiwan has perhaps been the most gay-friendly country in Asia for over a decade. Taipei is home to a 1)**thriving** gay community and hosts Asia's largest gay pride parade. In 2019, the parade was even more 2)**festive** than usual, because lawmakers made Taiwan the first Asian nation to legalize same-sex marriage.

Since then, thousands of gay couples have wed. Many 3)**heterosexuals** also support gay marriage, stating that having one's union legally recognized is a human right for everyone. Many of the newly-wed gay couples were among Taipei's recent parade and celebration, with attendance 4)**estimated** to be over 200,000.

Not everyone is celebrating, though. As in the United States and elsewhere, many people **are** deeply **opposed to** gay marriage. Immediately after Taiwan's Constitutional Court made gay marriage legal, several groups organized **in opposition to** the ruling. Religious and 5)**conservative** groups favored same-sex unions that were limited **in nature** as opposed to true marriage. They 6)**launched** legal challenges, but were defeated in 7)**parliament**. Those opposed to marriage equality warned President Tsai Ing-wen that she would be voted out in the January elections. But most voters **were** more **concerned with** economic issues and Taiwan's strained relationship with China.

Still, gay marriage in Taiwan is not exactly 8)**equivalent** to heterosexual marriage. Gay couples can not adopt children, though they may raise any biological children they may have.

Also, Taiwan will not recognize marriage if one of the partners is a foreigner from a country that does not have gay marriage. But many are still excited for the future of gay rights in Taiwan.

Legalizing gay marriage is just a part of many socially progressive policies Taiwan has [9]**instituted** in recent years. Taiwan is seen as an example of [10]**democracy** in action within the region.

重要單字

1. **thrive** [θraɪv] *(vi.)* 興旺、繁榮
   → thrive **on** stress/pressure 擅長在壓力下工作
   → business thrives 生意興隆

2. **festive** [ˈfɛstɪv] *(adj.)* 歡宴的；歡樂的
   → festival *(n.)* [C] 節日；節慶
   → a festive mood/occasion 節日氣氛／喜慶場合
   → the festive season/period/holiday 聖誕節期間
   → a folk/pop/rock festival 民間音樂／流行音樂／搖滾音樂節

3. **heterosexual** [ˌhɛtərəˈsɛkʃuəl] *(n./adj.)* [C] 異性戀的（人）
   → bisexual 雙性戀；homosexual 同性戀者

4. **estimate** [ˈɛstəˌmet] *(vt./n.)* [C] 估計（數字）
   → make an estimate 估算
   → a(an) rough/approximate/accurate/conservative estimate 粗略／粗略／精確／保守估計

5. **conservative** [kənˈsɜvətɪv] *(adj.)* 保守的、守舊的 ↔ liberal *(adj.)* 自由開放的
   → a conservative society/outlook 保守的社會／觀念

6. **launch** [lɔntʃ] *(v.)* 開始；推出、啟用；猛力展開 *(n.)* 發表（會）
   → launch an artificial satellite 發射人造衛星
   → launch a strike/campaign/project 發起一場罷工／一場活動／一個計劃
   → launch an attack/assault 發起攻擊
   → launch into a new business 開始一個新生意

7. **parliament** [ˈpɑrləmənt] *(n.)*（英國）議會；國會
   → congress *(n.)*（美國）國會
   → in parliament 在議會上

8. **equivalent** [ɪˋkwɪvələnt] *(adj.)* 相等的、相同的
   → equivalence *(n.)* 相等；等值
   → be equivalent **to** sth. 跟某事物相當

9. **institute** [ˋɪnstətjut] *(vt.)* 創立、設立 *(n.)* [C] 學院
   → institute a search 開始搜查
   → institute a suit against sb. 對某人提起訴訟
   → institution *(n.)* [C] 制度，習俗；機構
   → a medical/educational/financial institution 醫療／教育／金融機構

10. **democracy** [dɪˋmɑkrəsɪ] *(n.)* [U] 民主；[C] 民主國
    → democratic *(adj.)* 民主的
    → democrat *(n.)* 民主主義者
    → a democratic country/constitution/election 民主國家／憲法／選舉

重要片語

1. **be opposed to + N** 反對…
2. **be in opposition to + N** 反對…
3. **in nature** 本質上
4. **be concerned with/about** 關心、擔憂…

相關文法句型

1. **分詞構句**

   例 Since then, thousands of gay couples have wed. Many **heterosexuals** also support gay marriage, **stating** that having one's union legally recognized is a human right for everyone.
   自那時開始，上千對的同性伴侶結為夫妻。許多異性戀也都支持同性婚姻，他們表示婚姻被合法認可是每個人都應享有的權利。
   → 本句「stating...」為 and they state 簡化而成的分詞構句，當前後對等子句主詞相同時，可刪掉連接詞 and 以及第二個子句的主詞，動詞主動改為現在分詞，被動改成過去分詞。

2. **is seen as 被視為…**

例 **Taiwan** is seen as **an example of democracy in action** within the region.
台灣在亞洲地區被視為一個將民主化為行動的典範。

「將 A 視為 / 認為 B」的句型：

$$\left.\begin{array}{l} \text{see} \\ \text{view} \\ \text{take} \\ \text{treat} \\ \text{regard} \\ \text{think of} \\ \text{refer to} \\ \text{look on/upon} \end{array}\right\} + A + as + B$$

第貳部分：非選擇題

一、中譯英 —— 政治腐敗

1. 如同眾所周知的，絕對的權力導致絕對的腐敗，也因此，強大的政府很難擺脫掉貪汙的指控。

As everyone knows,
As is known to everyone,　absolute power leads to absolute corruption,
As is widely known,

　　　 owing to this,
and　therefore,
　　　 it gets into a situation where

a powerful government cannot get rid of the accusation of being corrupt.

2. 如果這種混亂的政治風氣不改變的話，政府不只無法為人民服務，同時也會讓大眾對政府失去信心。

If the chaotic political climate
Provided the disorderly political atmospheredoesn't change　not only will it be
Supposing the confused political environment

impossible/difficult for the government to serve its people, but the people will also lose
faith/confidence in their government at the same time.

二、英文作文 —— 求職履歷

畢業季即將來臨，許多社會新鮮人及學生將陸續投入職場或工讀行列。網路大型求職平台廣大徵才，為多項專業領域開立職缺及廣泛開放人才招募。假設你是一位今年大學剛畢業的新鮮人，請在徵才平台上投遞英文求職信函，職務不拘。第一段簡單作自我介紹，並表明要應徵的職位，第二段表明為何你適任這份工作。信末署名請遵照規範，男生用 Xiao Ming，女生用 Hui Mei。文長至少 120 個單詞（words）。

作文範文

To Whom it May Concern,

My name is Xiao Ming, and I am currently a student at National Taiwan University. I was recently introduced to your company via the 1234 recruiting platform and am interested in applying for the position of editor. It is widely acknowledged that ABC News is a fast-moving global institution and pioneer in communications, poised to guide the future of print and online journalism. I have grown up reading your daily and weekly publications. I have long admired the institution of ABC News, not only because you produce high-quality, objective accounts of current events, but also because you provide room for discussion and critical thinking. Much of the public may have already been disillusioned by certain mass media outlets—print, broadcast, or digital—that have capitulated to their sponsors' political leanings and have become mere propaganda. In this era of disinformation, ABC News remains unbiased, nonpartisan, and firmly opposed to sensationalism. I hold your company in high esteem for its ethical journalism, and I am eager to contribute to this righteous pursuit of the truth.

I believe my extensive training as a media major makes me an ideal candidate for this position at your company. I have completed multiple internships, including Media Relations Coordinator Intern at Y Company. Through this experience, I enhanced my writing skills and became familiar with most of the editing tools such as PS and AI. I also served as president of the Media and Marketing Club at my university. During my term in office, we successfully developed and pitched an advertisement campaign for a local nonprofit organization, which helped increase donations to the nonprofit by 22%. I served as chief editor of our school's student newspaper on several occasions. Additionally, I operated our Facebook Fanpage that saw a significant increase in popularity, with a 30% increase in daily visitors and overall readership that soared 20% in six months. These strengths—together with deep and varied academic, internship, and employment experience—prepare me to make a strong and immediate impact on the ABC News company. I have enclosed a copy of my résumé for your reference. I am excited about the opportunity to join you. Thank you for your time and consideration, and I am looking forward to hearing from you.

Xiao Ming

譯文

敬啟者：

　　我的名字是小明，目前是國立台灣大學的學生。我最近透過 1234 招聘平台認識到貴公司，並對申請編輯職位感興趣。眾所周知，ABC 新聞是快速發展的全球機構，也是傳播界的先驅，已準備好帶領平面和網路新聞業的未來。我從小就一直閱讀你們的每日和每週刊物。長久以來我一直敬佩 ABC 新聞機構，不僅是因為你們針對時事製作高品質的客觀報導，也因為你們提供了討論和思辨的空間。多數民眾已對特定大眾媒體通路幻滅，例如平面、廣播或數位媒體，因為這些媒體屈服於贊助商的政治傾向，只成了宣傳工具。在不實訊息充斥的時代，ABC 新聞保持公正、無黨派和堅決反對嘩眾取寵。我對貴公司的新聞倫理懷抱崇高的敬意，並渴望為這種追求事實的正義做出貢獻。

　　我相信我在媒體主修方面的廣泛訓練讓我成為貴公司這個職位的理想人選。我已完成數個實習工作，包括 Y 公司的媒體關係統籌實習。透過此經驗，我提升了寫作技巧，並熟悉了修圖軟體 PS 和繪圖軟體 AI 等大部分編輯工具。我也曾在大學擔任媒體行銷社團的社長。我在擔任社長期間成功為當地一家非營利組織開發和宣傳一項廣告活動，並幫助這間非營利組織增加 22% 的捐款。我曾數次擔任過敝校校刊的總編輯。此外，我經營的臉書粉專的人氣有明顯增加，在六個月內每日造訪人數增加了 30%，整體閱讀率激增 20%。這些實力加上深厚多元的學術、實習和就職經驗，讓我準備好為 ABC 新聞公司帶來強力而直接的影響。隨信附上我的履歷供您參考。我很高興有機會加入你們。感謝您撥冗考慮，期待您的答覆。

小明

作文教學

To Whom it May Concern,

　　My name is Xiao Ming, and I am currently a student at National Taiwan University. I was recently introduced to your company 1)**via** the 1234 recruiting platform and am interested in applying for the position of editor. It is widely acknowledged that ABC News is a fast-moving global 2)**institution** and 3)**pioneer** in communications, poised to guide the future of print and online journalism. I have grown up reading your daily and weekly publications. I have long admired the institution of ABC News, not only because you produce high-quality, 4)**objective** 5)**accounts** of current events, but also because you provide room for discussion and 6)**critical thinking**. Much of the public may have already been disillusioned by certain mass media outlets—print, broadcast, or digital—that have capitulated to their 7)**sponsors'** 8)**political leanings** and have become mere 9)**propaganda**. In this era of 10)**disinformation**, ABC News remains 11)**unbiased**, nonpartisan, and firmly opposed to 12)**sensationalism**. I hold your company in high esteem for its 13)**ethical** journalism, and I am eager to contribute to this 14)**righteous** pursuit of the truth.

　　I believe my 15)**extensive** training as a media major makes me an ideal 16)**candidate** for this position at your company. I have completed multiple 17)**internships**, including Media Relations 18)**Coordinator** Intern at Y Company. Through this experience, I enhanced my writing skills and became familiar with most of the editing tools such as PS and AI. I also

served as president of the Media and Marketing Club at my university. During my term in office, we successfully developed and pitched an advertisement campaign for a local nonprofit organization, which helped increase donations to the nonprofit by 22%. I served as chief editor of our school's student newspaper on several occasions. Additionally, I operated our Facebook Fanpage that saw a significant increase in popularity, with a 30% increase in daily visitors and overall readership that soared 20% in six months. These strengths— together with deep and varied academic, internship, and employment experience—prepare me to make a strong and immediate impact on the ABC News company. I have [19]**enclosed** a copy of my [20]**résumé** for your [21]**reference**. I am excited about the opportunity to join you. Thank you for your time and consideration, and I am looking forward to hearing from you.
Xiao Ming

重要單字

1. **via** [vɪə] *(prep.)* 藉由、經由 = by way of, by means of

2. **institution** [ˌɪnstɪˈtuʃən] *(n.)* [C] 機構
   → institute *(n.)* 學會、協會；學院

3. **pioneer** [ˌpaɪəˈnɪr] *(n.)* [C] 先驅、開拓 *(vt.)* 當先驅、開拓出

4. **objective** [əbˈdʒɛktɪv] *(adj.)* 客觀的 *(n.)* [C] 目標

5. **account** [əˈkaʊnt] *(n.)* [C] 記述、描述 (+ of)；帳戶 *(vi.)* 說明 (+ for)

6. **critical thinking** [ˈkrɪtɪkl ˈθɪŋkɪŋ] *(n.)* 批判性思考
   → independent thinking 獨立思考

7. **sponsor** [ˈspɑnsə] *(n.)* [C] 贊助者 *(vt.)* 贊助、支持

8. **political leaning** [pəˈlɪtɪkl ˈlinɪŋ] *(n.)* 政治傾向

9. **propaganda** [ˌprɑpəˈgændə] *(n.)* [U] 政治宣傳（貶義）

10. **disinformation** [dɪsˌɪnfəˈmeʃən] *(n.)* [U] 假消息

11. **unbiased** [ʌnˈbaɪəst] *(adj.)* 無偏頗的 = unprejudiced, impartial, nonpartisan
    → bias *(n.)* 偏見（常用單數）*(v.)* 對⋯抱有偏見
    → bias against N 反對、討厭⋯的偏見；bias in favor of N 偏好⋯的偏見
    → biased *(adj.)* 充滿偏見的

12. **sensationalism** [sɛnˈseʃənəlɪzəm] *(n.)* [U] 譁眾取寵、追求社會轟動性

13. **ethical** [ˈɛθɪkl] *(adj.)* 倫理道德的；合乎道德的

14. **righteous** [ˋraɪtʃəs] *(adj.)* 正當的、正義的

15. **extensive** [ɪkˋstɛnsɪv] *(adj.)* 廣泛的

16. **candidate** [ˋkændɪˌdet] *(n.)* [C] 求職者；候選人

17. **internship** [ˋɪntɝnˌʃɪp] *(n.)* [U] 實習（資格）
    → intern *(n.)* [C] 實習生

18. **coordinator** [koˋɔrdɪˌnetɚ] *(n.)* [C] 協調者
    → coordinate *(vt./vi.)* 使協調、調和 *(adj.)* 動作協調的

19. **enclose** [ɪnˋkloz] *(vt.)* 封入（信件、公文內）；夾帶檔案；圍住、包圍住

20. **résumé** [ˌrɛzuˋme] *(n.)* [C] 履歷

21. **reference** [ˋrɛf(ə)rəns] *(n.)* [U, C] 參考；提及、涉及；推薦
    → for one's reference 供…參考

重要片語

1. **be poised to + V$_R$** 準備好要…；志在…

2. **hold sb. in high esteem** 敬重某人

3. **serve as** 充當…；有…的功能 = act as, function as

相關文法句型

1. **It is widely acknowledged that S + V** …是廣為人認知、是公認的

    例 **It is widely acknowledged that** ABC News is a fast-moving global institution and pioneer in communications.
    眾所周知，ABC 新聞是快速發展的全球機構，也是傳播界的先驅。
    → 類似的用法還有：
    「It is widely accepted/assumed/held/known/recognized/agreed on that S + V」
    表「某件事是被廣為接受／認知／認為／公認／認可／認同的」

2. **推測過去情況**

例 The public **may have** already **been disillusioned** by certain mass media outlets.
民眾或許已經對特定大眾媒體通路幻滅。

$$
\left.\begin{array}{l}
\text{must} \\
\text{may} \\
\text{might} \\
\text{cannot}
\end{array}\right\} + \text{have} + \text{Vpp}
\qquad
\begin{array}{ll}
\text{以前必定…} & \text{（可能性 99\%）} \\
\text{以前可能…} & \text{（可能性 70\%）} \\
\text{以前或許…} & \text{（可能性 50\%）} \\
\text{以前不可能…} & \text{（可能性 0\%）}
\end{array}
$$

3. **表達「見證」的說法**

例 Fanpage **saw** a significant increase in popularity.
臉書粉專見證了人氣的增加。

→ 「**人 / 事 / 時 / 地 + see/saw/have seen + N**」表「見證」：

例 This winter vacation **has seen tourism** hit its rock bottom because of the newly-found virus.
由於新發現的病毒，今年寒假見證了觀光業的最低潮。

第壹部分：選擇題

一、綜合測驗

第 1 至 10 題為題組 ── 生態保育

The leopard cat, commonly ___1___ "shi hu" in Chinese, is the only remaining wild cat in Taiwan now that the Formosan clouded leopard is thought to be extinct. Leopard cats are roughly the size of housecats with black-spotted fur and thrive at elevations of around 500 meters. Sadly, leopard cats are frequently lost to road kills and poisoning, and there are now approximately 500 animals ___2___ in Taiwan.

The habitats of leopard cats are at risk partly ___3___ economic development. In Chuolan, an urban town in Miaoli County, ___4___, a wetland park was established to provide space for locals to relax in their free time. As it turns out, however, the park was built ___5___ this endangered species of wild cat. The greatest ___6___ of this situation is that the public is calling this "nature park" a "memorial park" for leopard cats, ___7___ part of their habitat was destroyed in the process of creating a recreation space for humans.

Aside from habitat destruction, leopard cats also suffer from pesticide ingested through their prey, as well as road deaths ___8___ increased traffic in rural areas. Perhaps the most shocking deaths are those ___9___ hunting and trapping, especially in Miaoli, where the cats pose a threat to farmers' free-range chickens. When these chickens become part of leopard cats' diet, farmers set up traps and hire hunters to kill these predators, ___10___ understanding the negative impact their actions may have on the natural world.

譯文

豹貓在中文裡以「石虎」之名為人所知，是台灣目前僅存的山貓，因為台灣雲豹被認為已經滅絕了。石虎大約與家貓體型一致，身上有豹斑黑毛，常出沒於海拔 500 公尺地區。令人難過的是，石虎常常死於交通意外或是毒殺，而現在台灣只剩下約莫 500 隻的石虎。

石虎棲地瀕危，部分原因是因為經濟的發展。舉例來說，在一個苗栗的城鎮卓蘭，建了一座濕地公園，以方便當地居民休憩。但最後，這座公園的建造卻犧牲了石虎這種瀕臨滅絕的野貓。最大的諷刺是大眾開始稱這座自然公園「石虎紀念公園」，因為牠們部分的棲地在公園建設的過程中被破壞掉，只為了滿足人類的休閒之需。

除了棲地破壞外，石虎也會因獵物身上的殺蟲劑而遭毒害，或是由於鄉村地區漸增的交通量而橫屍路口。或許最令人震驚的死法是因被獵殺或捕捉，尤其是在苗栗縣，因為石虎會對放養雞圈構成威脅。當這些雞隻成為石虎的大餐時，農夫們就會架設起重重陷阱並聘僱獵人去獵殺這些侵略者，卻對他們此番行為會帶來的環境浩劫渾然不知。

1. (A) known　　　(B) called as　　　**(C) known as**　　　(D) called for

2. (A) leave　　　**(B) left**　　　(C) leaving　　　(D) having left

3. **(A) because of**　　　(B) in spite of　　　(C) instead of　　　(D) regardless of
　　(A) 由於　　　(B) 儘管　　　(C) 而非　　　(D) 不論

4. (A) on the contrary　　　(B) in addition　　　**(C) for instance**　　　(D) after all
　　(A) 反之　　　(B) 此外　　　**(C) 例如**　　　(D) 畢竟

5. (A) in accordance with　　　(B) with the exception of　　　(C) in terms of　　　**(D) at the expense of**
　　(A) 與…一致　　　(B) 以…為例外　　　(C) 就…方面而言　　　**(D) 犧牲了**

6. **(A) irony**　　　(B) insight　　　(C) prospect　　　(D) provision
　　(A) 諷刺　　　(B) 洞察力、理解　　　(C) 願景　　　(D) 提供

7. (A) on　　　(B) in　　　(C) with　　　**(D) as**

8. (A) accused of　　　**(B) associated with**　　　(C) removed from　　　(D) mistaken for
　　(A) 被指控　　　**(B) 與…有關**　　　(C) 由…移除　　　(D) 被誤認

9. **(A) resulting from**　　　(B) resulting in　　　(C) resulted from　　　(D) resulted in

10. (A) for　　　**(B) without**　　　(C) beyond　　　(D) upon

原文

　　The leopard cat, commonly known as "shi hu" in Chinese, is the only remaining wild cat in Taiwan **now that** the Formosan clouded leopard is thought to be [1]**extinct**. Leopard cats are roughly the size of housecats with black-spotted fur and [2]**thrive** at [3]**elevations** of around 500 meters. Sadly, leopard cats are frequently lost to road kills and poisoning, and there are now approximately 500 animals left in Taiwan.

　　The [4]**habitats** of leopard cats **are at risk** partly because of economic development. In Chuolan, an urban town in Miaoli County, for instance, a wetland park was established to provide space for locals to relax in their free time. As it turns out, however, the park was built at the expense of this [5]**endangered** species of wild cat. The greatest irony of this situation is that the public is calling this "nature park" a "memorial park" for leopard cats, as part of their habitat was destroyed **in the process of** creating a [6]**recreation** space for humans.

　　Aside from habitat destruction, leopard cats also suffer from pesticide [7]**ingested** through their prey, as well as road deaths associated with increased traffic in rural areas. Perhaps the most shocking deaths are those resulting from hunting and trapping, especially in Miaoli, where the cats pose a threat to farmers' free-range chickens. When these chickens become part of leopard cats' diet, farmers set up traps and hire hunters to kill these [8]**predators**, without understanding the negative impact their actions may have on the natural world.

重要單字

1. **extinct** [ɪk `stɪŋkt] *(adj.)* 滅絕的、絕種的；（火山）死的、不活躍的
    → become extinct 絕種、消失的
    → extinction *(n.)* [U] 滅絕、絕種
    → face/in danger **of**/be threatened **with** extinction 面臨絕種危機
    → be **on** the brink/verge of extinction 處在絕種邊緣、快滅絕

2. **thrive** [θraɪv] *(vi.)* 成長茁壯；繁榮、興旺
    → thrive **on** sth. 以某物為養分成長、在某情況下茁壯
    → thriving *(adj.)* 蓬勃發展的；生意興旺的
    → thriving economy/industry/business 蓬勃發展的經濟／產業／事業

3. **elevation** [.ɛlə`veʃən] *(n.)* [U] 海拔、高度；高處、高地；拔擢、晉升
    → at high/low elevation 在高／低海拔地區
    → at/above an elevation of (number) meter 位於／高於海拔…公尺
    → elevate *(vt.)* 提升、提高、改進；抬高、使上升
    → be elevated **to** sth. 被晉升為…、被拔擢為…

→ elevated *(adj.)* 提高的、抬高的；地位高的、重要的

→ elevator *(n.)* [C] 電梯

→ escalator *(n.)* [C] 手扶梯

4. **habitat** [ˋhæbətæt] *(n.)* [C, U]（動植物的）棲息地、生長地

→ habitable *(adj.)* 可居住的、適合居住的

→ habitant *(n.)* [C] 居民、居住者 = inhabitant

→ inhabit *(vt.)* 居住於（常用被動語態）

→ native/natural habitat 原生地／自然生長地

→ a woodland/wetland/grassland/marine/coastal habitat
樹林／濕地／草原／海洋／沿岸棲息地

→ habitat protection/conservation 棲地保護、保育

5. **endanger** [ɪnˋdendʒə] *(vt.)* **使處於困境；危及、危害**

→ endangered *(adj.)* 瀕臨滅絕的、有危險的

→ endangered species/creatures/animals 瀕危的種類／生物／動物

→ put sth./sb. **in danger/at risk** 使某人事物陷入危險

6. **recreation** [ˌrɛkrɪˋeʃən] *(n.)* [C, U] **娛樂、消遣（方式）；再現；重做**

→ a recreation center/area/ground 娛樂中心

→ recreation facilities 娛樂設備、設施

→ a recreation **of** N …的再現

→ recreate *(vt.)* 使重現；再創造

→ recreational *(adj.)* 消遣的；娛樂的；休閒的

7. **ingest** [ɪnˋdʒest] *(vt.)* **攝取、嚥下（食物）**

→ ingestion *(n.)* [U] 攝取（營養、藥物）

→ digest *(vt./vi.)*（使）消化；理解、吸收（資訊）*(n.)* [C] 文摘、簡報

→ digestion *(n.)* [C, U] 消化（能力）

→ digestive *(adj.)* 消化的

→ digestive system/track/organ 消化系統／道／器官

8. **predator** [ˋprɛdətə] *(n.)* [C] **掠食者、天敵**

→ prey *(n.)* [C] 獵物

→ predatory *(adj.)* 掠食性的；（人或組織）掠奪成性的

→ apex/alpha/top predator 最高級掠食者

→ predatory pricing *(n.)* 惡意削價競爭

1. **now that** 既然；由於

2. **be at risk (of...)** 處於（…）危險之中

3. **in the process of** 在…的過程中

4. **aside from** 除了…之外 = apart from

相關文法句型

1. **省略關係代名詞的用法**

   例 The leopard cat, **(which is)** commonly known as "shi hu" in Chinese, is the only remaining wild cat in Taiwan now.

   豹貓在中文裡以「石虎」之名為人所知，是台灣目前僅存的野貓。

   → 此處省略了關係代名詞 which 與 be 動詞。注意，若要省略主格關代，必須與 be 動詞一起省略！

2. **as it turns out 出乎意料、沒想過結果竟然是…**

   例 **As it turns out**, however, the park was built at the expense of this endangered species of wild cat.

   但最後，這座公園的建造卻犧牲了石虎這種瀕臨滅絕的野貓。

   → 作為一個副詞片語，後面要接續一個句子前，必須在副詞片語後加上逗點隔開。

第 11 至 20 題為題組 —— 恐怖攻擊

Visitors to top hotels in India encounter ___11___ has now become a daily routine: a body scan and a ___12___ inspection of their belongings. For those who arrive by car, guards look inside the vehicle's trunk and under the hood. These ___13___ were put in place after Nov. 26, 2008, when terrorists attacked several of Mumbai's most famous sites, including the city's iconic Taj Mahal Palace Hotel.

The 2008 attacks, widely ___14___ to members of one of the most notorious terrorist organizations in South Asia, Lashkar-e-Taiba, ___15___ in the news again because of the recent suicide bombings in Sri Lanka, which ___16___ more than 300 lives. India's 2008 experience is also back in the public consciousness because of the new film *Hotel Mumbai*. Starring famous international actors and actresses, the movie provides a powerful ___17___ of the assault that gripped the country's financial capital for nearly 72 hours. ___18___ the attacks targeted several locations—a crowded railway ___19___, a Jewish community center, and two hotels—the movie focuses on three days and nights of horror mostly within one hotel, the glamorous Taj. ___20___ the bravery of local police officers and the selfless deeds of the Taj's staff, the death toll of the attacks could have been much higher.

譯文

　　到印度頂級酒店住宿的遊客，會遇到現已成為日常例行的事情：全身安檢以及隨身行李的徹底檢查。開車來的人甚至會被警衛檢查後車廂以及引擎蓋下方。這些做法都是在 2008 年 11 月 26 日之後才開始實施的，那天孟買的許多著名景點都遭受恐怖攻擊，包括該城市的地標：泰姬瑪哈酒店。

　　南亞最惡名昭彰的恐攻組織虔誠軍，廣泛參與 2008 年恐怖襲擊，虔誠軍近日又再度出現於新聞版面，因為日前在斯里蘭卡發生了奪走 300 條人命的自殺爆炸事件。也因為新上映電影《失控危城》，印度 2008 年的恐攻記憶又再度浮現群眾腦海。本電影由多位國際巨星主演，細膩呈現了劫持印度金融中心長達七十二小時的恐攻事件。雖然當年的恐攻波及許多地點 —— 擁擠的地鐵站、猶太聚集中心、及兩間飯店，這部電影聚焦在發生在壯麗泰姬瑪哈酒店中慘絕人寰的三天三夜。如果不是當時當地警方的英勇以及酒店職員的無私，死亡人數應該會更高。

11. (A) which   (B) that   **(C) what**   (D) where

> **解說** 本格前後皆有動詞（encounter 以及 has）且前後皆不完整，故選擇 what。也可將本句改寫成 Visitors to top hotels in India encounter **the thing that** has become a daily routine。

12. (A) through   (B) thought   (C) though   **(D) thorough**
   (A) 藉由   (B) 想法   (C) 雖然   **(D) 徹底的**

13. **(A) practices**   (B) effects   (C) strategies   (D) approaches
   (A) 措施；習慣   (B) 效果   (C) 策略   (D) 方法

14. (A) attributed   (B) contributed   (C) admitted   **(D) referred**
   (A) attribute A to B 將 A 歸因於 B   (B) contribute to 導致
   (C) admit (to) + Ving 承認做過…   **(D) refer to A as B 將 A 稱作 B**

15. (A) is   **(B) are**   (C) being   (D) has been

> **解說** 本句的主詞為 The 2008 attacks，為複數名詞。故選擇動詞 are。

16. **(A) claimed**   (B) reared   (C) stated   (D) pained
   (A) 奪走（人命）   (B) 撫養   (C) 陳述   (D) 使疼痛

> **解說** 本句指斯里蘭卡的自殺爆炸攻擊奪走 300 人性命。

17. **(A) account**   (B) division   (C) conduct   (D) harmony
   (A) 描述   (B) 分歧   (C) 行為 [ˈkɑndʌkt]   (D) 和諧

18. **(A) While**   (B) However   (C) Besides   (D) Since
   (A) 雖然   (B) 無論如何   (C) 除了…之外   (D) 自從；因為

19. (A) arrival   (B) denial   **(C) terminal**   (D) commercial
   (A) 抵達   (B) 否決   **(C) 航站**   (D) 商業廣告

20. (A) Were it not for   **(B) Had it not been for**   (C) Should it not for   (D) Were it to be

> **解說** 本題考「與過去事實相反的假設語氣」，Had it not been for + N. 指「如果當時不是、若非」。

原文

Visitors to top hotels in India [1]**encounter** what has now become a daily routine: a body scan and a thorough [2]**inspection** of their belongings. For those who arrive by car, guards look inside the vehicle's [3]**trunk** and under the hood. These practices were put in place after Nov. 26, 2008, when terrorists attacked several of Mumbai's most famous sites, including the city's [4]**iconic** Taj Mahal Palace Hotel.

The 2008 attacks, widely referred to members of one of the most notorious terrorist organizations in South Asia, Lashkar-e-Taiba, are in the news again because of the recent suicide bombings in Sri Lanka, which claimed more than 300 lives. India's 2008 experience is also back in the public [5]**consciousness** because of the new film *Hotel Mumbai*. [6]**Starring** famous international actors and actresses, the movie provides a powerful account of the assault that gripped the country's financial capital for nearly 72 hours. While the attacks targeted several locations—a crowded railway terminal, a Jewish community center, and two hotels—the movie focuses on three days and nights of horror mostly within one hotel, the [7]**glamorous** Taj. Had it not been for the bravery of local police officers and the selfless deeds of the Taj's staff, the death toll of the attacks could have been much higher.

重要單字

1. **encounter** [ɪn`kaʊntɚ] *(vt.)* 遇到；偶然遇見
   → encounter/come across difficulties 遇到困難
   → encounter/come up against opposition 遭遇反對
   → encounter sb. 偶遇某人

2. **inspection** [ɪn`spɛkʃən] *(n.)* [C] 檢查、檢驗
   → inspect *(vt.)* 檢查、檢驗
   → carry out/make/perform/conduct an inspection 進行檢查
   → safety/medical/annual/daily inspection 安全／醫療／年度的／每天的檢查
   → inspect sth. for... 因⋯而檢查某事

3. **trunk** [trʌŋk] *(n.)* [C] 汽車車尾的行李箱；軀幹；樹幹；象鼻
   → tree trunk 樹幹

4. **iconic** [aɪ`kɑnɪk] *(adj.)* 代表性的；偶像的；圖像的
   → icon *(n.)* [C] 偶像；畫像；（電腦上的）圖示
   → iconic figure 偶像人物
   → iconic memory 圖像記憶

5. **consciousness** [ˈkɑnʃəsnɪs] *(n.)* [U] 意識；知覺
   → conscious *(adj.)* 意識到的；有知覺的
   → be conscious/sensible/aware of 意識到⋯
   → health-conscious/self-conscious 有健康意識的；有自我意識的
   → lose/regain consciousness 失去／恢復意識
   → public/collective consciousness 公眾／集體意識
   → bring sb. back to consciousness 喚醒某人的知覺

6. **star** [stɑr] *(vt.)* 由⋯主演 *(n.)* 星星
   → have stars in sb's eyes 某人眼中充滿希望的亮光
   → sth. is written in the stars 某事物是命中注定

7. **glamorous** [ˈglæmərəs] *(adj.)* 有魅力的、迷人的
   → glamor *(n.)* [U] 魅力
   → lead/live a glamorous/frugal life 過著光鮮亮麗的／簡樸的生活

重要片語

1. **put sth. in place** 實施、執行某計畫
2. **be referred to...** 涉及到⋯、與⋯相關

相關文法句型

1. **複合關係代名詞 what**
   what 為複合關係代名詞，可理解為 what = the thing(s) that。複合關係代名詞 what 與一般關係代名詞的差異在於：它前方沒有先行詞，且其後所引導的子句並非關係子句，而是名詞子句。

   例 Visitors to top hotels in India encounter **what** has now become a daily routine.
   到印度頂級酒店住宿的遊客會遇到現已成為日常例行的事情。

2. **假設語氣**
   與過去相反的假設語氣的句型為：
   If + S + had + Vpp, S + **would/could/should/might** + have + Vpp

   例 **Had it not been** for the bravery of local police officers and the selfless deeds of the. Taj's staff, the death toll of the attacks **could have been** much higher.
   如果不是當時當地警方的英勇以及酒店職員的無私，死亡人數應該會更高。
   → 此句為「與過去事實相反的假設語氣」的倒裝句，其原來的句子為：**If it had not been** for the bravery of local police officers and the selfless deeds of the Taj's staff, the death toll of the attacks <u>could have been</u> much higher.

二、文意選填

第 21 至 30 題為題組 —— 年長者照護

When it comes to home care for the elderly, there are several factors that should be taken into ___21___. First, every senior has their own needs. It's common knowledge that the greater a person's ___22___, the greater his or her needs. When seniors have needs that can't be met by themselves or their caregivers, they may become impatient and irritated. Some seniors, however, ___23___ that they are content with what they have, though this is less common. All in all, there is a large gap that caregivers have to ___24___.

Second, when faced with the task of caring for a senior citizen, you should bear in mind that every senior is human and should be treated as such. They are ___25___ to the same level freedom that adults enjoy. That is the ___26___ you should take when providing care to the elderly. You can help them ___27___ their dignity by always treating them with respect. Elder people should be encouraged to complete tasks on their own when possible, but shouldn't be criticized when they fail. Moreover, make it a ___28___ to be understanding. They may sometimes act like babies, but this kind of behavior is never ___29___.

Finally, you should try to be a good confidant to the senior you care for. Make sure to spend time talking to them and be a good listener when they share things with you. It is vital to be like a friend to the person you are caring for. Caring for the elderly can be challenging, but if you listen to their needs and are ___30___, you're sure to have a rewarding experience.

譯文

當提到年長者的居家照護，有些因素必須被納入考慮。首先，每位年長者都有自己的需求。眾所周知，這個人的殘疾越多，他的需求就越多。當年長者有自己或照護者無法滿足的需要時，他們可能會變得沒耐心或是暴躁易怒。但也有部分年長者表示他們已經滿足，雖然比較少見。整體來說，照護者要加強補足的還有很大空間。

再者，當要照顧年長者的時候，你必須知道年長者也是人，該被妥善對待。他們有權享有成人應得的自由。這就是為年長者提供照顧時應採取的觀點。以尊重對待他們，可以讓他們保有尊嚴。應鼓勵長者盡可能地自己完成任務，但當他們失敗時也不該被批評指責。而且要將體貼理解他們視為要務。他們有時可能舉止像個嬰兒，但這樣的行為絕非是故意的。

最後，你也要成為你所照顧的長者密友。務必要抽出時間跟他們聊天，而當他們與你分享時，要當個好的傾聽者。當你照顧對象的朋友是很重要的。照顧老人家可能很有挑戰性，但如果你傾聽他們的需求、讓他們信賴你，你一定會獲得值得的經驗。

(A) fill	(B) entitled	(C) consideration	(D) priority	(E) perspective
(A) 填滿、滿足	(B) 有資格的	(C) 考量	(D) 優先事項	(E) 觀點、立場
(F) disability	(G) retain	(H) intentional	(I) indicate	(J) reliable
(F) 缺陷	(G) 保留	(H) 故意的	(I) 表現、顯示	(J) 可靠的

原文

　　When it comes to home care for the elderly, there are several factors that should be taken into consideration. First, every senior has their own needs. It's common knowledge that the greater a person's 1)**disability**, the greater his or her needs. When seniors have needs that can't be met by themselves or their caregivers, they may become impatient and 2)**irritated**. Some seniors, however, indicate that they are 3)**content** with what they have, though this is less common. All in all, there is a large gap that caregivers have to fill.

　　Second, when faced with the task of caring for a senior citizen, you should bear in mind that every senior is human and should be treated as such. They are entitled to the same level freedom that adults enjoy. That is the perspective you should take when providing care to the elderly. You can help them retain their dignity by always treating them with respect. Elder people should be encouraged to complete tasks on their own when possible, but shouldn't be 4)**criticized** when they fail. Moreover, make it a priority to be understanding. They may sometimes act like babies, but this kind of behavior is never 5)**intentional**.

　　Finally, you should try to be a good 6)**confidant** to the senior you care for. Make sure to spend time talking to them and be a good listener when they share things with you. It is vital to be like a friend to the person you are caring for. Caring for the elderly can be challenging, but if you listen to their needs and are reliable, you're sure to have a 7)**rewarding** experience.

重要單字

1. **disability** [ˌdɪsə`bɪləti] *(n.)* [C, U] 殘疾、殘障、缺陷
   → learning/physical/mental disabilities 學習障礙、身體上／心理上殘疾
   → disability insurance 傷殘保險
   → disable *(vt.)*（常用被動語態）使喪失能力、使傷殘；使故障、使失靈
   → disabled *(adj.)* 殘疾的、喪失能力的
   → the disabled *(n.)* 殘疾人士，視為複數名詞 = people with disabilities

2. **irritate** [`ɪrətet] *(vt.)* 激怒、使惱火；使發炎；刺激 (+ **at/with**)
   → irritation *(n.)* [C, U] 激怒、惱怒；使人惱怒之事；發炎；疼痛
   → minor irritation 瑣事
   → skin/throat/eyes irritation 皮膚／喉嚨／眼睛發炎
   → irritated *(adj.)*（形容人）被激怒的、惱怒的 (+ **at** N)
   → irritating *(adj.)*（形容事）惱人的、煩人的、令人感到厭煩的
   → irritant *(n.)* [C] 令人煩惱的事；麻煩事；刺激物

3. **content** [kən `tent] *(adj.)* 滿意的、滿足的 (+ **with**) *(vt.)* 使滿足、使滿意
   [`kɑntɛnt] *(n.)* [C] 內容、內容物；目錄；內含量
   → content oneself **with** sth. 使某人滿足／甘心於某事
   → fat/protein/alcohol content 脂肪／蛋白質／酒精含量
   → to one's heart's content 盡興地、盡情地
   → contented *(adj.)* 高興的、滿足的

4. **criticize** [`krɪtɪsaɪz] *(vt./vi.)* 批評、指責；評論（書、影片等）
   → be heavily/strongly/sharply criticized 被大肆批評
   → criticism *(n.)* [C, U] 批評、指責；（對書、電影等的）評價
   → critical *(adj.)* 批判的、批評的；關鍵的、決定性的；（對書、電影）評論的
   → critical thinking 批判性思考
   → in a critical condition 受重傷、情況危急
   → critique *(n.)* [C] 文章評論（多為負面）*(vt.)* 評論（電影、文學等）

5. **intentional** [ɪn`tenʃənəl] *(adj.)* 故意的、有意的
   → intend *(vt.)* 打算、計畫（+ to V$_R$）
   → intention *(n.)* [C] 意圖、打算 (+ **to** V$_R$ / **of** Ving)
   → intentionally *(adv.)* 故意地、有意地 = on purpose, by design
   → intentional killing/murder/crime 蓄意殺人／謀殺／犯案

6. **confidant** [`kɑnfɪdænt] *(n.)* [C] 知心朋友、知己
   → a close confidant 親密好友

7. **rewarding** [rɪ`wɔrdɪŋ] *(adj.)* 值得做的；有意義的；有回報的
   → rewarding experience/adventure 可貴的經驗／收益良多的冒險
   → reward *(n.)* [C] 酬勞（+ **of** 金錢）；獎賞（+ **for** 原因）
           (vt.) 報答、獎賞（+ **with** 物）
   → financial/economic/monetary reward 經濟、金錢上的報酬
   → reap the reward 得到回報

重要片語

1. **take (sth./sb.) into consideration**（把某人事物）列入考量

2. **fill the gap** 補足、填補空缺

3. **bear in mind** 記在心裡、記住

4. **be entitled to sth./V$_R$** 被賦予…資格；有權利…

1. **使役動詞**

make 為使役動詞，接續受詞後除了可加**原型動詞**，也可以加**形容詞**和**名詞**作為受詞補語。

例 Moreover, **make** **it a priority** to be understanding. They may sometimes act like babies, but this kind of behavior is never intentional.

而且要將體貼理解他們視為要務。他們有時可能舉止像個嬰兒，但這樣的行為絕非是故意的。

→ 此句的受詞為虛受詞 it，真正的受詞為後面的不定詞 to be understanding 這一件事情。

第 31 至 35 題為題組 —— 氣候變遷

Time is running out for the inhabitants of Pacific Island nations. Research suggests that climate change will spell disaster for the islands—, and many others—by the end of this century. ___31___ But the famously scenic islands may face an even more immediate threat.

As sea levels rise, more salt water will enter the islands' aquifers. ___32___ It acts as a kind of reservoir and can be tapped into via wells. When the aquifer is inundated with ocean water, its purity is affected, and the water is rendered undrinkable. This is bad news for those who depend on this source of fresh water.

If this bleak projection proves true, islanders will be forced to collect rainfall or rely on expensive imported freshwater. ___33___ Many will be forced to leave their homelands behind and emigrate to distant countries. This disturbance in the lives of Pacific Islanders will be a great climate injustice. The Pacific Island nations are small and have contributed only 0.03 percent of the greenhouse gasses which are causing climate change. ___34___

Climate experts say this doomsday scenario is not yet inevitable. But we must act soon. ___35___ The collective human race must stage a global intervention on behalf of all humanity. The clock is ticking.

譯文

　　對太平洋島國居民來說，他們的時日已無多。研究指出氣候變遷將在本世紀結束前為這些島嶼帶來災難，包含斐濟、東加、密克羅尼西亞以及馬紹爾群島和許多其他小島。(D) **上升的海平面意味著浪潮將深入更多這種內陸島嶼，有些低窪島嶼甚至會被完全吞沒。**而這些知名風景名勝島可能會面臨到更加急迫的威脅。

　　隨著海平面上升，更多鹽水將入侵到島嶼的含水層。(A) **含水層指的是當雨降落時會收集雨水的大片多孔岩。**它是種蓄水層，可以藉由井口抽水。當蓄水層被海水淹沒時，水純度會受到影響，水也會變成無法飲用。這對仰賴含水層作飲用的居民來說可謂一大悲劇。

　　若這晦暗的預想成真，島民就會被迫收集雨水或是購買昂貴進口的淡水。(E) **同樣地，水將會成為短缺商品，而島嶼上的生活品質將會大幅惡化。**很多人也會被迫離開他們的家鄉、搬遷到遙遠的國家去。這種窘境對太平洋島民來說是一種氣候不公。因為太平洋島嶼面積都很小，僅占會導致氣候變遷的溫室氣體排放中的 0.03 %。(B) **然而，他們卻是第一批受到危害的國家。**

　　專家指出這種末日景象並非不可避免的，但我們必須立刻採取行動。(C) **世界強國必須同心協力，想出決定性的行動方針。**全體人類必須為了人類而起身干預。須儘速行動。

(A) An aquifer is a mass of porous rock that collects freshwater when it falls as rain.
含水層指的是當雨降落時會收集雨水的大片多孔岩。

(B) Yet, they are among the first countries to be dramatically endangered.
然而，他們卻是第一批受到危害的國家。

(C) The more powerful nations of the world must cooperate with a decisive plan of action.
世界強國必須同心協力，想出決定性的行動方針。

(D) Rising sea levels means waves will ravage more of the inland areas, and some of the low-lying islands will be submerged completely.
上升的海平面意味著浪潮將深入更多這種內陸島嶼，有些低窪島嶼甚至會被完全吞沒。

(E) Likely, water will become a scarce commodity, and the standard of living on the islands will deteriorate.
同樣地，水將會成為短缺商品，而島嶼上的生活品質將會大幅惡化。

原文

　　Time is running out for the inhabitants of Pacific Island nations. Research suggests that climate change will spell disaster for the islands—Fiji, Tonga, Micronesia, The Marshall Islands, and many others—by the end of this century. Rising sea levels means waves will ¹⁾**ravage** more of the inland areas, and some of the low-lying islands will be submerged completely. But the famously ²⁾**scenic** islands may face an even more immediate threat.

　　As sea levels rise, more salt water will enter the islands' aquifers. An aquifer is a mass of porous rock that collects freshwater when it falls as rain. It **acts as** a kind of ³⁾**reservoir** and can be tapped into via wells. When the aquifer is inundated with ocean water, its ⁴⁾**purity** is affected, and the water is ⁵⁾**rendered** undrinkable. This is bad news for those who depend on this source of fresh water.

　　If this ⁶⁾**bleak** ⁷⁾**projection** proves true, islanders will be forced to collect rainfall or rely on expensive imported freshwater. Likely, water will become a scarce commodity, and the standard of living on the islands will ⁸⁾**deteriorate**. Many will be forced to leave their homelands behind and ⁹⁾**emigrate** to distant countries. This ¹⁰⁾**disturbance** in the lives of Pacific Islanders will be a great climate injustice. The Pacific Island nations are small and have contributed only 0.03 percent of the greenhouse gasses which are causing climate change, yet they are among the first countries to be dramatically endangered.

　　Climate experts say this doomsday scenario is not yet ¹¹⁾**inevitable**. But we must act soon. The more powerful nations of the world must cooperate with a decisive plan of action. The collective human race must stage a global ¹²⁾**intervention** on behalf of all humanity. **The clock is ticking**.

重要單字

1. **ravage** [ˋrævɪdʒ] *(vt.)* 毀滅、蹂躪、摧殘 = destroy, devastate, demolish, desolate, wreck
　　　　　　　　 (n.) 毀滅、大災難（固定用複數型式 ravages）

　→ a country ravaged by civil war 一個受內戰戰火摧殘的國家

---

2. **scenic** [ˋsinɪk] *(adj.)* 風景（秀麗）的；描繪景象的
   - → scenic spot 風景名勝
   - → scenic beauty 秀麗美景
   - → scene *(n.)* [C] 畫面；（電影、電視）一景、一鏡；（事發）地點
   - → scenery *(n.)* [U] 景象、風景

3. **reservoir** [ˋrɛzəˏvɔr] *(n.)* [C] 蓄水庫、儲水池；儲藏所
   - → a reservoir of + N. 源源不絕的⋯
   - → a reservoir of strength/energy/human experience 源源不絕的精力／能量／人類經驗

4. **purity** [ˋpjʊəˏrəti] *(n.)* [U] 純度、純淨、清白；純粹
   - → pure *(adj.)* 純白潔淨的
   - → purify *(vt.)* 使純淨、淨化；洗滌、清除
   - → purification *(n.)* [U] 淨化；滌罪

5. **render** [ˋrɛndə] *(vt.)* （書面用語）使得、使成為；給予、提供
   - → render sth. unfit/harmful/impossible 認為某事物不適合／有害的／不可能的
   - → render sb. speechless/ unconscious 使某人啞口無言／使某人失去意識
   - → render sb. assistance/an opinion/a decision 提供某人幫助／想法／一項決定
   - → render A (as) B 以 B 形式表現 A

6. **bleak** [blik] *(adj.)* 陰暗淒涼的、無希望的；荒涼的；單調乏味的
   - → a bleak future/prospect/projection 黯淡的未來／前景／預想

7. **projection** [prəˋdʒɛkʃən] *(n.)* [C] 預想、規劃；投射、投影；發射
   - → project *(vt.)* 計畫、預計；發射 *(n.)* [C] 方案、企劃、任務

8. **deteriorate** [dɪˋtɪrɪəˏret] *(vi.)* 惡化、（品質水準）下降 *(vt.)* 使惡化
   = get worse, go from bad to worse, worsen, degenerate, degrade
   - → deterioration *(n.)* [C, U] 惡化

9. **emigrate** [ˋɛməˏgret] *(vi./vt.)* 移居外地
   ↔ **immigrate** [ˋɪməˏgret] *(vi./vt.)* 遷入、（從外地）移居
   - → emigration *(n.)* 遷居外地 ↔ immigration 遷入
   - → emigrant *(n.)* 移出者 ↔ immigrant 移入者

10. **disturbance** [disˋtɝbəns] *(n.)* [C, U] 擾亂、打擾；混亂
    - → disturb *(vt.)* 煩擾、擾亂、使心神不寧；妨礙 = upset, trouble, worry, distress
    - → disturbing *(adj.)* 令人不安的 = upsetting, troubling, worrying, distressing
    - → disturbed *(adj.)* 心煩意亂的 = upset, worried, troubled, anxious, bothered, agitated, distressed

11. **inevitable** [ɪn`ɛvətəbəl] *(adj.)* 不可避免的、必然發生的 = unavoidable, unpreventable, inescapable
    (n.) 必然發生的事
    → inevitable result/consequence 不可避免的結果
    → inevitability *(n.)* 必然性；無法逃避之事

12. **intervention** [ˌɪntə`vɛnʃən] *(n.)* 干預、介入；調停、斡旋
    → intervene *(vi.)* 介入、干涉、干擾 (+ between/in)

重要片語

1. **time is running out** 時間所剩無多
2. **act as** 當作是、有…功能 = function as, serve as
3. **sth. proves (to be) true** 某事成真、某事被證實為真
4. **doomsday scenario** 世界末日或景象
5. **on behalf of...** 代表…，指少數代表多數
6. **the clock is ticking** 時間滴答地走，比喻時間緊迫，須儘速行動

相關文法句型

1. **關係代名詞 who**
   以關係子句表示「凡是…的人」，關代常用 who：

   例 This is bad news for **those** who depend on this source of fresh water.
   這對仰賴含水層作飲用的居民來說可謂一大悲劇。

people who those who they who	+ 複數動詞

anyone who he/one who whoever	+ 單數動詞

第貳部分：非選擇題

一、中譯英 —— 替代能源

1. 科學家們一直在尋求各種環保的方法來替代石油和煤炭，一些常見的方法包括了太陽能以及風力發電。

Scientists have been | seeking / looking for / searching for | all kinds of / various / a variety of | green / eco-friendly / environmentally-friendly |

ways/approaches / means/methods/measures | to | replace / take the place of / substitute (for) | oil and coal,

and some commonly-seen ones include / some common ones being | solar energy and wind power.

2. 然而，這些方法並不是沒有缺點的。舉例來說，核能發電廠會產生大量的廢料，而太陽能需要非常昂貴的器材。

However, / Nevertheless, / Nonetheless, | these methods are not without (their) | flaws; / defects; / downsides; / shortcomings; / drawbacks; |

for example/instance, nuclear power plants produce large amounts of waste, while solar energy requires/calls for extremely expensive equipment.

二、英文作文 —— 陳情訴求

以下是一個國際疾病救治網站，請參考網頁上的訊息，然後在下一頁的表格中，寫一封陳情書，為一個世界傳染病的防治發聲。寫陳情書時，請依據第一個箭號提示處的建議（Use strong language...），填入陳情書的標題，並依據第二個箭號提示處的建議（Describe what happened, why you're concerned, and what you want to happen now.），以 120 字寫一封陳情書。

EPIDEMIC PETITIONS
It's time to stand together on epidemic prevention!

Epidemics have threatened humans even before history, but the "precautions" and "conversations" that bring about a collective response are a relatively new phenomenon. International concerns help shape the global health landscape. And our actions today have a tremendous impact on the earth and our future!

Start a Petition

DENGUE FEVER

Worsening threats of global warming and climate change have made the insect rage on fiercely! Our actions today have a tremendous impact on the earth and our future!

33,437 SUPPORTING   Sign NOW

RABIES

A vaccine-preventable viral disease.
Dogs are the main source of human rabies deaths.

35,248 SUPPORTING   Sign NOW

START YOUR PETITION

In just minutes, we'll help you build your campaign.

SELECT A CATEGORY

Epidemic

TITLE OF YOUR PETITION

Use strong language to rally support, like "Demand an End to the Seal Hunt, NOW!"

EXPLAIN THE ISSUE AND OFFER A SOLUTION

Describe what happened, why you're concerned, and what you want to happen now.

PHONE NUMBER Optional and NEVER published

100% private. We may contact you with urgent petition matters or media opportunities.

疫情陳情書
是時候站出來一起抗疫了！

早在有歷史記載之前，流行病就一直威脅著人類，但集體應變發起「預防措施」和「對話」，相對來說是一種新現象。國際關注有助於塑造全球衛生格局。我們今日的行動，對地球和我們的未來都將產生巨大影響！

簽署陳情書

登革熱

全球暖化和氣候變遷的威脅日益嚴峻，使昆蟲更加肆虐！

33,437 人支持　　立刻簽署

狂犬病

有疫苗可預防的病毒性疾病。
狗是人類感染狂犬病而死亡的主要來源。

35,248 人支持　　立刻簽署

開始撰寫陳情書

只需幾分鐘，我們就能幫您發起活動。

選擇類別

傳染病

你的陳情標題

使用強而有力的言詞號召大家支持，例如「立刻要求終結海豹狩獵！」

說明問題並提供解決方案

描述情況、你為何關心此議題，以及現在你想怎麼做。

電話號碼 非強制，絕不會公布

絕對隱密，我們可能會在緊急請願或有媒體報導機會時與您聯繫。

範文 A：Dengue Fever 登革熱

START YOUR PETITION

In just minutes, we'll help you build your campaign.

SELECT A CATEGORY

Epidemic

TITLE OF YOUR PETITION

Use strong language to rally support, like "Demand an End to the Seal Hunt, NOW!"

Controlling Dengue Fever, Improving Lives

EXPLAIN THE ISSUE AND OFFER A SOLUTION

Describe what happened, why you're concerned, and what you want to happen now.

Dengue fever is a virus spread by the bite of an infected mosquito. There are approximately 75 million cases around the world every year. Symptoms can be quite mild, flu-like ones, to extremely severe symptoms of bleeding, and an aching pain in the bones, nicknamed breakbone fever for that very reason, and more striking forms of dengue fever (dengue shock syndrome and hemorrhagic fever) can be fatal.

Dengue fever has made a comeback ever since the global temperature keeps rising and extreme weather patterns have made mosquitoes more likely to reproduce and transmit the virus onto people. To keep it at bay, vector control is needed in the most productive habitats. Moreover, clothing that minimizes skin exposure when mosquitoes are most active is encouraged during outbreaks. Repellents may be applied, and insecticide-treated mosquitoes nets afford ideal protection. With collaborated efforts, we can control dengue fever, and improves lives hence.

PHONE NUMBER Optional and NEVER published

100% private. We may contact you with urgent petition matters or media opportunities.

譯文

開始撰寫陳情書
只需幾分鐘，我們就能幫您發起活動。

選擇類別

傳染病

你的陳情標題
使用強而有力的言詞號召大家支持，例如「立刻要求終結海豹狩獵！」

控制登革熱，改善生活

說明問題並提供解決方案
描述情況、你為何關心此議題，以及現在你想怎麼做。

登革熱是一種經由蚊子叮咬傳播的病毒。每年全球約有 7,500 萬病例。症狀可以很輕微，類似流感，嚴重則會出現出血症狀，骨頭疼痛，因此有個別名為「斷骨熱」，還有其他症狀更明顯的登革熱類型會致命（登革休克症候群和登革出血熱）。

自全球氣溫持續升高，登革熱便捲土重來，極端氣候型態也使蚊子更容易繁殖並將病毒傳給人類。為阻止這種情況，需要在最容易繁殖的棲息地進行病媒控制。此外在疫情爆發期間，在蚊子最活躍時應鼓勵盡量穿著少暴露皮膚的衣服。可以使用驅蟲劑，而經過殺蟲劑處理的蚊帳可提供理想的保護。我們可以透過共同努力控制登革熱，從而改善生活。

電話號碼 非強制，絕不會公布
絕對隱密，我們可能會在緊急請願或有媒體報導機會時與您聯繫。

範文 B：Rabies 狂犬病

START YOUR PETITION
In just minutes, we'll help you build your campaign.

SELECT A CATEGORY

Epidemic

TITLE OF YOUR PETITION
Use strong language to rally support, like "Demand an End to the Seal Hunt, NOW!"

Rabies: The Modern-day Hades

EXPLAIN THE ISSUE AND OFFER A SOLUTION
Describe what happened, why you're concerned, and what you want to happen now.

What if I told you we could eliminate one of the oldest diseases known to humankind, a disease that still kills a person every nine minutes? We CAN prevent rabies, by vaccinating dogs, by washing dog bite wounds thoroughly with soap and water, and by immediately seeking medical care after a dog bite. No child should die of rabies nor be orphaned by the disease. No family should suffer from rabies. To end the modern-day Hades, Rabies, our time to act is now.

Simply eradicating the dog species alone has never had a significant impact on dog population densities or the spread of rabies, let alone the fact that such radical measures may be considered unacceptable. Instead, mass vaccination campaigns have proved to be the most effective method to control canine rabies. High vaccination coverage can be attained through comprehensive strategies. Surveillance of rabies and immediate submission of reports of suspected animal cases are also necessary. We really can stop the modern-day hades, starting from now!

PHONE NUMBER Optional and NEVER published
100% private. We may contact you with urgent petition matters or media opportunities.

譯文

開始撰寫陳情書
只需幾分鐘，我們就能幫您發起活動。

選擇類別

傳染病

你的陳情標題
使用強而有力的言詞號召大家支持，例如「立刻要求終結海豹狩獵！」

狂犬病：現代煉獄

說明問題並提供解決方案
描述情況、你為何關心此議題，以及現在你想怎麼做。

　　我若告訴你，我們可以消除人類已知的最古老疾病之一，也就是平均每九分鐘仍能殺死一個人的疾病呢？我們可以預防狂犬病，方法包括讓狗接種疫苗、用肥皂水徹底清洗狗咬過的傷口，並在被狗咬傷後立刻就醫。任何兒童都不應該死於狂犬病，也不應該因這種疾病而成為孤兒。任何家庭都不應該因狂犬病而受苦。為終結有現代煉獄之稱的狂犬病，我們該立刻行動了。

　　光是撲滅狗，從來就無法對狗的數量密度或狂犬病的傳播產生重大影響，更不用說這種激進措施可能讓人無法接受。反之，大規模疫苗接種運動已證實是控制狂犬病的最有效方法。透過綜合策略可獲得高疫苗接種覆蓋率。狂犬病的監控和立即提交可疑動物病例報告也是必要的。從現在開始，我們真的可以終止現代煉獄！

電話號碼 非強制，絕不會公布
絕對隱密，我們可能會在緊急請願或有媒體報導機會時與您聯繫。

START YOUR PETITION

In just minutes, we'll help you build your campaign.

SELECT A CATEGORY

Epidemic

TITLE OF YOUR 1)**PETITION**

Use strong language to rally support, like "Demand an End to the Seal Hunt, NOW!"

Controlling 2)**Dengue Fever**, Improving Lives

EXPLAIN THE 3)**ISSUE AND OFFER A SOLUTION**

Describe what happened, why you're concerned, and what you want to happen now.

Describe what happened, why you're concerned, and what you want to happen now.

Dengue fever is a virus spread by the bite of an infected mosquito. There are 4)**approximately** 75 million cases around the world every year. 5)**Symptoms** can be quite mild, flu-like ones, to extremely severe symptoms of bleeding, and an aching pain in the bones, 6)**nicknamed** breakbone fever for that very reason, and more 7)**striking** forms of dengue fever (dengue shock 8)**syndrome** and 9)**hemorrhagic** fever) can be fatal.

Dengue fever has made a comeback ever since the global temperature keeps rising and extreme weather patterns have made mosquitoes more likely to 10)**reproduce** and 11)**transmit** the virus onto people. To keep it at bay, 12)**vector** control is needed in the most 13)**productive** habitats. Moreover, clothing that 14)**minimizes** skin exposure when mosquitoes are most active is encouraged during outbreaks. 15)**Repellents** may be applied, and insecticide-treated mosquitoes nets 16)**afford** ideal protection. With 17)**collaborated** efforts, we can control dengue fever, and improves lives hence.

PHONE NUMBER Optional and NEVER published

100% private. We may contact you with urgent petition matters or media opportunities.

1. **petition** [pəˋtɪʃən] *(n.)* [C] 請願書

2. **dengue fever** [ˋdɛŋgɪ ˋfivə] *(n.)* 登革熱，可簡稱 dengue

3. **issue** [ˋɪʃu] *(n.)* [C] 議題、問題；（刊物）期數 *(vt.)* 核發、開立；發布、發行

4. **approximately** [əˋprɑksəmɪtli] *(adv.)* 約略、大約 = about, around, roughly

5. **symptom** [ˋsɪmptəm] *(n.)* [C] 症狀
   → have/show/display/exhibit/experience/suffer symptoms 出現⋯症狀

6. **nickname** [ˋnɪk͵nem] *(vt.)* 為⋯取綽號 *(n.)* [C] 綽號

7. **striking** [ˋstraɪkɪŋ] *(adj.)* 顯著的、突出的
   → striking contrast/similarity/parallel 非常鮮明的對比／非常驚人的相似度

8. **syndrome** [ˋsɪn͵drom] *(n.)* [C] 症候群、綜合症狀

9. **hemorrhagic** [hɛməˋrædʒɪk] *(adj.)* 出血性的

10. **reproduce** [͵riprəˋdus] *(vt./vi.)* 繁殖

11. **transmit** [trænsˋmɪt] *(v.)* 傳染；傳遞、傳送、播送（光、電、熱、訊息、聲音、疾病）
    → transmission *(n.)* [U, C] 傳染；傳遞、傳送

12. **vector** [ˋvɛktə] *(n.)* [C] 傳染媒介、帶菌者

13. **productive** [prəˋdʌktɪv] *(adj.)* 富饒的、多產的；（蚊蟲）容易孳生的

14. **minimize** [ˋmɪnəmaɪz] *(vt.)* 最小化、將⋯降到最少 ↔ maximize

15. **repellent** [rɪˋpɛlənt] *(n.)* [C, U] 驅蟲劑
    → insect/mosquito repellent 殺蟲劑／驅蚊劑
    → repel *(vt.)* 驅除，擊退

16. **afford** [əˋford] *(vt.)* 提供、給予；付得起
    → affordable *(adj.)* 負擔得起的、買得起的

17. **collaborated** [kəˋlæbə͵retɪd] *(adj.)* 協力的
    → collaborate *(vi.)* 共同合作

重要片語

1. **make a comeback** 捲土重來、強勢回歸

2. **keep N at bay** 遠離⋯、阻止⋯靠近 = fend off, hold off, keep off, keep away

作文教學 —— 範文 B：Rabies 狂犬病

START YOUR PETITION
In just minutes, we'll help you build your campaign.

SELECT A CATEGORY

Epidemic

TITLE OF YOUR PETITION
Use strong language to rally support, like "Demand an End to the Seal Hunt, NOW!"

Rabies: The Modern-day [1)]**Hades**

EXPLAIN THE ISSUE AND OFFER A SOLUTION
Describe what happened, why you're concerned, and what you want to happen now.

What if I told you we could [2)]**eliminate** one of the oldest diseases known to humankind, a disease that still kills a person every nine minutes? We CAN prevent rabies, by [3)]**vaccinating** dogs, by washing dog bite wounds thoroughly with soap and water, and by immediately seeking medical care after a dog bite. No child should die of rabies nor be [4)]**orphaned** by the disease. No family should suffer from rabies. To end the modern-day Hades, Rabies, our time to act is now.

Simply [5)]**eradicating** the dog species alone has never had a significant impact on dog population [6)]**densities** or the spread of rabies, let alone the fact that such [7)]**radical** measures may be considered unacceptable. Instead, mass [3)]**vaccination** campaigns have proved to be the most effective method to control [8)]**canine** rabies. High vaccination [9)]**coverage** can be attained through [10)]**comprehensive** strategies. [11)]**Surveillance** of rabies and immediate [12)]**submission** of reports of suspected animal cases are also necessary. We really can stop the modern-day hades, starting from now!

PHONE NUMBER Optional and NEVER published
100% private. We may contact you with urgent petition matters or media opportunities.

1. **Hades** [ˋhediz] *(n.)* 冥界、地獄（希臘神話中掌管地獄的神稱 Hades，延伸指地獄）

2. **eliminate** [ɪˋlɪməˌnet] *(vi.)* 消滅、消除；終結；淘汰 (+ from)
   = get rid of, eradicate, exterminate, put an end to
   → eliminate a need/possibility/risk/problem 終結…的需求／可能性／風險／問題
   → elimination *(n.)* [U] 終結、排除；淘汰

3. **vaccinate** [ˋvæksəˌnet] *(vt.)* 注射、接種疫苗
   → vaccine *(n.)* 疫苗
   → vaccination *(n.)* 疫苗接種

4. **orphan** [ˋɔrfə] *(vt.)* 使成為孤兒（常用被動語態）*(n.)* [C] 孤兒
   → orphaned *(adj.)* 孤兒的
   → orphaned children 孤兒
   → orphanage *(n.)* 孤兒院
   → nursing home 養老院、療養院

5. **eradicate** [ɪˋrædɪˌket] *(vt.)* 根除、消滅、杜絕
   → eradication *(n.)* 根除、消滅

6. **density** [ˋdɛnsətɪ] *(n.)* 密度、稠密度
   → dense *(adj.)* 稠密的、濃密的
   → densely-populated *(adj.)* 人口稠密的、密度高的 ↔ sparsely-populated 人跡罕至的

7. **radical** [ˋrædɪkəl] *(adj.)* 激進的、極端的

8. **canine** [ˋkenaɪn] *(adj.)* 犬科的 *(n.)* [C] 犬科動物

9. **coverage** [ˋkʌvərɪdʒ] *(n.)* 覆蓋（範圍）；保險項目；新聞報導
   → media/press coverage 新聞版面

10. **comprehensive** [ˌkɑmprɪˋhɛnsɪv] *(adj.)* 全面的、詳盡的
    → comprehend *(vt.)* 充分理解、領悟
    → comprehension *(n.)* [U] 理解力、領悟力

11. **surveillance** [sɝˋveləns] *(n.)* [U] 監督、檢查、看守

12. **submission** [səbˋmɪʃən] *(n.)* [C, U] 提交；[U] 屈從、歸順；謙恭
    → submit *(vt.)* 提交 = hand in *(vt./vi)* 使服從

EZ TALK
108 課綱林熹老師帶你學測英文拿高分：
6 回試題＋詳解

作　　　者：林熹、Luke Farkas
責任編輯：鄭莉璇
校　　　對：鄭莉璇、許宇昇
封面設計：比比司
內頁設計：白日設計
內頁排版：張靜怡
行銷企劃：陳品萱

發 行 人：洪祺祥
副總經理：洪偉傑
副總編輯：曹仲堯
法律顧問：建大法律事務所
財務顧問：高威會計事務所

出　　　版：日月文化出版股分有限公司
製　　　作：EZ 叢書館
地　　　址：臺北市信義路三段 151 號 8 樓
電　　　話：(02) 2708-5509
傳　　　真：(02) 2708-6157
網　　　址：www.heliopolis.com.tw
郵撥帳號：19716071 日月文化出版股分有限公司

總 經 銷：聯合發行股分有限公司
電　　　話：(02) 2917-8022
傳　　　真：(02) 2915-7212
印　　　刷：中原造像股分有限公司
初　　　版：2021 年 3 月
定　　　價：360 元
ＩＳＢＮ：978-986-248-947-5

108 課綱林熹老師帶你學測英文拿高分：
6 回試題＋詳解／林熹、Luke Farkas 著.
-- 初版 . -- 臺北市：日月文化，2021.03
216 面；19×25.7 公分（EZ Talk）
ISBN 978-986-248-947-5（平裝）

1. 英語教學 2. 讀本 3. 中等教育

524.38　　　　　　　　　110002318